Dante and Aquinas

A Study of Nature and Grace in the *Comedy*

Christopher Ryan

Revised with an Introduction
by
John Took

UCL
Arts & Humanities Publications
2013

]u[

ubiquity press
London

Published by
Ubiquity Press Ltd.
Gordon House
29 Gordon Square
London WC1H 0PP
www.ubiquitypress.com

and

The Faculty of Arts and Humanities
University College London
Gower Street, London WC1E 6BT

First published 2013

Cover illustration by John Took

Printed in the UK by Lightning Source Ltd.

ISBN (paperback): 978-1-909188-03-7
ISBN (EPUB): 978-1-909188-07-5
ISBN (PDF): 978-1-909188-11-2

DOI: http://dx.doi.org/10.5334/bad

Suggested citation:
Ryan, C. 2013 *Dante and Aquinas*. London: University College London
Arts & Humanities Publications / Ubiquity Press. DOI: http://dx.doi.
org/10.5334/bad

To read the online open access version of this
book, either visit http://dx.doi.org/10.5334/bad
or scan this QR code with your mobile device:

Contents

Foreword

In his Introduction to the book *Dante and Aquinas: A Study in Nature and Grace in the Comedy* which my husband, Christopher Ryan, left in draft at his death in 2004, he speaks of his debt to Kenelm Foster, 'who alone of the major *dantisti* of the twentieth century made the comparative study of Dante and Aquinas a significant and sustained part of his scholarly activity'. Christopher further speaks of his 'debt of affection to both the poet and his critic'.

Nine years after Christopher's death John Took has brought the manuscript to publication. His belief in the importance of Christopher's discussion of the originality of Dante's theology – as studied in the context of that of Thomas Aquinas – prompted Professor Took to undertake his meticulous re-shaping and revision of Christopher's typescript. Had Christopher had any inkling of the future course of events, I am quite sure that he would have wanted his debt of affection to be extended to John.

Christopher's hope was that his discussion might help to signal 'the achievement of [Dante's] distinctive intellectual vision and mark culturally a major point in the transition from the medieval to the early modern period'. Fundamental to this was his deep belief in 'the poet's respect for, and delight in, the dynamics of nature and of finite being'. Ultimately Christopher hoped to bring his understanding of this delight to his readership. The adoption and re-presentation by John Took of a text which Christopher had worked on for many years will allow access to this area of his work by future generations of *dantisti*. That John should have devoted so much of his time, energy and scholarship in this cause is a matter for which my children and I are enormously grateful.

Henrietta Ryan
Cambridge, April 2013

Preface

Professor Christopher Ryan's book on Dante and Aquinas remained incomplete at the time of his death on 20 February 2004. Turning on what he saw as the importance for Dante of free will as the power in man to significant self-affirmation, the book had long been on the stocks, its original proposal dating from 1990. The proposal comes straight to the point. Noting the continuing tendency among scholars to gloss the Dantean by way of the Thomist text, and the need, therefore, if only for the sake of confirming Dante as his own man, it settles on the question of nature and grace as the main area of contention between them – on, more precisely, Dante's commitment (*a*) to the possibility irrespective of Eden of man's in some degree making good from out of his ordinary power to moral self-determination, and (*b*) to the efficacy of revelation, independently of any further movement of grace, as a principle of new life:

> In modern Dante studies, particularly in the light of the work of Nardi, Gilson and Foster, it is widely accepted in principle that Dante was not on all points in agreement with Thomas Aquinas. Despite this, commentators (notably Singleton in the English-speaking world) have continued to interpret difficult theological passages in the *Divine Comedy* by quoting without qualification passages from Aquinas on the same subjects. A major desideratum in present day Dante studies is a detailed comparison of Dante and Aquinas on central theological topics. The present work offers one such study. It argues that while Aquinas and Dante work within a common doctrinal framework, from within the notion that grace in co-operation with nature is necessary for salvation, they differ significantly in the roles they ascribe to nature, and in their conception of the operation of grace. Briefly, Dante gives greater weight than Aquinas to the power inherent in nature, even in sinful man, and he attributes an overriding importance to external revelation, in contrast to Aquinas, who radically subordinates such revelation to the internal operation of grace.[1]

---

[1] I quote here and in what follows from the correspondence and other papers made available to me by Professor Ryan's widow, Henrietta Ryan, whose generosity in this

Ryan, then, sets out his plan of action. His book, he says, will consist of seven chapters. The first chapter will focus on Dante's idea of pagan righteousness, on the situation of those living either before or beyond the Christian dispensation but according to their lights. A second chapter will address the question of man's natural desire for God, a notion which, while acknowledged by Thomas albeit with some qualification, is espoused by Dante as a property of human being in act. A third chapter will look at original justice as a feature of human nature in its prelapsarian state, while a fourth chapter will be concerned with original sin as a matter of man's alienation from God at the point of fundamental willing. The fifth chapter, focusing on the question of election, will set out to confirm Dante's commitment to explicit faith in the Christ either as to come or else as already with us, while the sixth chapter will address the question of grace, nature, and their relationship one with the other within the economy of personality. A final chapter will look at the question of predestination, and there will be two appendices, one on Thomas and Dante in relation to Augustine, and especially to the Augustine of the anti-Pelagian controversy, and one on aspects of what Kenelm Foster used to call Dante's brand of Christian humanism, the Peripatetic moment of his spirituality. The whole thing would be ready for publication by the end of December 1990.

Christopher must have been pleased by the Press's initial response, for while noting that, were it to stand any chance of doing well, the book would need to be pitched at the level of the 'professional Dante scholar' rather than the 'educated general reader and undergraduate', it was nonetheless encouraging in its sense of a text designed to appeal at one and the same time to both Dantists and theologians. The timetable, however, turned out to be sanguine, the next round of correspondence dating from the beginning of the new century. Having, then, been in touch with the Press in the early part of 2000, Ryan was invited to submit a fresh specification for the book and to provide draft copy of the whole thing by the end of that September. This could then go to the Press's readers with a view to finalizing in the summer of 2001. The new description represents a considerable advance over the 1990 version. Noting once again the continuing tendency among scholars – Nardi, Gilson and Foster

respect has made it possible for me, not only to reconstruct the history and pre-history of the text, but to re-shape it with a view to bringing out as clearly and convincingly as possible its leading ideas. Persuaded as I am both of the correctness of its central contentions, and thus of its transparency to some of the main features of Dante's mature spirituality, it has been a privilege to oversee its coming at last to fruition, and for this I am, once again, grateful to Henrietta both for her courage and for her co-operation in this matter.

notwithstanding – to measure Dante up against Thomas in key areas
of philosophical and theological concern, Ryan turns at last to his own
project, one, he says, designed to confirm in Dante 'a quite individual and
distinctive configuration of moral and religious beliefs' and leading him
on in the *Commedia* to 'unrivalled creative heights':

> The present study is designed to make a substantial response to the
> need both for an account of the fundamentals of the theology of the
> *Comedy,* and for an assessment of how, exactly, Dante's religious
> thought compares to that of Aquinas. This study is in the first
> place comparative: it sets out to show that, contrary to common
> assumptions, in major areas of religious concern Dante took up a
> stance which differed significantly from that of Aquinas. Its first
> line of argument, then, is that the *Comedy* does not merely echo the
> views even of the greatest of the scholastic theologians, but, within
> the broad bounds of the Christianity of its time, champions a quite
> individual and distinctive configuration of moral and religious
> beliefs, a configuration whose particular emphases helped in no
> small measure to shape the *Comedy* and to fuel the passion that drove
> the poet to unrivalled creative heights.

True, the proposal set out here, and as developed in the introduction
to the volume as submitted to the Press, is couched still in terms of pagan
nobility and the problems thereof in Dante, Ryan himself conceding that
the 'present study may in fact be described as a sustained reflection on the
wider implications of Dante's Limbo'. But addressing as it does a range of
soteriological and grace-theological issues over and above that of antique
righteousness, the book is even so more amply conceived than this, less
constrained by a τόπος of Dante scholarship:

> The present study may in fact be described as a sustained reflection
> on the wider implications of Dante's Limbo. A common-sense
> response to the eternal fate which the poet ascribes to the virtuous
> pagans might well be: how could he? Or even how could He?
> [...] This study replies to that question, not only by probing what
> immediately underlies Dante's conception of Limbo, but by carrying
> forward the lines of thought to show that a grasp of what Dante's
> Limbo implies helps to illuminate other aspects of the poem. It
> transpires (so the study will argue) that in the creation of Limbo the
> reverence Dante shows for the moral integrity of the pagans who
> had not been granted Christian grace is but one manifestation of a
> much more pervasive feature of the *Comedy*: the poet's respect for,
> and delight in, the dynamics of nature and of finite being generally,
> even when grace is present. The distinctiveness of Dante's attitude

will be brought out by showing that, in contrast to the emphasis
the poet places on the human and the finite even in the context of
salvation, Aquinas accords a dominant and irreplaceable role to the
direct interior operation of grace in the soul.

Proceeding, then, on the basis of a revised specification, Ryan
undertakes now (*a*) to review the relationship between nature and grace
among those living *within* the Christian καιρός; (*b*) to consider Dante's
position as regards the question of explicit and implicit faith as conditions
of salvation; (*c*) to visit afresh the question of man's natural desire for
God as conceived by Dante; and (*∂*) to look afresh at the Augustinian
dimension of the argument, the neo-Augustinianism of the *Prima secundae*
consituting the background or 'control' for his account in the book
of Dante's thinking in the areas of salvation and election theology. He
himself sums up thus:

> It will be no small gain if awareness of the significant differences
> between Dante and Aquinas in their views of nature and grace, and
> of the roots of those differences in their contrasting attitude to the
> immensely influential later works of Augustine, helps to highlight the
> fact that the *Comedy* [...] signals also the achievement of a distinctive
> intellectual vision and marks culturally a major point in the transition
> from the medieval to the early modern world.

Again, the Press was encouraging, observing only that it would be
desirable to preserve a balance in the book between the detailed exegetical
and the more generally interpretative moment of the text, between
that aspect of it designed for the specialist and that aspect intended to
commend it, if not to the man in the street, then to the medievalist without
any special interest or competence in Dante. Ryan, as always, took note,
and returning to the matter at the beginning of 2001 following a delay
for health reasons, confirmed first that the introduction to the volume
would be expanded to include an account of the current state of play in
Dante and Aquinas studies, and secondly that there would be a further
short chapter on the virtuous pagans in the theological and the romance-
vernacular literature of the time. In the event, the full draft, wanting only
for further footnoting and bibliographical refinement, was submitted
to the Press on 22 January 2001, the Press in turn undertaking on 24
January to inaugurate a peer review prior to any recommendation to the
Syndicate. The results of this, communicated by one of the Press officials
and accompanied by extracts from the peer reviews commissioned by
them, were, however, mixed, and Ryan must have been dispirited. On the

substantial side, reservations were expressed as to (*a*) his overall estimate
of the soteriological situation in Aquinas, a situation no less responsive,
even in the relatively late *Summa theologiae*, to its Aristotelian than to its
Augustinian component; (*b*) his proposal of the question of Dante and
Aquinas in terms more or less exclusively of the grace-theological; (*c*)
the propriety of approaching Dante's complex spirituality by way of just
one of his *auctores* (Thomas); and (*∂*) the scant regard in Ryan's book
for the poetic dimension of Dante's undertaking in the *Commedia*, for
his proceeding in the text, not so much ideologically, as imaginatively,
a notion precluding any straight comparison of Dante and Thomas as
theological spirits. On the technical and expressive side there was a sense
(*a*) of the diffuse structure of the book, of its articulation by way of a series
of short and at times inconclusive chapters; and (*b*) of a certain in-built
antipathy towards Thomas, a touch of *parti pris* having no part to play in
an enterprise of this kind. Again, Ryan must have been dismayed, not
least in the sense of being constrained now, not only to a fresh review of
his leading emphases in the book, but to a rebuilding of the whole project
along lines quite other than those he had originally intended. Diligent to
a fault in taking on board the suggestions put to him by his critics, but
overwhelmed by the implications of it all, he set the project aside in favour
of something more manageable, the whole thing thus living on by way
only of the melancholy of its incompletion, of its destiny not actually to
make any difference in this area of Dante studies.

For myself, I had for some time been aware of a book on the way
about Dante and Aquinas and thus about one of the great encounters
in our tradition. I therefore made contact in the spring of 2005 with
Christopher's widow, Henrietta, with a view to looking again at the text
and seeing it through to publication. Thanks to her enthusiasm and good
will, I had access, not only to the text itself, but to much of the ancillary
material (correspondence, notes, revisions and so on) making for a sense
of its conception and development. Having consulted a number of friends
and colleagues, including Professor Corinna Lonergan-Salvadori of
Dublin and Dr Stephen Bemrose of Exeter, spirits as generous as they
are discriminating in matters of this kind, I decided in consultation with
Henrietta that what was required was a revision of the text in such a way
as (*a*) to honour its central contention relative to Dante's sense of – albeit
within the context of God's original and continuing work in Christ – the
moral and ontological viability of the human project; (*b*) to preserve intact
its method, its close reading of the primary text as a point of departure;
(*c*) to remedy the fragmentary structure of the original by condensing
the argument into just four chapters; and (*∂*) to refresh the footnoting

and update the bibliography.[2] The result is a text as much rewritten as it is revised, but rewritten in such a way as to confirm the substance and strength of Professor Ryan's own intuitions and emphases in this area; for his, I believe, was a fully justified sense of what might be described as the 'incarnational' Dante, of a Dante who, while sensitive to the power in man to self-annihilation and thus to his forever standing in the dimension of grace, remains committed to the equality of human nature as quickened in Christ to its own high calling.

John Took
University College London

---

[2] Further to the third of these points, the remedying and reorganization of Christopher's text in response to its, at times, fragmentary and inconclusive development, I should for the record indicate those areas in which I have most amply supplemented the argument for the sake both of completing it and of confirming what I see to be its persuasiveness. This has occurred most conspicuously in the conclusion to Chapter 2 (where I have suggested how it is that Dante himself might have intuited a solution to the otherwise stark severity of his soteriological position in the *Commedia*), in the conclusion to Chapter 3 (where again I have brought to Professor Ryan's emphases a sense of how, pressed on the point, Dante might have wished to resolve the question of destiny and of predestination as features of the soteriological scheme generally), and in Chapter 4 wherever the argument touches on the interplay of reception and repudiation characteristic of Dante's approach to Augustine. At no stage, however, have I ventured beyond or sought in any way to qualify what I see as Christopher's main contention in the book, namely his sense of how it stands with Dante as representative of a certain kind of moral and ontological heroism, of commitment to the human project in its power to significant self-determination on the plane of properly human being and doing. Expertly nuanced as it is in his text (for the *Commedia*, whatever else it is, is a meditation, not only upon God's dealings with man, but upon man's dealings with God), the thesis seems to me unexceptionable.

The publication of this volume has been made possible by the kind generosity of a group of Christopher Ryan's friends and colleagues.

Introduction

> We have often been shown how Dante
> followed Aquinas; it would be of interest
> to have an exhibition of their differences.
>
> Charles Williams[1]

In a more than ordinarily gracious moment of the *Paradiso*, Thomas
Aquinas introduces Dante one by one to those most accomplished in
the way of Judeo-Christian wisdom, including, among the ancients,
King Solomon, and, among the moderns, Albert the Great of Cologne,
Dionysius the Areopagite, Gratian, Peter Lombard, Bede, Richard of St
Victor ('more than man in contemplation') and his old antagonist Siger of
Brabant. But Dante, as yet a stranger in paradise and thus to their now
radiant configuration, needs no introduction, for the souls he discovers
there and in whose company he now rejoices had long since been his
companions as a philosophical and theological spirit. From Albert, he
had learnt how it might be possible to reconcile the Platonic and the
Peripatetic elements of his spirituality,[2] while from the Areopagite he had
come to appreciate something of the graduated character of the cosmos in
general (the *De hierarchia*) and of the art of predication in particular (the

---

[1] Charles Williams, *The Descent of the Dove. A Short History of the Holy Spirit in the Church*
(London: Longmans, 1939), p. 123.

[2] B. Nardi, 'Raffronti fra alcuni luoghi di Alberto Magno e di Dante', in *Saggi di filosofia
dantesca*, 2nd edn (Florence: La Nuova Italia, 1967), pp. 63-72; C. Vasoli, 'L'immagine
di Alberto Magno in Bruno Nardi', in *Freiburger Zeitschrift für Philosophie und Theologie* 32
(1985), 1-2, 45-64 (and in *Otto saggi per Dante* (Florence: Le Lettere, 1995), pp. 117-32);
idem, 'Dante, Alberto Magno e la scienza dei peripatetici', in P. Boyde and V. Russo
(eds), *Dante e la scienza. Atti del Convegno Internazionale di Studi, Ravenna 28-30 maggio 1995*
(Ravenna: Longo, 1995), pp. 55-70; idem, 'Fonti albertiane nel *Convivio* di Dante', in M.
J. F. M. Hoenene and A. De Libera (eds), *Albertus Magnus und der Albertismus. Deutsche
philosophische kultur des Mittelalters* (Leiden, New York and Cologne: Brill, 1995), pp.
33-49; G. Fioravanti, 'Dante e Alberto Magno', in *Il pensiero filosofico e teologico di Dante
Alighieri* (Milan: V&P Università, 2001), pp. 93-102; A. Kablitz, '*Alberto è di Cologna*'.
Albertus ist es, aus Köln. Dantes "Göttliche Komödie" und die Scholastik (Cologne: Fritz-
Thyssen-Stiftung, 2002).

De divinis nominibus), of affirmation and of negation as means of theological understanding.[3] In Solomon he had contemplated the substance of kingship,[4] while in Richard of St Victor he had pondered the psychology of ecstasis.[5] But the wisdom he gleaned from these figures both severally and in the round pales in relation to what he had discovered and come to admire in Thomas, for here was the archetypal representative of the kind of precision and piety proper to those looking into things human and divine, and for this he could not help but love him, and, in loving him, proposing and celebrating him as spokesman for those in paradise most gifted in things of the mind.

[3] E. Grether, *Geistige Hierarchien. Der Mensch und die übersinnliche Welt in der Darstellung großer Seher des Abendlandes. Dionysus Areopagita, Dante Alighieri, Rud*, 2nd edn (Freiburg: Die Kommenden, 1977); U. Gamba, '"Il lume di quel cero ...": Dionigi Areopagita fu l'ispiratore di Dante?', *Studia Patavina* 32 (1985), 1, 101-14; D. Giuliotti, 'San Dionigi e Dante', in M. Baldini (ed.), *Tizzi e fiamme* (Siena: Cantagalli, 1999; originally 1921), pp. 182-89; M. Ariani, '"E sì come di lei bevve la gronda / de le palpebre mie" (*Par.* XXX. 88): Dante e lo pseudo Dionigi Areopagita', in L. Battaglia Ricci (ed.), *Leggere Dante* (Ravenna: Longo, 2004), pp. 131-52; D. Sbacchi, *La presenza di Dionigi Areopagita nel Paradiso di Dante* (Florence: Olschki, 2006); idem, 'Il linguaggio superlativo e gerarchico del *Paradiso*', *L'Alighieri*, n.s. 31 (2008), 5-22; S. Prandi, 'Dante e lo Pseudo-Dionigi: una nuova proposta per l'immagine finale della *Commedia*', *Lettere Italiane* 61 (2009), 1, 3-29.

[4] P. Nasti, 'Autorità, topos e modello: Salomone nei commenti trecenteschi alla *Commedia*', *The Italianist* 19 (1999), 5-49; eadem, 'The Wise Poet: Solomon in Dante's Heaven of the Sun', *Reading Medieval Studies* 27 (2001), 103-38; eadem, *Favole d'amore e 'saver profondo'. La tradizione salomonica in Dante* (Ravenna: Longo, 2007); E. Peters, 'The Voyage of Ulysses and the Wisdom of Solomon: Dante and the "vitium curiositatis"', *Majestas* 7 (1999), 75-87; M. Mills Chiarenza, 'Solomon's Song in the *Divine Comedy*', in *Sparks and Seeds. Medieval Literature and its Afterlife. Essays in Honour of John Freccero*, ed. D. E. Stewart and A. Cornish (Turnhout: Brepols, 2000), pp. 199-208; R. Herzman, 'From Francis to Solomon: Eschatology in the Sun', in *Dante for the New Millennium*, ed. T. Barolini and H. W. Storey (New York: Fordham University Press, 2003), pp. 320-33; P. Williams, 'Dante's Heaven of the Sun and the Wisdom of Solomon', *Italica* 82 (2005), 2, 165-79; A. Rossini, *Il Dante sapienziale. Dionigi e la bellezza di Beatrice* (Pisa and Rome: Fabrizio Serra, 2009) (various essays). More generally, M. Bose, 'From Exegesis to Appropriation: the Medieval Solomon', *Medium Aevum* 65 (1996), 2, 187-210.

[5] B. Nolan, 'The *Vita Nuova* and Richard of St Victor's Phenomenology of Vision', *Dante Studies* 92 (1974), 35-52; P. Amargier, *Saint Bernard, Richard de Saint-Victor, Dante* (Marseille: Robert-Amargier, 1984); M. Colombo, 'L'ineffabilità della "visio mystica": il XXIII canto del *Paradiso* e il *Benjamin major* di Riccardo da San Vittore', *Strumenti critici*, n.s. 1, 51 (1986), 2, 225-39 (subsequently in *Dai mistici a Dante. Il linguaggio dell'ineffabilità* (Florence: La Nuova Italia, 1987), pp. 61-71); M. Mocan, 'Ulisse, Arnaut, e Riccardo di SanVittore: convergenze figurali e richiami lessicali nella *Commedia*', *Lettere Italiane* 57 (2005), 2, 173-208; S. Distefano, 'La mistica della *Vita Nova* secondo Riccardo di San Vittore', in S. Cristaldi and C. Tramontana (eds), *L'opera di Dante fra Antichità, Medioevo ed epoca moderna* (Catania: Cooperativa Universitaria Editrice catanese di Magistero, 2008), pp. 285-327.

But for all Dante's espousal of Aquinas as among the most cherished of his *auctores* the differences between them are as great as the similarities, one of the great accomplishments of the twentieth century in the area of Dante scholarship being the retrieval of Dante from Thomas, or, more exactly, from Thomism, as decisive for his emergence as a philosopher and theologian. First, then, there was Bruno Nardi with his sense of Dante's combination of radicalism and eclecticism in philosophy and of this as quite other than anything envisaged by Aquinas.[6] Then there was Etienne Gilson with his sense, not so much of his radicalism, as of his enthusiasm, of his discovering in the Philosopher a means of confirming the periodic structure of human understanding and desiring, their susceptibility to contemplation in terms of the soul's progression from one peak of perfection and satisfaction to the next.[7] And then, as impressed by both but with an approach entirely his own, there was Kenelm Foster with his sense of the tension in Dante between the Christian and the Peripatetic aspects of his spirituality, of his 'simultaneous attachment both to Christianity and to paganism'.[8] True, the *Commedia* as it goes on, Kenelm thought, witnesses

[6] B. Nardi, *Note critiche di filosofia dantesca* (Florence: Olschki, 1938); *Nel mondo di Dante* (Rome: Edizioni di Storia e Letteratura, 1944); *Saggi e note di critica dantesca* (Milan: Ricciardi, 1966); *Saggi di filosofia dantesca*, 2nd edn (Florence: La Nuova Italia, 1967); *Dante e la cultura medievale*, ed. P. Mazzantini with an introduction by T. Gregory (Rome and Bari: Laterza, 1983; originally Bari: Laterza, 1942); *Dal 'Convivio' alla 'Commedia': sei saggi danteschi*, with a preface by O. Capitani (Rome: Istituto storico italiano per il Medio Evo, 1992; originally 1960). For a general bibliography of Nardi, see his *Saggi sulla cultura veneta del Quattro e Cinquecento*, ed. P. Mazzantini (Padua: Antenore, 1971), pp. ix-xlix (also, idem, 'Gli scritti di Bruno Nardi', in B. Nardi, *'Lecturae' e altri studi danteschi*, ed. R. Abardo (Florence: Le Lettere, 1990), pp. 285-312).

[7] Etienne Gilson, *Dante and Philosophy*, trans. D. Moore (New York, Evanston and London: Harper and Row, 1963; originally *Dante et la philosophie*, Paris: Vrin, 1939, second edn, 1953). Also 'Dante's Notion of a Shade: *Purgatorio* XXV', *Medieval Studies* 29 (1967), 14-42; 'Dante's *Mirabile Visione*', *Cornell Library Journal* 5 (1968), 1-17 (from a lecture delivered in May 1965 at the Italian Cultural Institute in Paris, with an Italian version by V. Cappelletti, Istituto italiano di cultura, quaderni 1); *Dante et Beatrice: études dantesques* (Paris: Vrin, 1974). Fundamental in respect of Aquinas, *The Christian Philosophy of St. Thomas Aquinas*, trans. L. K. Shook (New York: Octagon Books, 1983; originally New York: Random House, 1956); *Thomism: the Philosophy of Thomas Aquinas*, trans. L. K. Shook and A. Maurer (Toronto: Pontifical Institute of Mediaeval Studies, 2002; from *Le Thomisme: introduction à la philosophie de Saint Thomas d'Aquin*, 6th edn rev., Paris: Vrin, 1965). For a general bibliography, *Etienne Gilson: a bibliography / une bibliographie* (*The Etienne Gilson Series*, 3), ed. M. McGrath (Toronto: Pontifical Institute of Mediaeval Studies, 1982).

[8] K. Foster, O.P., 'The Two Dantes (I): Limbo and Implicit Faith', in *The Two Dantes and Other Studies* (London: Darton, Longman and Todd, 1977), p. 156 ('Dante was attached, simultaneously, to Christianity and to paganism'). Otherwise, idem, *The Mind in Love*, Aquinas Society of London 25 (London: Blackfriars, 1956); *God's Tree: Essays on Dante*

to a mutual accommodation of these things, but never in such a way or in such a degree as to resolve the problems by which it is beset at the level of root intentionality. The present volume, then, mindful as it is of all these emphases and, above all, of the difficulty everywhere engendered in the area of grace theological consciousness by the need to balance one set of considerations with another, seeks to develop the argument by way of a sense in Dante of the human project as made equal by grace to a species of moral and ontological self-actualization. Needless to say, the proposition requires careful statement, since for Dante too grace subsists both as the *prius* and as the encompassing of all righteousness in man. But at the same time, and on the basis of what amounts to an unusually developed sense of the coalescence of human and divine purposefulness at the core of existence, his was a desire to confirm the power in man to being and becoming *ex seipso*, from out of his connatural power to moral determination, at which point his redistribution of emphases is complete.

The argument proceeds as follows. Chapter 1, entitled 'Morality and Merit', offers an account of the nature and aetiology of righteousness in Thomas and Dante, while Chapter 2, entitled 'Faith and Facticity', considers the implications for a theology of election of the latter's preoccupation with the status of the revelatory instant as a channel of grace in its own right. Chapter 3, entitled 'Desire and Destiny', has to do with Dante's commitment (*a*) to the co-extensivity of being and of yearning in man, and (*b*) to a resolving of the question of destiny in terms pre-eminently of the individual's laying hold of what he already has it in himself to be and become, while Chapter 4, entitled 'The Augustinian Dimension: Narratives of Succession and Secession', develops the argument in terms of the nature of Augustine's presence to the Aquinas of the great *summae* and to the Dante of the *Commedia*, his presence to Dante being simultaneously one of everywhereness and nowhereness, of reception and repudiation. Three appendices address a number of details which, had they been incorporated in the body of the text, would have made for an unnecessarily complicated line of argument.

and Other Matters (London: Blackfriars, 1957) (with, at pp. 141-49, an essay entitled 'The Tact of St Thomas'); 'Religion and Philosophy in Dante', in *The Mind of Dante* (Cambridge: Cambridge University Press, 1965), pp. 47-78; 'Tommaso d'Aquino', in the *Enciclopedia dantesca*, 6 vols (Rome: Istituto della Enciclopedia Italiana, 1970-76), vol. 5, pp. 626-49; *Dante e San Tommaso* (Rome: Casa di Dante, 1975; lecture of 17 November 1974 at the Casa di Dante in Rome); 'St Thomas and Dante', in *The Two Dantes and Other Studies*, cit., pp. 56-65). Also (ed. and trans.), *The Life of Saint Thomas Aquinas: Biographical Documents* (London: Longmans, 1959) and, with P. Boyde, *Dante's Lyric Poetry*, 2 vols (Oxford: Oxford University Press, 1967).

Chapter 1
Morality and Merit

> e non voglio che dubbi, ma sia certo,
> che ricever la grazia è meritorio
> secondo che l'affetto l'è aperto.

(*Par.* XXIX.64-66)[1]

1. Preliminary considerations: Aquinas, grace and grace-consciousness. 2. Patterns of doing and deserving I: Aquinas and movement. 3. Patterns of doing and deserving II: Dante and the coalescence of human and divine willing at the core of existence. 4. Dante, maturity in the flame of love, and primordial possibility.

In a startling passage near the beginning of the *Inferno*, Virgil announces that both he and those with whom he is destined to pass all eternity in Limbo were without sin:

> Lo buon maestro a me: "Tu non dimandi
> che spiriti son questi che tu vedi?
> Or vo' che sappi, innanzi che più andi,
>   ch'ei non peccaro; e s'elli hanno mercedi,
> non basta, perché non ebber battesmo,
> ch'è porta de la fede che tu credi;
>   e s'e' furon dinanzi al cristianesmo,
> non adorar debitamente a Dio:
> e di questi cotai son io medesmo.
>   Per tai difetti, non per altro rio,
> semo perduti, e sol di tanto offesi
> che sanza speme vivemo in disio".

(*Inf.* IV.31-42)[2]

---

[1] and I would not have you doubt, but be assured that to receive grace is meritorious, in proportion as the affection is open to it. Translations (occasionally amended) from the *Commedia* are from *The Divine Comedy*, trans. C. S. Singleton, second printing (Princeton, NJ: Princeton University Press, 1970-) by permission.

[2] The good master said to me: "Do you not ask what spirits are these that you see? Now, before you go farther, I will have you know that they did not sin; but if they have merit,

The passage raises a number of issues relative to those living before or beyond the Christian dispensation and thus innocent of Christ and clergy, but striking above all is the 'ei non peccaro' moment of the argument, for it is straightaway a question of what exactly Dante meant by this. Did he mean that the pagan spirits of whom Virgil is one and for whom he is spokesman in the poem were untouched by the catastrophe of Eden and by the forces of destruction unleashed by that catastrophe?[3] Or did

that does not suffice, for they did not have baptism, which is the portal of the faith you hold; and if they were before Christianity, they did not worship God aright, and I myself am one of these. Because of these shortcomings, and for no other fault, we are lost, and only so far afflicted that without hope we live in longing."

[3] On Dante and the 'virtuous pagans' (in addition to commentaries and *lecturae* on *Inferno* IV), G. Rizzo, 'Dante and the Virtuous Pagans', in W. De Sua and G. Rizzo (eds), *Dante Symposium in Commemoration of the 700th Anniversary of the Poet's Birth (1265-1965)* (Chapel Hill: University of North Carolina Press, 1965), pp. 115-39; K. Foster, O.P., 'The Two Dantes (III). The Pagans and Grace', in *The Two Dantes and Other Studies* (London: Darton, Longman and Todd, 1977), pp. 220-53 (also, in the same volume, pp. 137-55, 'The Son's Eagle: *Paradiso* XIX'); D. Thompson, 'Dante's Virtuous Romans', *Dante Studies* 96 (1978), 145-62, and subsequently in R. Lansing (ed.), *The Critical Complex* (New York and London: Routledge, 2003), vol. 2, pp. 345-62; H.A. Mason, 'A Journey through Hell: Dante's *Inferno* Revisited. Virtuous Pagans – "gente di molto valore". Canto IV', *The Cambridge Quarterly* 16 (1987), 3, 187-211; M. Picone, 'La "viva speranza" di Dante e il problema della salvezza dei pagani virtuosi. Una lettura di *Paradiso* 20', *Quaderni di Italianistica* 10 (1989), 1-2, 251-68 (a monographic volume entitled *Dante Today*); C. L. Vitto, 'The Virtuous Pagan in Legend and in Dante', in *The Virtuous Pagan in Middle English Literature. Transactions of the American Philosophical Society* 79, part 5 (Philadelphia: The American Philosophical Society, 1989), pp. 36-49; M. L. Colish, 'The Virtuous Pagan: Dante and the Christian Tradition', in W. Caferro and D. G. Fisher (eds), *The Unbounded Community. Papers in Christian Ecumenism in Honor of Jaroslav Pelikan* (New York: Garland, 1996), pp. 43-91 (subsequently in *The Fathers and Beyond. Church Fathers Between Ancient and Medieval Thought* (Aldershot and Burlington: Ashgate, 2008), pp. 1-40); G. Inglese, 'Il destino dei non credenti. Lettura di *Paradiso* XIX', *La Cultura. Rivista trimestrale di filosofia letteratura e storia* 42 (2004), 2, 315-29.

On Virgil (Dante's Virgil) in particular, and in addition to the *Enciclopedia dantesca* ad voc. (Rome: Istituto dell'Enciclopedia Italiana, 1970-76), vol. 5, pp. 1030-48, E. Auerbach, 'Dante und Virgil', *Das Humanistisches Gymnasium* 42 (1931), 136-44 (and as 'Dante e Virgilio', in *San Francesco Dante Vico e altri saggi di filologia romanza* (Rome: Ed. Riuniti,1987), pp. 27-37); idem, *Dante Poet of the Secular World*, trans. R. Manheim (Chicago and London: University of Chicago Press, 1961; originally 1929 but now with an introduction by M. Dirda (New York: New York Review Books, 2007)); D. Consoli, *Significato del Virgilio dantesco* (Florence: Le Monnier, 1967); E. Moore, *Studies in Dante. First Series: Scripture and Classical Authors in Dante* (Oxford: Oxford University Press, 1969; originally 1896), pp. 166-97; R. Hollander, *Il Virgilio dantesco: tragedia nella 'Commedia'* (Florence: Olschki, 1983); T. Barolini, *Dante's Poets. Textuality and Truth in the Comedy* (Princeton NJ: Princeton University Press, 1984); see also her 'Q. Does Dante hope for Virgil's salvation? A. Why do we care? For the very reason we should not ask the question (response to Mowbray Allan [*MLN* 104])', *Modern Language Notes* 105 (1990), 1, 138-44 and 144-47 (and in *Dante and the Origins of Italian Literary Culture* (New

he understand by the term 'sin' ('peccare') something theologically less drastic than this, something more like 'moral aberration' or 'indiscretion'? Or is Virgil speaking strictly in character here, as one for whom the notion of sin as understood by those living in Christ had no meaning as a principle of self-interpretation? Or did he mean – somewhat after the manner of the 'man on the banks of the Indus' passage of *Paradiso* XIX[4] – that though the pagans may, like all men, be said to have participated in the original sin of Adam, and thus to have incurred God's wrath as visited both upon him and upon his progeny, they lived according to their lights and were to that extent morally irreproachable? Or was he just speaking hyperbolically, in a manner designed to convey forcefully, but no more than that, a sense of the spiritual nobility of those now assembled in Limbo?

Whatever he meant by this, Thomas, everywhere cherished by Dante for his particular kind of intellectual and expressive discerning,[5] would have none of it, the twilight pages of the *Prima secundae* in particular offering a sustained account of his sense of the indispensabilty of grace to a life of moral and intellectual integrity. Amost any article in the text would suffice as a point of departure, but let us take to begin with, as going straight to the heart of the matter, 109.8 on 'whether or not man needs grace to avoid sin' ('utrum homo sine gratia possit non peccare'). The 'objections' or antitheses in this article, turning as they do on the

York: Fordham University Press, 2006), pp. 151-57). More generally, D. Comparetti, *Virgil in the Middle Ages*, trans. E. F. M. Benecke (Hamden, Conn.: Archon Books, 1967; originally 1872).

On the Dantean limbo, G. Busnelli, 'La colpa del "non fare" degli infedeli negativi', *Studi danteschi* 23 (1938), 79-97; K. Foster, O.P., 'The Two Dantes (I). Limbo and Implicit Faith', in the *Two Dantes* (above), pp. 156-89; G. Padoan, 'Il limbo dantesco', *Lettere italiane* 21 (1969), 4, 369-88 (and in *Il pio Enea, l'impio Ulisse* (Ravenna: Longo, 1977), pp. 103-24); A. A. Iannucci, 'Limbo: the Emptiness of Time', *Studi danteschi* 52 (1979-80), 69-128.

[4] *Par.* XIX.70-75: 'ché tu dicevi: "Un uom nasce a la riva / de l'Indo, e quivi non è chi ragioni / di Cristo né chi legga né chi scriva; / e tutti suoi voleri e atti buoni / sono, quanto ragione umana vede, / sanza peccato in vita o in sermoni.' On the living out among the pagans of moral (as distinct from theological) virtue in its entirety, *Purg.* VII.34-36: 'quivi sto io con quei che le tre sante / virtù non si vestiro, e sanza vizio / conobber l'altre e seguir tutte quante.'

[5] K. Foster, O.P., 'St Thomas and Dante', in *The Two Dantes* (note 3 above), p. 61: 'what distinguishes the motive and manner of his regard for St Thomas? A fine subject for a book which no one has written! But if I were to try and write it I would begin by distinguishing, in the poet's devotion (the expression is not too strong) to "il buon frate Tommaso", two basic motives: (*a*) gratitude to the Aristotelian scholar, the author of the commentaries, and (*b*) esteem for the thinker as a model of intellectual probity and finesse. And I would show that the former attitude appears chiefly in the *Convivio* and the latter above all in cantos X-XIII of the *Paradiso*.'

propriety of speaking about 'sin' at all if it is something that cannot be avoided, insist that man without grace *can* avoid sin, anything less than this not only making a nonsense of the moral issue generally (for how, without the power to choose either way, *can* there be a moral issue?) but flying in the face of Scripture.[6] In reply, however, Thomas, having cited Augustine to the effect that those thinking along these lines 'ought without doubt to be removed beyond all hearing and to be anathematized by the tongues of all' ('ab auribus omnium removendum, et ore omnium anathematizandum esse non dubito'),[7] proceeds by way of a distinction between the before and after of justifying grace to affirm that, while before justification man can indeed abstain from mortal sin (though not from the kind of venial sin arising from the waywardness of his lower appetites), he cannot do this for long, his general disorderliness conspiring eventually, in the words of Gregory on Ezekiel, to 'drag him down' ('suo pondere ad aliud trahit') and destroy him:

> Similiter etiam antequam hominis ratio, in qua est peccatum mortale, reparetur per gratiam iustificantem, potest singula peccata mortalia vitare, et secundum aliquod tempus, quia non est necesse quod continuo peccet in actu. Sed quod diu maneat absque peccato mortali, esse non potest. Unde et Gregorius dicit, super Ezech., quod 'peccatum quod mox per poenitentiam non deletur, suo pondere ad aliud trahit'. Et huius ratio est quia, sicut rationi subdi debet inferior appetitus, ita etiam ratio subdi debet Deo, et in ipso constituere finem suae voluntatis. Per finem autem oportet quod regulentur omnes actus humani, sicut per rationis iudicium regulari debent motus inferioris appetitus. Sicut ergo, inferiori appetitu non totaliter subiecto rationi, non potest esse quin contingant inordinati motus in appetitu sensitivo; ita etiam, ratione hominis non totaliter existente subiecta Deo, consequens est ut contingant multae inordinationes in ipsis actibus rationis. Cum enim homo non habet cor suum firmatum in Deo, ut pro nullo bono consequendo vel malo vitando ab eo separari vellet; occurrunt multa propter quae consequenda vel

[6] *ST* Ia IIae.109.8, objs 1-3: 'Videtur quod homo sine gratia possit non peccare. "Nullus enim peccat in eo quod vitare non potest"; ut Augustinus dicit, in libro de Duab. Animab., et de Lib. Arb. Si ergo homo existens in peccato mortali non possit vitare peccatum, videtur quod peccando non peccet. Quod est inconveniens. Praeterea, ad hoc corripitur homo ut non peccet. Si igitur homo in peccato mortali existens non potest non peccare, videtur quod frustra ei correptio adhibeatur. Quod est inconveniens. Praeterea, Eccli. XV dicitur, "ante hominem vita et mors, bonum et malum, quod placuerit ei, dabitur illi". Sed aliquis peccando non desinit esse homo. Ergo adhuc in eius potestate est eligere bonum vel malum. Et ita potest homo sine gratia vitare peccatum.'

[7] *De perfectione justitiae hominis* xxi.44, ult.

vitanda homo recedit a Deo contemnendo praecepta ipsius, et ita
peccat mortaliter ...

(ST Ia IIae.109.8 resp.)[8]

Without grace, then, the situation is hopeless. Called upon to submit the
lower to the higher appetites, this being the way of a properly structured
act of existence in man, the individual never – or never for long – succeeds
in this, nature being forever in the grip of its frailty. True, a man on guard
against his old ways may on occasion forestall them and act virtuously;
but rarely, short of a movement of grace, can he be equal to his readiness to
sin again: 'Sed quia homo non potest semper esse in tali praemeditatione,
non potest contingere ut diu permaneat quin operetur secundum
consequentiam voluntatis deordinatae a Deo, nisi cito per gratiam ad
debitum ordinem reparetur' (ibid).[9] Reading between the lines, it is not
hard to discern something of Thomas's misgiving here, his doubts about
having yet again to resolve the Aristotelian in the Augustinian moment
of his spirituality; for not only is it clear from the body of the article that

---

[8] So, too, before man's reason, wherein is mortal sin, is restored by justifying grace,
he can avoid each mortal sin, and for a time, since it is not necessary that he should
be always actually sinning. But it cannot be that he remains for a long time without
mortal sin. Hence Gregory says (Super Ezech. Hom. xi) that "a sin not at once taken
away by repentance, by its weight drags us down to other sins"; and this because, as
the lower appetite ought to be subject to the reason, so should the reason be subject to
God, and should place in him the end of its will. Now it is by the end that all human acts
ought to be regulated, even as it is by the judgment of the reason that the movements of
the lower appetite should be regulated. And thus, even as inordinate movements of the
sensitive appetite cannot help occurring since the lower appetite is not subject to reason,
so likewise, since man's reason is not entirely subject to God, the consequence is that
many disorders occur in the reason. For when man's heart is not so fixed on God as to be
unwilling to be parted from him for the sake of finding any good or avoiding any evil,
many things happen for the achieving or avoiding of which a man strays from God and
breaks his commandments, and thus sins mortally. (Translation here and throughout
by the Fathers of the English Dominican Province, 20 vols, New York: Benziger, 1911-
25). On the difficulty of withstanding, at least for any length of time, venial sin, ST
Ia IIae.109.8 resp.: 'Non autem potest homo abstinere ab omni peccato veniali, propter
corruptionem inferioris appetitus sensualitatis, cuius motus singulos quidem ratio
reprimere potest (et ex hoc habent rationem peccati et voluntarii), non autem omnes, quia
dum uni resistere nititur, fortassis alius insurgit; et etiam quia ratio non semper potest
esse pervigil ad huiusmodi motus vitandos .'

[9] But because a man cannot always be in this state of heightened attentiveness, it cannot
be but that he sometimes acts in accordance with a will turned aside from God, unless, by
grace, he is quickly brought back to due order; cf. ScG III.clx.2: 'Non est autem possibile
mentem hominis continue in ea vigilantia esse ut per rationem discutiat quicquid debet
velle vel agere. Unde consequitur quod mens aliquando eligat id ad quod est inclinata,
inclinatione manente. Et ita, si inclinata fuerit in peccatum, non stabit diu quin peccet,
impedimentum gratiae praestans, nisi ad statum rectitudinis reducatur.'

man *can* resist mortal sin from out of his reasonableness as man ('in quo quidem statu potest homo abstinere ab omni peccato mortali quod in ratione consistit'),[10] but the reply to Objection 3, an objection turning on a passage from *Ecclesiasticus* to the effect that man will sooner or later reap his proper reward ('ante hominem vita et mors, bonum et malum; quod placuerit ei, dabitur illi'),[11] works by way only of introducing into that passage a distinction quite foreign to the plain sense of the text: 'Ad tertium dicendum quod, sicut Augustinus dicit, in Hypognost., verbum illud intelligitur de homine secundum statum naturae integrae, quando nondum erat servus peccati, unde poterat peccare et non peccare. Nunc etiam quodcumque vult homo, datur ei. Sed hoc quod bonum velit, habet ex auxilio gratiae.'[12] Somewhere, in other words, between the uncluttered substance of what the text actually says, its straightforward sense of the choice in human experience between good and evil, and Thomas's invocation of it for the purposes of securing a position in grace theology, comes the severity of Augustine's anti-Pelagian cast of mind, his sense of grace as a condition, not only of doing good, but of willing to do good in the first place.

The grace-theological resolution of 109.8 is foreshadowed in Articles 2 and 4 of the same question, articles bearing respectively on whether man can will and do good without grace ('utrum homo possit velle et facere bonum absque gratia'), and whether, again without grace, he can fulfil the precepts of the law ('utrum homo sine gratia per sua naturalia legis possit praecepta implere'). Article 2 especially has something about it of the 'retractation', of thinking through afresh earlier emphases, for previously in the *Summa* (Ia IIae.65.2 resp.) Thomas had taken the view that the sort of virtue required of man for the accomplishment of his natural as distinct from his supernatural end lies within his reach, a position plain from the situation of the gentiles: 'virtutes morales prout sunt operativae boni in ordine ad finem qui non excedit facultatem naturalem hominis, possunt

---

[10] In this state man can abstain from all mortal sin, which takes its stand in his reason.

[11] Before man are life and death, good and evil; whichever he pleases will be given to him (Eccles. 15:18).

[12] In reply to the third point, as Augustine says in the *Hypognosticon*, this saying is to be understood of man in the state of perfect nature, when as yet he was not a slave of sin. Hence he was able to sin and not to sin. Now, too, whatever a man wills, is given to him; but his willing good, he has by God's assistance. The *Hypognosticon* (also *Hypomnesticon*, a spurious text but close in inspiration to the *De gratia et libero arbitrio*) has at III.ii.2 (*PL* 45, 1621), and following on from the passage from Ecclesiasticus (15:14-18): 'Quid est autem, "Et reliquit illum in manu consilii sui", nisi, dimisit eum in possibilitate liberi arbitrii sui? In manu enim possibilitas intelligitur. Ipsa enim est prima gratia, qua primus homo stare potuisset, si servare mandata Domini voluisset.'

per opera humana acquiri. Et sic acquisitae sine caritate esse possunt, sicut fuerunt in multis gentilibus.'[13] Now, however, in Ia IIae.109, he is not so sure; for if *before* the Fall man was equal to his natural end by natural means ('per sua naturalia'), *after* the Fall even this eludes him. Certain things, like building houses, planting vineyards and the like ('sicut aedificare domos, plantare vineas, et alia huiusmodi'), are indeed still possible, but these, important as they are for man's well-being in the round, are matters of technical rather than moral concern, matters of moral concern requiring of him more than he himself can provide:

> natura hominis dupliciter potest considerari, uno modo, in sui integritate, sicut fuit in primo parente ante peccatum; alio modo, secundum quod est corrupta in nobis post peccatum primi parentis. Secundum autem utrumque statum, natura humana indiget auxilio divino ad faciendum vel volendum quodcumque bonum, sicut primo movente, ut dictum est. Sed in statu naturae integrae, quantum ad sufficientiam operativae virtutis, poterat homo per sua naturalia velle et operari bonum suae naturae proportionatum, quale est bonum virtutis acquisitae, non autem bonum superexcedens, quale est bonum virtutis infusae. Sed in statu naturae corruptae etiam deficit homo ab hoc quod secundum suam naturam potest, ut non possit totum huiusmodi bonum implere per sua naturalia. Quia tamen natura humana per peccatum non est totaliter corrupta, ut scilicet toto bono naturae privetur; potest quidem etiam in statu naturae corruptae, per virtutem suae naturae aliquod bonum particulare agere, sicut aedificare domos, plantare vineas, et alia huiusmodi; non tamen totum bonum sibi connaturale, ita quod in nullo deficiat.
>
> (*ST* Ia IIae.109.2 resp.)[14]

---

[13] it is possible by means of human works to acquire moral virtues, in so far as they produce good works that are directed to an end not surpassing the natural power of man; and when they are acquired thus, they can be without charity, even as they were in many of the gentiles.

[14] man's nature may be looked at in two ways: first, in its integrity, as it was in our first parent before sin; secondly, as it is corrupted in us after the sin of our first parent. Now in both states human nature needs the help of God as first mover to do or to wish any good whatsoever, as stated above [art. 1]. But in the state of integrity, as regards the sufficiency of the operative power, man by his natural endowments could wish and do the good proportionate to his nature, such as the good of acquired virtue; but not surpassing good, as the good of infused virtue. But in the state of corrupt nature, man falls short of what he could do by his nature, so that he is unable to fulfil it by his own natural powers. Yet because human nature is not altogether corrupted by sin, so as to be shorn of every natural good, even in the state of corrupted nature it can, by virtue of its natural endowments, work some particular good, such as building houses, planting vineyards, and the like; yet it cannot do all the good natural to it, so as to fall short in nothing.

Thus just as an invalid may have some movement of his own, Thomas goes on, there can even so be no healing without a physician ('Sicut homo infirmus potest per seipsum aliquem motum habere, non tamen perfecte potest moveri motu hominis sani, nisi sanetur auxilio medicinae'), at which point his theologization of the moral issue, its referral to grace as the *prius* of every significant inflexion of the spirit in the areas of right doing and of right being, is complete. And what applies in Article 2 on the willing and doing of good applies also in Article 4 on obedience to the law generally and to the gospel imperative in particular, where again it is a question of grace as a condition of fulfilment. Now obedience to the law, Thomas maintains, has two aspects to it, a material aspect relating to the *what* of obedience, to the precise nature of the obligation laid by the law upon those subject to it, and a psychological aspect relating to the *how* of obedience, to the mood or disposition of the one who obeys. If, then, materially or as regards the *what* of obedience, man in his innocence had no need of grace (his, at this stage, being an integral act of existence), psychologically or as regards the *how* of obedience he did, the *how* of obedience, both prior to and following the Fall, being a matter of grace as facilitative:

> Respondeo dicendum quod implere mandata legis contingit dupliciter. Uno modo, quantum ad substantiam operum, prout scilicet homo operatur iusta et fortia, et alia virtutis opera. Et hoc modo homo in statu naturae integrae potuit omnia mandata legis implere, alioquin non potuisset in statu illo non peccare, cum nihil aliud sit peccare quam transgredi divina mandata. Sed in statu naturae corruptae non potest homo implere omnia mandata divina sine gratia sanante. Alio modo possunt impleri mandata legis non solum quantum ad substantiam operis, sed etiam quantum ad modum agendi, ut scilicet ex caritate fiant. Et sic neque in statu naturae integrae, neque in statu naturae corruptae, potest homo implere absque gratia legis mandata. Unde Augustinus, in libro de Corrept. et Grat., cum dixisset quod sine gratia nullum prorsus bonum homines faciunt, subdit, "non solum ut, monstrante ipsa quid faciendum sit, sciant; verum etiam ut, praestante ipsa, faciant cum dilectione quod sciunt". Indigent insuper in utroque statu auxilio Dei moventis ad mandata implenda, ut dictum est.

> (*ST* Ia IIae.109.4 resp.)[15]

---

[15] I answer that there are two ways of fulfilling the commandments of the Law. The first regards the substance of the works, as when a man does works of justice, fortitude, and of other virtues. And in this way man in the state of perfect nature could fulfil all the commandments of the Law; otherwise he would have been unable not to sin in that state, since to sin is nothing other than to transgress the divine commandments. But in the

Here too, therefore, commitment at one level of consciousness to the viability of the human project as such, to what man as man may accomplish *ex naturalibus* on the plane of right being and right doing, is at another level resolved in a sense of the priority of grace as enabling in respect of the whole.

2. The basic question here is the relationship within the totality of human experience of the divine and the human initiative, of what God does for man and of what man does for himself. Inasmuch as these things are understood to relate extrinsically, in terms of the latter as made possible by the former as radically other than self, then the viability of that being, its power in any sense or degree to function from out of itself, is called into question. In so far, however, as they are understood to relate intrinsically, in terms of the coalescence of human and divine willing at the core of existence, then the human project commends itself from out of itself, from out of its adequacy to the business in hand. Now here we must be careful, for Thomas's too is a species of intrinsicism, for in thinking about grace and the nature of its presence to the individual as graced, he is inclined to see it in terms of something placed in the soul, of a superadded principle of existence apt from within to quicken it in the interests of its supernatural finality. Eloquent in their expression of this idea – of grace as a matter of superadditionality – are, for example, these lines from the *Prima secundae* at 110.2 resp., secure in their sense of grace as a matter of infused formality and of this as the condition of every morally and eschatologically significant inflexion of the spirit in man:

> Creaturis autem naturalibus sic providet ut non solum moveat eas ad actus naturales, sed etiam largiatur eis formas et virtutes quasdam, quae sunt principia actuum, ut secundum seipsas inclinentur ad huiusmodi motus. Et sic motus quibus a Deo moventur, fiunt creaturis connaturales et faciles; secundum illud Sap. VIII, *et disponit*

state of corrupted nature man cannot fulfil all the divine commandments without healing grace. Secondly, the commandments of the law can be fulfilled, not merely as regards the substance of the act, but also as regards the mode of acting, i.e. its being done out of charity. And in this way, neither in the state of perfect nature, nor in the state of corrupt nature can man fulfil the commandments of the law without grace. Hence, Augustine having stated that without grace men can do no good whatever, adds: 'Not only do they know by its light what to do, but by its help they do lovingly what they know' [*De corrept. et grat.* ii]. Beyond this, in both states they need the help of God's motion in order to fulfil the commandments. Augustine himself, in the *De corrept. et gratia* at ii.3, has: 'Intellegenda est enim gratia Dei per Iesum Christum Dominum nostrum, qua sola homines liberantur a malo, et sine qua nullum prorsus sive cogitando, sive volendo et amando, sive agendo faciunt bonum: non solum ut monstrante ipsa quid faciendum sit sciant, verum etiam ut praestante ipsa faciant cum dilectione quod sciunt.'

omnia suaviter. Multo igitur magis illis quos movet ad consequendum bonum supernaturale aeternum, infundit aliquas formas seu qualitates supernaturales, secundum quas suaviter et prompte ab ipso moveantur ad bonum aeternum consequendum. Et sic donum gratiae qualitas quaedam est.[16]

---

[16] Now he so provides for natural creatures, that not merely does he move them to their natural acts, but he bestows upon them certain forms and powers, which are the principles of acts, in order that they may of themselves be inclined to these movements, and thus the movements whereby they are moved by God become natural and easy to creatures, according to Wisdom 8 [v. 1]: 'she orders all things sweetly.' Much more, therefore, does he infuse into such as he moves towards the acquisition of supernatural good, certain forms or supernatural qualities, whereby they may be moved by him sweetly and promptly to acquire eternal good; and thus the gift of grace is a quality. Cf. *ScG* III.cl. 3 and 6: 'Oportet autem hanc gratiam aliquid in homine gratificato esse, quasi quandam formam et perfectionem ipsius. Quod enim in aliquem finem dirigitur, oportet quod habeat continuum ordinem in ipsum: nam movens continue mutat quousque mobile per motum finem sortiatur. Cum igitur auxilio divinae gratiae homo dirigatur in ultimum finem, ut ostensum est, oportet quod continue homo isto auxilio potiatur, quousque ad finem perveniat. Hoc autem non esset si praedictum auxilium participaret homo secundum aliquem motum aut passionem, et non secundum aliquam formam manentem, et quasi quiescentem in ipso: motus enim et passio talis non esset in homine nisi quando actu converteretur in finem; quod non continue ab homine agitur, ut praecipue patet in dormientibus. Est ergo gratia gratum faciens aliqua forma et perfectio in homine manens, etiam quando non operatur ... Oportet quod homo ad ultimum finem per proprias operationes perveniat. Unumquodque autem operatur secundum propriam formam. Oportet igitur, ad hoc quod homo perducatur in ultimum finem per proprias operationes, quod superaddatur ei aliqua forma, ex qua eius operationes efficaciam aliquam accipiant promerendi ultimum finem.' R. W. Gleason, S.J., *Grace* (London and New York: Sheed and Ward, 1962), p. 132: 'Since this gift of grace is added to a nature already substantially complete, we know that, philosophically speaking, it cannot be a substance but must be an accident. We know also from revelation that this created grace *inheres* in the soul, as Trent teaches, is capable of increase, and is therefore an absolute accident. We may conclude, therefore, that grace is a created, spiritual, absolute, qualitative accident, an accident which inheres in the soul, empowering the soul to supernatural acts, and which bears a proportion to man's end – the happiness proper to God, the beatific vision of heaven' (italics original).

On Thomas and grace (in addition to Gleason), R. Garrigou-Lagrange, O.P., *La Prédestination des saints et la grâce: doctrine de Saint Thomas comparée aux autres systèmes théologiques* (Paris: Desclée de Brouwer, 1936); idem, *Grace: Commentary on the* Summa Theologica *of St Thomas, Ia IIae, 109-14*, trans. from the Commentarius of 1947 (Rome: Pontificium Institutum Internationale 'Angelicum') by the Dominican Nuns of the Corpus Christi Monastery, Menlo Park, California (St. Louis: B. Herder, 1952); B. J. F. Lonergan, S.J., 'St Thomas's Thought on Gratia Operans', *Theological Studies* 2 (1941), 289-324; 3 (1942), 69-88, 375-402 and 533-78; idem, *Grace and Freedom. Operative Grace in the Thought of St Thomas Aquinas*, ed. F. E. Crowe and R. M. Doran (Toronto: University of Toronto Press, 2000; originally 1971); H. Bouillard, *Conversion et grâce chez s. Thomas d'Aquin: étude historique* (Paris: Aubier, 1944); M. Flick, *L'attimo della giustificazione secondo S. Tommaso* (Rome: Apud aedes Universitatis Gregorianiae, 1947); P. Wehbrink (trans.), *Thomas von Aquin. Die menschliche Willensfreiheit* (Düsseldorf: L. Schwann, 1954; selections

In so far, then, as it is a question of grace as incoming and thus as inclining the soul from deep within itself to its sublime finality we must speak of the immanentism of Thomist grace-theology. But – and this now is the point – to read over this and similar passages both in and beyond the *Summa theologiae* is to become aware that immanence is not the sole nor even the dominant model in Thomas's mind; for *immanence*, as a means of conceiving and of expressing the relationship of grace and nature within the economy of this or that instance of specifically human being, at once gives way to *movement* as a way of seeing and exploring this issue, to a sense of that being as constrained *ab extra* to its proper good; so, in the 110.2 passage just quoted, the 'ut non solum *moveat* eas ad actus naturales' moment of the argument, the 'Et sic *motus* quibus a Deo *moventur*' moment, the 'illis quos *movet* ad consequendum bonum supernaturale aeternum' moment, and the 'prompte ab ipso *moveantur* ad bonum aeternum consequendum' moment, each alike turning on a sense of grace as a matter, less of coalescence, than of coercion in respect of man's proper good as man. And this, notable as it is in 110.2, is by and large the way with the grace treatise generally of the *Prima secundae*, Thomas's sense of what needs to be said here, and certainly of how it needs to be said, being causal and kinetic rather than immanentist or inwardly operative in kind. Take, for example, as further evidence of this situation, these lines from 113.6 on the question of justification as that whereby the lower powers of the soul are by grace ordered to the higher powers, and the higher powers of the soul to God himself as to their proper end.[17] There are, Thomas says, four things involved in the justification or making righteous of the

from the *Quaestiones disputatae de malo and de veritate* with an introduction by G. Siewerth); C. Ernst, O.P. (ed. and comm.), St Thomas Aquinas. *Summa theologiae*, vol. 30 (*The Gospel of Grace*. 1a 2a. 106-114) (London: Eyre and Spottiswoode, 1972); J. P. Wawrykow, *God's Grace and Human Action. 'Merit' in the Theology of Thomas Aquinas* (Notre Dame, Ind.: University of Notre Dame Press, 1995); idem, 'Grace', in R. Van Nieuwenhove and J. P. Wawrykow (eds), *The Theology of Thomas Aquinas* (Notre Dame, Ind.: University of Notre Dame Press, 2005), pp. 192-221; J. F. Wippel, 'Natur und Gnade (S.th. I-II, qq. 109-114)', in A. Speer (ed.), *Thomas von Aquin: Die Summa theologiae. Werkinterpretationen* (Berlin: de Gruyter, 2005), pp. 246-70. More generally on grace theology (but with reference still to Thomas), J. Auer, *Die Entwicklung der Gnadenlehre in der Hochscholastik*, 2 vols (Freiburg: Herder, 1951); N. P. Williams, The *Grace of God* (London: Hodder and Stoughton, 1966, originally 1930).

[17] *ST* Ia IIae.113.1 resp.: 'Alio modo dicitur iustitia prout importat rectitudinem quandam ordinis in ipsa interiori dispositione hominis, prout scilicet supremum hominis subditur Deo, et inferiores vires animae subduntur supremae, scilicet rationi.' In addition to Bouillard and Flick (previous note), M. G. Lawler, 'Grace and Free Will in Justification: a Textual Study in Aquinas', *The Thomist* 35 (1971), 601-30; A. E. McGrath, *Iustitia Dei. A History of the Christian Doctrine of Justification*, vol. 1 (*The Beginnings to the Reformation*) (Cambridge: Cambridge University Press, 1986), pp. 78 ff.

wicked, namely, an in-breathing of grace, a turning of the will towards God, a turning of the will from sin, and a setting aside of guilt, the process as a whole, however, lending itself to contemplation under the aspect of causality, of one thing's being moved by another until at last there is nothing more to be moved:

> quatuor enumerantur quae requiruntur ad iustificationem impii, scilicet gratiae infusio; *motus* liberi arbitrii in Deum per fidem; et *motus* liberi arbitrii in peccatum; et remissio culpae. Cuius ratio est quia, sicut dictum est, iustificatio est quidam *motus* quo anima *movetur* a Deo a statu culpae in statum iustitiae. In quolibet autem *motu* quo aliquid ab altero *movetur*, tria requiruntur, primo quidem, *motio ipsius moventis*; secundo, *motus mobilis*; et tertio, consummatio *motus*, sive perventio ad finem. Ex parte igitur *motionis* divinae, accipitur gratiae infusio; ex parte vero liberi arbitrii *moti*, accipiuntur duo *motus* ipsius, secundum recessum a termino a quo, et accessum ad terminum ad quem; consummatio autem, sive perventio ad terminum huius *motus*, importatur per remissionem culpae, in hoc enim iustificatio consummatur.

> (*ST* Ia IIae.113.6 resp.)[18]

But that is not all, for his preoccupation with grace as a matter of movement affects Thomas's sense, not only of justification as the pivotal point of human experience under its soteriological aspect, but of preparation and of perseverance as leading up to and following on from justification thus understood.[19] As far, then, as the moment of preparation

---

[18] there are four things which are accounted to be necessary for the justification of the ungodly, namely the infusion of grace, the *movement* of free will towards God by faith, the *movement* of free will in the matter of sin, and the remission of sin. The reason for this is that, as stated above [art. 1], the justification of the ungodly is a *movement* whereby the soul is *moved* by God from a state of sin to a state of justice. Now in the *movement* whereby one thing is *moved* by another, three things are required: first, the *motion of the mover*; secondly, the *movement of the moved*; thirdly, the consummation of the *movement*, or the attainment of the end. On the part of the divine *motion*, there is the infusion of grace; on the part of the free will which is *moved*, there are two *movements* – of departure from the term 'whence', and of approach to the term 'whereto'; but the consummation of the *movement* or the attainment of the end of the *movement* is implied in the remission of sin; for in this is the justification of the ungodly completed.

[19] A. E. McGrath, 'The Influence of Aristotelian Physics upon St Thomas Aquinas's Discussion of the "Processus Iustificationis"', *Recherches de théologie ancienne et médiévale* 51 (1984), 223-29. In Thomas himself, *ST* Ia IIae.110.2 resp. 'Dictum est autem supra quod dupliciter ex gratuita Dei voluntate homo adiuvatur. Uno modo, inquantum anima hominis movetur a Deo ad aliquid cognoscendum vel volendum vel agendum. Et hoc modo ipse gratuitus effectus in homine non est qualitas, sed motus quidam animae, actus enim moventis in moto est motus, ut dicitur in III Physic.'; 113.8 ad 3: 'sicut philosophus

is concerned, there can, Thomas thinks, be no such thing short of the grace whereby the soul is inspired in the first place to embark on the way of spiritual renewal. To be more exact, if the soul's preparation for the grace of justification is nothing but preparation for *habitual* grace as a steady disposition of the spirit towards God, then we need to be thinking here, not of a still further act of habitual gracing (for otherwise we would be committed to infinite regression), but of something closer to what we would now call a form of *actual* gracing, a transient efflux of grace designed to set the whole thing in motion:

> duplex est praeparatio voluntatis humanae ad bonum. Una quidem qua praeparatur ad bene operandum et ad Deo fruendum. Et talis praeparatio voluntatis non potest fieri sine habituali gratiae dono, quod sit principium operis meritorii, ut dictum est. Alio modo potest intelligi praeparatio voluntatis humanae ad consequendum ipsum gratiae habitualis donum. Ad hoc autem quod praeparet se ad susceptionem huius doni, non oportet praesupponere aliquod aliud donum habituale in anima, quia sic procederetur in infinitum, sed oportet praesupponi aliquod auxilium gratuitum Dei interius animam moventis, sive inspirantis bonum propositum ... Hoc autem est praeparare se ad gratiam, quasi ad Deum converti, sicut ille qui habet oculum aversum a lumine solis, per hoc se praeparat ad recipiendum lumen solis, quod oculos suos convertit versus solem. Unde patet quod homo non potest se praeparare ad lumen gratiae suscipiendum, nisi per auxilium gratuitum Dei interius moventis.
>
> (*ST* Ia IIae.109.6 resp.)[20]

dicit, in II Physic., in motibus animi omnino praecedit motus in principium speculationis, vel in finem actionis, sed in exterioribus motibus remotio impedimenti praecedit assecutionem finis. Et quia motus liberi arbitrii est motus animi, prius naturae ordine movetur in Deum sicut in finem, quam ad removendum impedimentum peccati', etc.

[20] the preparation of the human will for good is twofold: the first, whereby it is prepared to operate rightly and to enjoy God; and this preparation of the will cannot take place without the habitual gift of grace, which is the principle of meritorious works, as stated above [art. 5]. There is a second way in which the human will may be taken to be prepared for the gift of habitual grace itself. Now in order that man may prepare himself to receive this gift, it is not necessary to presuppose any further habitual gift in the soul, otherwise we should go on to infinity. But we must presuppose a gratuitous gift of God, who moves the soul inwardly or inspires the good wish ... Now to prepare oneself for grace is, as it were, to be turned to God; just as, whoever has his eyes turned away from the light of the sun, prepares himself to receive the sun's light by turning his eyes towards the sun. Hence it is clear that man cannot prepare himself to receive the light of grace except by the gratuitous help of God moving him inwardly. On actual gracing and the Tridentine and post-Tridentine development generally of Thomist positions in grace theology see especially, B. J. F. Lonergan, S.J., *Grace and Freedom. Operative Grace in the Thought of St Thomas Aquinas* (note 16 above), especially pp. 117-38.

The moment of preparation, meaning by this the moment in which the soul first contemplates turning towards God as the first and final cause of all turning in human experience, is, therefore, a matter of special or extraordinary gracing, habitual grace as a matter of God's steady presence to the individual presupposing a special or dedicated movement of divine assistance ('aliquod auxilium gratuitum Dei') as its prior condition. And this, as a general proposition, is confirmed in 112.3 by way of Thomas's particular take on the old adage to the effect that 'to anyone who does what he can, God does not deny grace' ('facienti quod in se est, Deus non denegat gratiam'), a formula presupposing the idea that man *can* actually do what he has it in himself to do, that he *is* in some degree empowered to his own good, this being something that God will always seek to honour. That, at any rate, is the substance of the first 'objection' in this article, decisive in its sense of God's not only honouring, but, as a matter of elementary justice, of his *having* to honour the efforts of those doing their best:

> Videtur quod ex necessitate detur gratia se praeparanti ad gratiam, vel facienti quod in se est. Quia super illud Rom. V, 'iustificati ex fide pacem habeamus' etc., dicit Glossa, 'Deus recipit eum qui ad se confugit, aliter esset in eo iniquitas'. Sed impossibile est in Deo iniquitatem esse. Ergo impossibile est quod Deus non recipiat eum qui ad se confugit. Ex necessitate igitur gratiam assequitur.
>
> (*ST* Ia IIae.112.3 obj. 1)[21]

Thomas, however, committed as he is in the *Summa* to a high-theological account of this matter, to a steady referral of free will to grace as the ground and guarantee of its efficacy, is not persuaded. What we have to say, therefore, is (*a*) that grace does not, and cannot, follow necessarily upon a movement of human willing, since the gift of grace exceeds every kind of preparation man can possibly make for it, and (*b*) that if a man does what he can, and this in such a way that God honours him for it, then this must be looked upon as yet a further instance of his prior intentionality for that man, his gracing of him, therefore, being a matter, not of necessity, but of infallibility, as nothing but the outworking of what God had it in mind to do all along:

---

[21] It would seem that grace is necessarily given to whoever prepares himself for grace, or to whoever does what he can, because, on Romans 5:1 – 'Being justified ... by faith, let us have peace' etc. – the Gloss says 'God welcomes whoever flies to him, otherwise there would be injustice with him'. But it is impossible for injustice to be with God. Therefore, it is impossible for God not to welcome whoever takes refuge in him. Hence he receives grace of necessity.

Respondeo dicendum quod, sicut supra dictum est, praeparatio ad
hominis gratiam est a Deo sicut a movente, a libero autem arbitrio
sicut a moto. Potest igitur praeparatio dupliciter considerari. Uno
quidem modo, secundum quod est a libero arbitrio. Et secundum hoc,
nullam necessitatem habet ad gratiae consecutionem, quia donum
gratiae excedit omnem praeparationem virtutis humanae. Alio modo
potest considerari secundum quod est a Deo movente. Et tunc habet
necessitatem ad id ad quod ordinatur a Deo, non quidem coactionis,
sed infallibilitatis, quia intentio Dei deficere non potest; secundum
quod et Augustinus dicit, in libro de Praedest. Sanct., 'quod per
beneficia Dei certissime liberantur quicumque liberantur'. Unde si
ex intentione Dei moventis est quod homo cuius cor movet, gratiam
consequatur, infallibiliter ipsam consequitur; secundum illud Ioan.
VI, 'omnis qui audivit a patre et didicit, venit ad me'.

(*ST* Ia IIae.112.3 resp.)[22]

---

[22] I answer that, as stated above [art. 2], man's preparation for grace is from God as
mover and from free will as moved. Hence the preparation may be looked at in two ways:
first, as it is from free will, and thus there is no necessity that it should obtain grace, since
the gift of grace exceeds every preparation of human power. But it may be considered,
secondly, as it is from God the mover, and thus it has a necessity – not indeed of coercion,
but of infallibility – as regards what it is ordained to by God, since God's intention cannot
fail, according to the saying of Augustine in his book on the Predestination of the Saints
to the effect that 'by God's good gifts whoever is liberated, is most certainly liberated' [*De
dono persev.* xiv]. Hence if God intends, while moving, that the one whose heart he moves
should attain to grace, he will infallibly attain to it, according to John 6 [v. 45]: 'Every
one who has heard of the Father, and who has learned, comes to me.' McGrath (note 17
above), p. 86, glosses as follows: 'Whilst Thomas continues to insist upon the necessity
of a preparation for justification, and continues to discuss this in terms of man's *quod in se
est*, he now considers that this preparation lies outside man's purely natural powers. As
he now understands the matter, man is not even capable of his full *natural* good, let alone
the *supernatural* good required of him for justification. The preparation for justification
is itself a work of grace, in which God is active and man passive. For Thomas, the axiom
facienti quod in se est now assumes the meaning that God will not deny grace to the man
who does his best, in so far as he is moved by God to do this: "Cum dicitur homo facere
quod in se est, dicitur hoc esse in potestate hominis secundum quod est motus a Deo."'
See, however, as evidence, perhaps, of a certain unease at this point, 114.3 resp. on the
notion of merit *de congruo* in respect of a man's living by his lights: 'opus meritorium
hominis dupliciter considerari potest, uno modo, secundum quod procedit ex libero
arbitrio; alio modo, secundum quod procedit ex gratia spiritus sancti. Si consideretur
secundum substantiam operis, et secundum quod procedit ex libero arbitrio, sic non
potest ibi esse condignitas, propter maximam inaequalitatem. Sed est ibi congruitas,
propter quandam aequalitatem proportionis, videtur enim congruum ut homini operanti
secundum suam virtutem, Deus recompenset secundum excellentiam suae virtutis.' R.-
C. Dhont, *Le Problème de la préparation à la grâce. Débuts de l'école franciscaine* (Paris: Editions
franciscaines, 1946).

Reluctant, then, in his pursuit of a grace-theological position to make
any concession to the efficacy of human willing in and for itself, Thomas
manages to turn upside down a formula as gentle as it is generous in
inspiration, a formula inclined to see in every integral movement of the
spirit a moment of salvific significance. True, free will as such, as a power
of the rational soul to moral determination, is not abolished, and neither
can it be, for free will as the principle in man of accountability is part of
what and how he actually *is*. But within the economy of the moral and
religious life as a whole it stands to be contemplated in terms of the divine
initiative by which it is moved from beforehand, herein alone lying its
power to make any difference.[23]

What applies, moreover, at the point of preparation or of man's
preliminary turning towards God, applies also in respect of his persisting
in the way of righteousness, where even as graced habitually he is
dependent on a continual process of actual gracing as the condition of
his at last coming home. The key article here is Ia IIae.109.10, where in
the circumstances we might have been forgiven for expecting an easing
of the argumentative line, a sweetening of the severity of it all; for while
preparation as preliminary in respect of everything coming next by way

[23] For an earlier and alternative view of the 'facienti quod in se est' issue, II *Sent.*
28.1.4 resp.: 'Quidam enim dicunt, quod nullus potest se ad gratiam gratum facientem
praeparare, nisi per aliquod lumen menti infusum, quod est donum gratiae gratis datae.
Istud autem non videtur conveniens: quia praeparatio quae est ad gratiam, non est per
actus qui sint ipsi gratiae aequandi aequalitate proportionis, sicut meritum aequatur
praemio; et ideo non oportet ut actus quibus homo se ad gratiam habendam praeparat sint
naturam humanam excedentes: sicut enim natura humana se habet in potentia materiali
ad gratiam, ita actus virtutum naturalium se habent ut dispositiones materiales ad ipsam;
unde non exigitur ad hoc ut homo ad gratiam se praeparet, aliquod aliud lumen gratiae
praecedens. Et praeterea secundum hoc esset abire in infinitum: quia illud etiam lumen
gratiae gratis datae non datur alicui nisi qui ad illud recipiendum se praeparavit; alias
omnibus daretur: quod non potest intelligi; nisi forte gratia gratis data dicatur naturale
lumen rationis, quod pertinet ad bona naturalia, et non ad gratuita, nisi large accepta.
Si autem praeparatione indiget talis gratia gratis data, tunc redibit quaestio de ista
praeparatione, utrum in eam possit homo ex se, vel non: et sic vel abiretur in infinitum,
vel erit devenire ad aliquam gratiam ad quam homo per se praeparare potest se. Sed non
est ratio efficax quare hoc magis in una gratia sit quam in alia. Et ideo aliis consentiendo
dicimus, quod ad gratiam gratum facientem habendam ex solo libero arbitrio se homo
potest praeparare: faciendo enim quod in se est, gratiam a Deo consequitur. Hoc
autem solum in nobis est quod in potestate liberi arbitrii constitutum est.' Among the
ancients, Origen, *Contra Celsum* vii.2; Irenaeus, *Adv. haer.* IV.xxxix.2, etc., and, among
the moderns, J. Rivière, 'Quelques antécédents patristiques de la formule "facienti quod
in se est"', *Revue des sciences religieuses* 7 (1927), 93-97; A. M. Landgraf, *Dogmengeschichte der
Frühscholastik*, 8 vols (Regensburg: Friedrich Pustet, 1952-56), vol. 1, part 1, pp. 249-64;
H. A. Oberman, '"Facientibus quod in se est Deus non denegat gratiam"; Robert Holcot,
O.P. and the Beginning of Luther's Theology', *Harvard Theological Review* 55 (1962), 317-
42; A. McGrath, *Iustitia Dei* (note 17 above), pp. 83 ff.

of justification may reasonably be said to involve a movement of grace as facilitative, *perseverance*, as belonging to a subsequent phase of the soul's journey into God, might de deemed more self-sufficient, more properly adequate to the matter in hand. But again Thomas will have none of it, for though by habitual grace man is healed and made adequate to his high calling, he still needs God's special assistance in keeping him safe along the way ('ipsum dirigente et protegente'):

> perseverantia tripliciter dicitur. Quandoque enim significat habitum mentis per quem homo firmiter stat, ne removeatur ab eo quod est secundum virtutem, per tristitias irruentes, ut sic se habeat perseverantia ad tristitias sicut continentia ad concupiscentias et delectationes ut philosophus dicit, in VII Ethic. Alio modo potest dici perseverantia habitus quidam secundum quem habet homo propositum perseverandi in bono usque in finem. Et utroque istorum modorum, perseverantia simul cum gratia infunditur sicut et continentia et ceterae virtutes. Alio modo dicitur perseverantia continuatio quaedam boni usque ad finem vitae. Et ad talem perseverantiam habendam homo in gratia constitutus non quidem indiget aliqua alia habituali gratia, sed divino auxilio ipsum dirigente et protegente contra tentationum impulsus, sicut ex praecedenti quaestione apparet. Et ideo postquam aliquis est iustificatus per gratiam, necesse habet a Deo petere praedictum perseverantiae donum, ut scilicet custodiatur a malo usque ad finem vitae. Multis enim datur gratia, quibus non datur perseverare in gratia.
>
> (*ST* Ia IIae.109.10 resp.)[24]

a passage to which, as serving to point up the specifically Peripatetic moment of the argument, its accountability to the dynamics of movement as described by Aristotle in the *Physics*, we might add these lines from the *Contra gentiles* at III.clv.5:

---

[24] perseverance is taken in three ways. First, to signify a habit of the mind whereby a man stands steadfastly, lest he be moved by the assault of sadness from what is virtuous. And thus perseverance is to sadness as continence is to concupiscence and pleasure, as the Philosopher says in the seventh book of the *Ethics* [1150a9 ff.]. Secondly, perseverance may be called a habit, whereby a man has the purpose of persevering in good unto the end. And in both these ways perseverance is infused together with grace, even as continence and the other virtues are. Thirdly, perseverance is called the abiding in good to the end of life. And in order to have this perseverance man does not, indeed, need another habitual grace, but he needs divine assistance to guide and to guard him against the attacks of the passions, as appears from the preceding article. And hence after anyone has been justified by grace, he still needs to beseech God for the aforesaid gift of perseverance, that he may be kept from evil till the end of his life. For to many grace is given to whom perseverance in grace is not given.

Si sunt plura agentia successive, quorum scilicet unum agat post actionem alterius; continuitas actionis istorum non potest causari ex aliquo uno ipsorum, quia nullum eorum semper agit; nec ex omnibus, quia non simul agunt; unde oportet quod causetur ab aliquo superiori quod semper agat: sicut philosophus probat, in VIII Phys., quod continuitas generationis in animalibus causatur ab aliquo superiori sempiterno. Ponamus autem aliquem perseverantem in bono. In eo igitur sunt multi motus liberi arbitrii tendentes in bonum, sibi invicem succedentes usque ad finem. Huius igitur continuationis boni, quod est perseverantia, non potest esse causa aliquis istorum motuum: quia nullus eorum semper durat. Nec omnes simul: quia non simul sunt, non possunt igitur simul aliquid causare. Relinquitur ergo quod ista continuatio causetur ab aliquo superiori. Indiget igitur homo auxilio superioris gratiae ad perseverandum in bono.[25]

Once again, then, there is a steady referral of the ordinary or connatural powers of the soul – of, in this case, the power of the soul to persistence – to God himself as the mainstay of human nature in the inadequacy of that nature. If, therefore, in one part of his being, Thomas's is a commitment to the notion of grace as, by way of its superadditionality, an intrinsically operative principle of righteousness, then in an alternative inflexion of the spirit he is happy to settle for the causal as distinct from the co-immanent as a way of seeing and setting up the grace-theological issue.

[25] Moreover, suppose that there are several agents in succession, such that one of them acts after the action of another; the continuation of the action of these agents cannot be caused by any one of them, for no one of them acts forever; nor can it be caused by all of them, since they do not act together. Consequently, the continuity must be caused by some higher agent that always acts, just as the Philosopher proves, in Physics VIII [vi; 258b10 ff.], that the continuity of the generative process in animals is caused by some higher, external agent. Now, let us suppose the case of someone who is persevering in the good. There are, then, in his case many movements of free choice tending toward the good, successively following each other up to the end. So, for this continuation in the good, which is perseverance, no one of these movements can be the cause, since none of them lasts forever. Nor can all of them together, for they are not together, and so they cannot cause something together. It remains, then, that this continuation is caused by some higher being. Therefore, man needs the help of higher grace to persevere in the good. Similarly, ibid. 6: 'Si sint multa ordinata ad unum finem, totus ordo eorum quousque pervenerint ad finem, est a primo agente dirigente in finem. In eo autem qui perseverat in bono, sunt multi motus et multae actiones pertingentes ad unum finem. Oportet igitur quod totus ordo istorum motuum et actionum causetur a primo dirigente in finem. Ostensum est autem quod per auxilium divinae gratiae diriguntur in ultimum finem. Igitur per auxilium divinae gratiae est totus ordo et continuatio bonorum operum in eo qui perseverat in bono.' J. P. Wawrykow, '"Perseverance" in 13th-century Theology: the Augustinian Contribution', *Augustinian Studies* 22 (1991), 125-40.

The consequences of this referral of the human to the divine initiative for the question of merit are far-reaching, though here too there is in Thomas an element of ambiguity – a hint of misgiving even – about his delivering himself in quite the way he does to the sombre substance of Augustine's anti-Pelagian spirituality. To begin with, then, all is well with man and his proper deserving, Thomas's, on the threshold of the *Prima secundae*, being a sense even of the final vision as in some degree merited, as accruing to the individual by way of his well doing. True, the angels or separate substances have an easier time of it in that theirs, in the immateriality of their being, is a relatively speaking untroubled implementation of self, whereas man in his psychosomaticity is forever caught up in a conflict of willing, in a constraining of the lower to the higher parts of his nature; but this, confirming as it does the difficulty of the moral situation in man, confirms too the meritoriousness of it all, the completeness of man's deserving as man:

> Habere autem beatitudinem naturaliter est solius Dei. Unde solius Dei proprium est quod ad beatitudinem non moveatur per aliquam operationem praecedentem. Cum autem beatitudo excedat omnem naturam creatam, nulla pura creatura convenienter beatitudinem consequitur absque motu operationis, per quam tendit in ipsam. Sed angelus, qui est superior ordine naturae quam homo, consecutus est eam, ex ordine divinae sapientiae, uno motu operationis meritoriae, ut in primo expositum est. Homines autem consequuntur ipsam multis motibus operationum, qui merita dicuntur.
>
> (*ST* Ia IIae.5.7 resp.)[26]

Thus far, then, merit is meaningful, and, in its meaningfulness, enters into the soteriological scheme of things. But by the time we reach the other end of the *Prima secundae* the outlook is bleaker, such merit as man has being a matter of the grace by which it is everywhere inaugurated and sustained. There are, Thomas thinks, two questions here, the first turning on whether man can from out of himself merit eternal life, and the second on whether he can from out of himself merit anything at all. As far as the first is concerned, Thomas has no doubt, man as man being in no position to merit eternal life (*a*) because of its character as surpassing all that he is

---

[26] To have happiness naturally belongs to God alone. Therefore it belongs to God alone not to be moved towards happiness by any previous operation. Now since happiness surpasses every created nature, no pure creature can appropriately gain happiness, without the movement of operation, whereby it tends thereto. But the angel, who is above man in the natural order, obtained it, according to the order of divine wisdom, by one movement of a meritorious work, as was explained in the first part [qu. 62, art. 5]; whereas man obtains it by many movements of works which are called merits.

able to do and even to imagine unaided, and (*b*) because of his inveterate sinfulness, each of these things requiring a remedy – namely additionality and absolution – solely in the gift of God:

> Vita autem aeterna est quoddam bonum excedens proportionem naturae creatae, quia etiam excedit cognitionem et desiderium eius, secundum illud I ad Cor. II, 'nec oculus vidit, nec auris audivit, nec in cor hominis ascendit'. Et inde est quod nulla natura creata est sufficiens principium actus meritorii vitae aeternae, nisi superaddatur aliquod supernaturale donum, quod gratia dicitur. Si vero loquamur de homine sub peccato existente, additur cum hac secunda ratio, propter impedimentum peccati. Cum enim peccatum sit quaedam Dei offensa excludens a vita aeterna, ut patet per supradicta; nullus in statu peccati existens potest vitam aeternam mereri, nisi prius Deo reconcilietur, dimisso peccato, quod fit per gratiam.
>
> (*ST* Ia IIae.114.2 resp.)[27]

Now for the purpose of confirming this general position we need with Thomas to draw a distinction between *condign merit* or absolute worthiness (*meritum de condigno*) and *congruous merit* or relative worthiness (*meritum de congruo*). Condignly, there can be no question of man's meriting eternal life from out of himself (*ex naturalibus*), for eternal life is something wholly exceeding his power of willing. Inasmuch as he merits eternal life *ex condigno*, he merits it by way only of the Holy Spirit as fitting him for life everlasting.[28] But there is here room for manoeuvre in that, though there can be no question of man's meriting eternal life condignly, he may,

---

[27] Now everlasting life is a good exceeding the proportion of created nature; since it exceeds its knowledge and desire, according to 1 Corinthians 2 [v. 9]: 'Eye hath not seen, nor ear heard, neither has it entered into the heart of man.' And hence it is that no created nature is a sufficient principle of an act meritorious of eternal life, unless there is added a supernatural gift, which we call grace. But if we speak of man as existing in sin, a second reason is added to this, namely the impediment of sin. For since sin is an offence against God, excluding us from eternal life, as is clear from what has been said above [qu. 71, art. 6; qu. 113, art. 2], no one existing in a state of mortal sin can merit eternal life unless first he be reconciled to God, through his sin being forgiven, which is brought about by grace.

[28] *ST* Ia IIae. 114. 3 resp.: 'Si autem loquamur de opere meritorio secundum quod procedit ex gratia spiritus sancti, sic est meritorium vitae aeternae ex condigno. Sic enim valor meriti attenditur secundum virtutem spiritus sancti moventis nos in vitam aeternam; secundum illud Ioan. IV, "fiet in eo fons aquae salientis in vitam aeternam". Attenditur etiam pretium operis secundum dignitatem gratiae, per quam homo, consors factus divinae naturae, adoptatur in filium Dei, cui debetur hereditas ex ipso iure adoptionis, secundum illud Rom. VIII, "si filii, et heredes".' J. P. Wawrykow, 'On the Purpose of "Merit" in the Theology of Thomas Aquinas', *Medieval Philosophy and Theology* 2 (1992), 97-116; idem, *God's Grace and Human Action. 'Merit' in the Theology of Thomas Aquinas* (note 16 above).

if he does his best, be said to merit it congruously, by way of a certain proportionality, inequality, therefore, subsisting still, but not in such a way as to abolish all deserving whatever:

> opus meritorium hominis dupliciter considerari potest, uno modo, secundum quod procedit ex libero arbitrio; alio modo, secundum quod procedit ex gratia spiritus sancti. Si consideretur secundum substantiam operis, et secundum quod procedit ex libero arbitrio, sic non potest ibi esse condignitas, propter maximam inaequalitatem. Sed est ibi congruitas, propter quandam aequalitatem proportionis; videtur enim congruum ut homini operanti secundum suam virtutem, Deus recompenset secundum excellentiam suae virtutis.
>
> (*ST* Ia IIae.114.3 resp.)[29]

To this extent, then, Thomas's is a nod in the direction of deserving. But the spirit of accommodation does not last long, for, strictly speaking, Thomas tells us, all merit flows from charity, and charity in turn flows from God, the causal chain, therefore, brooking no interruption or qualification in favour of anything approaching human deserving. First, then, on the referability of merit to charity as to its first and final cause, we have these lines from the closing phase of the *Prima secundae*:

> sicut ex dictis accipi potest, humanus actus habet rationem merendi ex duobus, primo quidem et principaliter, ex divina ordinatione, secundum quod actus dicitur esse meritorius illius boni ad quod homo divinitus ordinatur; secundo vero, ex parte liberi arbitrii, inquantum scilicet homo habet prae ceteris creaturis ut per se agat, voluntarie agens. Et quantum ad utrumque, principalitas meriti penes caritatem consistit. Primo enim considerandum est quod vita aeterna in Dei fruitione consistit. Motus autem humanae mentis ad fruitionem divini boni, est proprius actus caritatis, per quem omnes actus aliarum virtutum ordinantur in hunc finem, secundum quod aliae virtutes imperantur a caritate. Et ideo meritum vitae aeternae primo pertinet ad caritatem, ad alias autem virtutes secundario, secundum quod eorum actus a caritate imperantur. Similiter etiam manifestum est quod id quod ex amore facimus, maxime voluntarie

---

[29] Man's meritorious work may be considered in two ways: first, as it proceeds from free will; secondly as it proceeds from the grace of the Holy Spirit. If it is considered as regards the substance of the work, and inasmuch as it springs from free will, there can be no condignity because of the very great inequality. But there is congruity, on account of an equality of proportion; for it would seem congruous that, if a man does what he can, God should reward him according to the excellence of his power.

facimus. Unde etiam secundum quod ad rationem meriti requiritur
quod sit voluntarium, principaliter meritum caritati attribuitur.

(ST Ia IIae.114.4 resp.)[30]

while on charity as a gift of the Spirit, as a species of friendship originating
with God himself as the beginning and end of all friendship, we have
these from the opening phase of the *Secunda secundae*:

caritas est amicitia quaedam hominis ad Deum fundata super
communicationem beatitudinis aeternae. Haec autem communicatio
non est secundum bona naturalia, sed secundum dona gratuita,
quia, ut dicitur Rom. VI, *gratia Dei vita aeterna*. Unde et ipsa
caritas facultatem naturae excedit. Quod autem excedit naturae
facultatem non potest esse neque naturale neque per potentias
naturales acquisitum, quia effectus naturalis non transcendit suam
causam. Unde caritas non potest neque naturaliter nobis inesse,
neque per vires naturales est acquisita, sed per infusionem spiritus
sancti, qui est amor patris et filii, cuius participatio in nobis est ipsa
caritas creata ...'

(ST IIa IIae.24.2 resp.)[31]

[30] as we may gather from what has been stated above [art. 1], human acts have the
nature of merit from two causes: first and chiefly from divine ordination, inasmuch as
acts are said to merit that good to which man is divinely ordained. Secondly, on the part
of free will, inasmuch as man, more than other creatures, has the power of voluntary acts
by acting by himself. And in both these ways does merit chiefly rest with charity. For we
must bear in mind that everlasting life consists in the enjoyment of God. Now the human
mind's movement to the fruition of the divine good is the proper act of charity, whereby
all the acts of the other virtues are ordained to this end, since all the other virtues are
commanded by charity. Hence the merit of life everlasting pertains first to charity, and
secondly, to the other virtues, inasmuch as their acts are commanded by charity. So,
likewise, is it manifest that what we do out of love we do most willingly. Hence, even
inasmuch as merit depends on voluntariness, merit is chiefly attributed to charity.

[31] charity is a friendship of man for God founded upon the fellowship of everlasting
happiness. Now this fellowship is in respect, not of natural, but of gratuitous gifts, for
according to Romans 6 [v. 23] 'the grace of God is life everlasting'; wherefore charity
itself surpasses our natural faculties. Now that which surpasses the faculty of nature
cannot be natural or acquired by natural powers, since a natural effect does not transcend
its cause. Therefore, charity can be in us neither naturally nor through acquistion by
natural powers, but by the infusion of the Holy Spirit, who is the love of the Father and
the Son, and the participation of whom in us is created charity. Cf. *ScG* III.cli, etc. Also,
however, I *Sent.* 17.1.3 resp. for a sense of infused perfection as proportionate to the
properties of personality, of nature as determined in this or that individual: 'Perfectiones
autem infusae sunt in natura ipsius animae sicut in potentia materiali et nullo modo
activa, cum elevent animam supra omnem suam actionem naturalem. Unde operationes
animae se habent ad perfectiones infusas solum sicut dispositiones. Dicendum est igitur,
quod mensura secundum quam datur caritas, est capacitas ipsius animae, quae est ex

Bit by bit, then, but in a manner faithful to the logic shaping each successive emphasis in the grace-theological moment of the *Summa theologiae*, the possibility of merit is qualified in favour of a sense, not so much of the indispensability of grace as the remote principle of each significant inflexion of the spirit, as of the ultimate *in*significance of that inflexion in itself, of – other than by way of its transparency to grace in its incomingness – its counting for next to nothing within the salvific scheme as a whole.

3. Dante's too is a theology of grace, of the grace whereby man is empowered as a creature of moral determination, and he too, above all in the *Commedia*, is at pains to stress its status as the ground of every significant movement of the mind and of the will in man.[32] Thus it is by grace that the penitent spirit knows itself in the henceforth unclouded

natura simul, et dispositione quae est per conatum operum: et quia secundum eumdem conatum magis disponitur natura melior; ideo qui habet meliora naturalia, dummodo sit par conatus, magis recipiet de perfectionibus infusis; et qui pejora naturalia, quandoque magis recipiet, si adsit major conatus.' Otherwise, as the deep ground of mature Thomist spirituality hereabouts, Augustine, *De gratia et lib. arb.* xviii.37: 'Haec omnia praecepta dilectionis, id est caritatis, quae tanta et talia sunt, ut quidquid se putaverit homo facere bene, si fiat sine caritate, nullo modo fiat bene; haec ergo praecepta caritatis inaniter darentur hominibus, non habentibus liberum voluntatis arbitrium; sed quia per legem dantur et veterem et novam (quamvis in nova venerit gratia quae promittebatur in vetere), lex autem sine gratia littera est occidens, in gratia vero spiritus vivificans, unde est in hominibus caritas Dei et proximi, nisi ex ipso Deo?'

[32] Most recently on Dante and grace: A. C. Mastrobuono, *Dante's Journey of Sanctification* (Washington D.C.: Regnery Gateway, 1990); S. Rossi, 'Il trionfo della grazia nell'episodio di Bonconte da Montefeltro', *L'Alighieri. Rassegna bibliografica dantesca*, 35, n.s. 3/4 (1994), 83-93; C. Ryan, '"Natura dividitur contra gratiam": concetti diversi della natura in Dante e nella cultura filosofico-teologica medievale', in P. Boyde and V. Russo (eds), *Dante e la scienza. Atti del Convegno Internazionale di Studi, Ravenna 28-30 maggio 1995* (Ravenna: Longo, 1995), pp. 363-73; L. Scorrano, '*Paradiso* XXXII. La legge, la grazia', *L'Alighieri. Rassegna bibliografica dantesca* 37, n.s. 7 (1996), 19-36, subsequently in *Tra il 'banco' e 'l'alte rote': Letture e note dantesche* (Ravenna: Longo, 1996), pp. 103-22; I. Biffi, *La poesia e la grazia nella Commedia di Dante* (Milan: Jaca Book, 1999), especially pp. 29-35: 'Un viaggio che parte dalla grazia'; J. T. Chiampi, 'The role of freely bestowed grace in Dante's journey of legitimation', in *Rivista di Studi Italiani* 17 (1999), 1, 89-111; J. Trabant, '"Gloria" oder "grazia". Oder: Wonach die "questione della lingua" eigentlich fragt', *Romanistisches Jahrbuch* 51 (2000), 29-52; P. Cherchi, '"Da me stesso non vegno" (*Inf.* X, 61)', *Rassegna europea di letteratura italiana* 18 (2001), 103-106. Notable prior to Mastrobuono are G. Getto, 'L'"epos" della grazia in *Paradiso*', in P. Pullega (ed.), *Scrittori e idee in Italia. Antologia della critica. (Dalle Origini al Trecento)* (Bologna: Zanichelli, 1982), pp. 209-14; G. Godenzi, 'Il viaggio spirituale di Dante dal peccato alla grazia', in *Quaderni Grigionitaliani. Rivista trimestrale delle valli Grigionitaliane* 56 (1987), 3-4, 234-39; B. Panvini, 'La concezione tomistica della grazia nella *Divina Commedia*', in *Letture classensi* 17 (Ravenna: Longo, 1988), pp. 69-85.

substance of self, in the now uncluttered character of conscience (the 'se
tosto grazia resolva le schiume / di vostra coscïenza sì che chiaro / per essa
scenda de la mente il fiume' of *Purg.* XIII.88-90),[33] and it is by grace that
it knows itself in its equality to the forces of reckless desiring (the 'Beati
cui alluma / tanto di grazia, che l'amor del gusto / nel petto lor troppo
disir non fuma' of *Purg.* XXIV.151-53).[34] It is by grace that it knows
itself as held by God in the love of God (the 'E se Dio m'ha in sua grazia
rinchiuso' of *Purg.* XVI.40),[35] and it is by grace that it knows itself in the
rapture of its proper self-surpassing on the plane of understanding (the
'Ringrazia, / ringrazia il Sol de li angeli, ch'a questo / sensibil t'ha levato
per sua grazia' moment of *Par.* X.52-54 and the 'Con tutto 'l core e con
quella favella / ch'è una in tutti, a Dio feci olocausto, / qual conveniesi a
la grazia novella' of XIV.88-90).[36] It is by grace, moreover, that the mind
is caressed by the truth to which it is now party (the 'Grazia, che donnea
/ con la tua mente' moment of *Par.* XXIV.118-19)[37] and it is by grace
that it rejoices in the knowledge of its spiritual sonship (the 'Figliuol
di grazia' of *Par.* XXXI.112). Grace, then, is everywhere present to
the pious spirit as both the beginning and the end of its piety, as that
whereby it is both encouraged and consummated in its seeking out of
God as the first and final cause of its every yearning. But there is here a
difference as regards the *Prima secundae*, for whereas Thomas, for all his
commitment to the notion of grace as a *something* placed by God in the
soul as the means of its proper righteousness, proceeds in terms first and
foremost of *causality*, Dante, for all his commitment to grace as by nature
adventitious, proceeds by way of *coalescence*, of the mutual indwelling
of the divine and of the human initiative at the core itself of existence,
all of which amounts to something more than a mere redistribution of
emphases, a modest tweaking of the argument as it stands; for Dante's
is a proposal of this issue in terms, not of the poverty of human nature
in its fallenness and thus of its dependence for the purposes of being

---

[33] so may grace soon clear the scum of your conscience that the stream of memory may
flow down through it.

[34] Blessed are they who are so illumined by grace that the love of taste kindles not too
great a desire in their breasts, and who hunger always so far as is just.

[35] And since God has received me so far into his grace [that he wills that I see his court
in a manner wholly outside modern usage, do not hide from me who you were before
death ...]

[36] Give thanks, give thanks to the sun of the angels who of his grace has raised you to
this visible one ... with all my heart, and with that speech which is one in all men, I made
a holocaust to God such as befitted the new grace.

[37] the grace that holds amorous discourse with your mind [till now has opened your lips
aright, so that I approve what has come from them].

and becoming on a ceaseless process of actual gracing, but of the fresh
sufficiency of that nature in Christ, at which point the severity of the
final phase of the *Prima secundae* gives way to something altogether more
radiant, to a sense of the human project as party once more to the process
of its own being and becoming.

Taking one by one, then, the successive moments of the argument
– the Christological moment of *Paradiso* VII, the volitional moment of
Paradiso III, and, as tending to confirm these things as the basis of every
kind of moral and ontological triumph in man, the covenantal moment
of *Paradiso* V – we may begin by saying that Dante's, for all his sense of
the propitiatory substance of Christ's work on Calvary, is pre-eminently
a sense of that work as one of re-empowerment, of making man equal
once again to his own high calling. Man's, then, in the moment of his first
disobedience, was a threefold forfeiture, a triple surrender of *eternal life*, of
freedom and of *God-likeness*, the loss of any one of which would have been
enough to confirm him in his now attenuated humanity and in the need
somehow to make good:

> Ciò che da lei sanza mezzo distilla
> non ha poi fine, perché non si move
> la sua imprenta quand' ella sigilla.
>   Ciò che da essa sanza mezzo piove
> libero è tutto, perché non soggiace
> a la virtute de le cose nove.
>   Più l'è conforme, e però più le piace;
> ché l'ardor santo ch'ogne cosa raggia,
> ne la più somigliante è più vivace.
>   Di tutte queste dote s'avvantaggia
> l'umana creatura, e s'una manca,
> di sua nobilità convien che caggia.
>   Solo il peccato è quel che la disfranca
> e falla dissimìle al sommo bene,
> per che del lume suo poco s'imbianca;
>   e in sua dignità mai non rivene,
> se non rïempie, dove colpa vòta,
> contra mal dilettar con giuste pene.

(*Par.* VII.67-84)[38]

---

[38] That which immediately derives from it thereafter has no end, because when it seals,
its imprint may never be removed. That which rains down from it immediately is wholly
free, because it is not subject to the power of the new things. It is the most conformed to it
and therefore pleases it the most; for the holy ardour, which irradiates everything, is most
living in what is most like itself. With all these gifts the human creature is advantaged,
and if one fails, it needs must fall from its nobility. Sin alone it is that disenfranchises

In a discourse turning on the precise *how* of this making good, Dante comes to the choices confronting God as the author and architect of the human project in all the now destitute character of that project, choices consisting either (*a*) of forgiving him outright, or (*b*) of leaving him to his own devices, or (*c*) of finding some way of involving him in his own redemption. Miraculously, or, rather, magnanimously, God chose all three, for in taking on man's humanity in Christ he made it possible for man as man somehow to make amends for Eden and the catastrophe thereof and to participate in his own resurrection:

> Ma perché l'ovra tanto è più gradita
> da l'operante, quanto più appresenta
> de la bontà del core ond' ell' è uscita,
>   la divina bontà che 'l mondo imprenta,
> di proceder per tutte le sue vie,
> a rilevarvi suso, fu contenta.
>   Né tra l'ultima notte e 'l primo die
> sì alto o sì magnifico processo,
> o per l'una o per l'altra, fu o fie:
>   ché più largo fu Dio a dar sé stesso
> per far l'uom sufficiente a rilevarsi,
> che s'elli avesse sol da sé dimesso;
>   e tutti li altri modi erano scarsi
> a la giustizia, se 'l Figliuol di Dio
> non fosse umilïato ad incarnarsi.

(Par. VII.106-20)[39]

And it is this which, to come now to the second and third moments of the argument identified above, enables Dante to speak (*a*) of the co-inherence of divine and human willing in the critical moment of moral and ontological deliberation (the burden of the 'Anzi è formale ad esto beato *esse*' sequence of *Paradiso* III), and (*b*) of man's actually striking a bargain with God, of doing a deal with him in respect of the divine

---

it and makes it unlike the supreme good, so that it is little illumined by its light; and to its dignity it never returns unless, where fault has emptied, it fill up with just penalties against evil delight.

[39] But because the deed is so much the more prized by the doer, the more it displays of the goodness of the heart whence it issued, the divine goodness which puts its imprint on the world, was pleased to proceed by all its ways to raise you up again; nor between the last night and the first day has there been or will there be so exalted and so magnificent a procedure, either by one or by the other; for God was more bounteous in giving himself to make man sufficient to uplift himself again, than if he solely of himself had remitted; and all other modes were scanty in respect to justice, if the Son of God had not humbled himself to become incarnate.

plan and of the working out of that plan (the burden of the 'Lo maggior don che Dio per sua larghezza' sequence of *Paradiso* V); on the one hand, then, these lines from *Paradiso* III on the mutual indwelling of divine and human intentionality within the economy of the moral instance:

> Frate, la nostra volontà quïeta
> virtù di carità, che fa volerne
> sol quel ch'avemo, e d'altro non ci asseta.
>   Se disïassimo esser più superne,
> foran discordi li nostri disiri
> dal voler di colui che qui ne cerne;
>   che vedrai non capere in questi giri,
> s'essere in carità è qui *necesse*,
> e se la sua natura ben rimiri.
>   Anzi è formale ad esto beato *esse*
> tenersi dentro a la divina voglia,
> per ch'una fansi nostre voglie stesse;
>   sì che, come noi sem di soglia in soglia
> per questo regno, a tutto il regno piace
> com' a lo re che 'n suo voler ne 'nvoglia.
>   E 'n la sua volontade è nostra pace:
> ell' è quel mare al qual tutto si move
> ciò ch'ella crïa o che natura face.

(Par. III.70-87)[40]

while on the other hand these lines from *Paradiso* V, settled in their sense of God's dealings with man and of man's with God as a matter, not of kinesis, but of co-operation, of mutual consent in the name and for the sake of a joint enterprise:

> Sì cominciò Beatrice questo canto;
> e sì com' uom che suo parlar non spezza,
> continüò così 'l processo santo:
>   "Lo maggior don che Dio per sua larghezza
> fesse creando, e a la sua bontate
> più conformato, e quel ch'e' più apprezza,

---

[40] Brother, the power of love quiets our will and makes us wish only for that which we have and gives us no other thirst. Did we desire to be more aloft, our longings would be discordant with his will who assigns us here, which you will see is not possible in these circles if to exist in charity here is of necessity, and if you well consider what is love's nature. Indeed, it is of the essence of this blessed existence to keep itself within the divine will, whereby our wills are made one; so that our being thus from threshold to threshold throughout this realm is a joy to all the realm as to the king, who inwills us with his will; and in his will is our peace. It is that sea to which all moves, both what it creates and what nature makes.

fu de la volontà la libertate;
di che le creature intelligenti,
e tutte e sole, fuoro e son dotate.
    Or ti parrà, se tu quinci argomenti,
l'alto valor del voto, s'è sì fatto
che Dio consenta quando tu consenti;
    ché, nel fermar tra Dio e l'omo il patto,
vittima fassi di questo tesoro,
tal quale io dico; e fassi col suo atto".

(*Par.* V.16-30)[41]

With this sense, then, (*a*) of the mutual inherence of divine and of human intentionality within the depths of the ontic instant, and (*b*) of God's dealings with man and of man's with God as a matter of contractual concern, we come once again to the question of merit, something which, on the face of it, Dante takes for granted; so, for example, the '"Perfetta vita e alto merto inciela / donna più sù", mi disse, "a la cui norma / nel vostro mondo giù si veste e vela, / perché fino al morir si vegghi e dorma / con quello sposo ch'ogne voto accetta / che caritate a suo piacer conforma"' passage of *Par.* III.97-102;[42] the 'Ma nel commensurar d'i nostri gaggi / col merto è parte di nostra letizia, / perché non li vedem minor né maggi' passage of *Par.* VI.118-20;[43] the 'Quell' uno e due e tre che sempre vive / e regna sempre in tre e 'n uno, / non circunscritto, e tutto circunscrive, / tre volte era cantato da ciascuno / di quelli spirti con tal melodia, / ch'ad ogne merto saria giusto muno' passage of *Par.* XIV.28-33;[44] the 'ora conosce il merto del suo canto, / in quanto effetto fu del suo consiglio, / per lo

---

[41] So Beatrice began this canto, and as one who does not interrupt her speech, she thus continued her discourse: "The greatest gift which God in his bounty bestowed in creating, and the most conformed to his own goodness and that which he most prizes, was the freedom of the will, with which the creatures who have intelligence, they all and they alone, were and are endowed. Now, if you argue from this, the high worth of the vow will appear to you, if it be such that God consents when you consent; for in establishing the compact between God and man, this treasure becomes the sacrifice, such as I pronounce it, and that by its own act."

[42] "Perfect life and high merit enheaven a lady more aloft", she said to me, "according to whose rule, in your world below, are those who take the robe and veil themselves that they, even till death, may wake and sleep with that spouse who accepts every vow which love conforms unto his pleasure."

[43] But in the equal measure of our rewards with our desert is part of our joy, because we see them neither less nor greater.

[44] That one, two and three which ever lives, and ever reigns in three, two and one, uncircumscribed, and circumscribing all things, was thrice sung by each of those spirits with such melody as would be adequate reward for each merit.

remunerar ch'è altrettanto' of *Par*. XX.40-42[45] and the 'nel trono che suoi merti le sortiro' passage of *Paradiso* XXXI (lines 64-69), where Bernard, in a proclamation faithful to the substance of a lifelong meditation, confirms the blessedness of the Virgin as nothing other than the fruit of her deserving:

> E "Ov' è ella?", sùbito diss' io.
> Ond' elli: "A terminar lo tuo disiro
> mosse Beatrice me del loco mio;
> e se riguardi sù nel terzo giro
> dal sommo grado, tu la rivedrai
> nel trono che suoi merti le sortiro".[46]

But what might appear here to be instances of theological simple-mindedness where merit and the problematics thereof are concerned is nothing of the kind, for at every point informing these passages is a sense of grace and merit as functioning less as *antecedence* than as *alongsidedness*, as a matter of intimate complementarity. Now here, clearly, we have again to be careful, since at a deeper level of awareness grace subsists and must be said to subsist as the *locus* or whereabouts of every significant movement of the spirit in man. But given that it is indeed a question here of layered consciousness, of the precise point of theological engagement, Dante, when it comes to the nature of the relationship between grace and

---

[45] now he knows the merit of his song, so far as it was the effect of his own counsel, by the reward which is proportioned to it.

[46] And "Where is she?", I said at once; whereon he: "to terminate your desire Beatrice urged me from my place; and if you look up to the circle which is third from the highest tier, you will see her again, in the throne her merits have allotted to her." Similarly on Beatrice and merit, though at an earlier stage of Dante's meditation, *VN* iii.1: 'per la sua ineffabile cortesia, la quale è oggi meritata nel grande secolo ...', with, in *Venite a intender li sospiri miei*, ll. 9-11 (xxxii.6): 'Voi udirete lor chiamar sovente / la mia donna gentil, che si n'è gita / al secolo degno del la sua vertute', and, in *Era venuta ne la mente mia* (primo cominciamento), ll. 1-4 (xxxiv.7): 'Era venuta ne la mente mia / la gentil donna che per suo valore / fu posta da l'altissimo signore / nel ciel de l'umiltate, ov'è Maria', etc. On Dante and Bernard, A. Masseron, *Dante et saint Bernard* (Paris: Michel, 1953); G. Petrocchi, 'Dante e la mistica di san Bernardo', in W. Binni et al. (eds), *Letteratura e critica: studi in onore di Natalino Sapegno*, 4 vols (Rome: Bulzoni, 1974-79), vol. 1, pp. 213-29 (originally 'Il canto XXXI del *Paradiso*', *Nuove Letture Dantesche* 7 (1974), 235-53 and as 'Dante e san Bernardo', in *L'ultima dea* (Rome: Bonacci, 1977), pp. 137-55); F. Montanari, 'L'ultima guida: San Bernardo', *Lectura Dantis Modenese. Paradiso* (Modena: Banca popolare dell'Emilia, 1986), pp. 279-86; S. Botterill, *Dante and the Mystical Tradition: Bernard of Clairvaux in the Commedia* (Cambridge: Cambridge University Press, 1994); F. Drago Rivera, *S. Bernardo e l'ascesa mistica del Paradiso*, 2nd edn (Lugano: Paradiso, 1975; originally 1965). In general, E. Gilson, *The Mystical Theology of Saint Bernard*, trans. A. H. C. Downes (Kalamazoo: Cistercian Publications, 1990 and London: Sheed and Ward, 1940 and 1955; originally Paris: Vrin, 1934).

nature *in re*, shows a preference for parallelism rather than for priority
as a way of configuring these things; so, for example, on the referability
of hope as a theological virtue both to grace *and* to merit as a matter of
companionship in the recesses of the spirit, these lines (67-69) from Canto
XXV of the *Paradiso*:

> "Spene", diss' io, "è uno attender certo
> de la gloria futura, il qual produce
> grazia divina e precedente merto".[47]

– to which, for the sake of confirming Dante's revised geometry of grace
and merit at this point, we may add these lines (40-42 and 106-14) from
Paradiso XIV and XXVIII as but further acknowledgement of the co-
inherence of nature and grace at the point of intellection:

> La sua chiarezza séguita l'ardore;
> l'ardor la visïone, e quella è tanta,
> quant' ha di grazia sovra suo valore
> ...
> e dei saper che tutti hanno diletto
> quanto la sua veduta si profonda
> nel vero in che si queta ogne intelletto.
> Quinci si può veder come si fonda
> l'esser beato ne l'atto che vede,
> non in quel ch'ama, che poscia seconda;
> e del vedere è misura mercede,
> che grazia partorisce e buona voglia:
> così di grado in grado si procede.[48]

and these (lines 49-66) from Canto XXIX on his commitment to the
notion of grace itself as meritorious *in casu*, in circumstances of a spirit
suitably disposed on the plane of loving:

> Né giugneriesi, numerando, al venti
> sì tosto, come de li angeli parte
> turbò il suggetto d'i vostri alimenti.
> L'altra rimase, e cominciò quest' arte

---

[47] "Hope", I said, "is a sure expectation of future glory, which divine grace produces,
and preceding merit."

[48] Its brightness follows our ardour, the ardour our vision, and that is in the measure
which each has of grace beyond his merit ... And you should know that all have delight in
the measure of the depth to which their sight penetrates the truth in which every intellect
finds rest; from which it may be seen that the state of blessedness is founded on the act
of vision, not on that of love, which follows after; and the merit, to which grace and good
will give birth, is measure of their vision; thus, from grade to grade the progression goes.

che tu discerni, con tanto diletto,
che mai da circüir non si diparte.
  Principio del cader fu il maladetto
superbir di colui che tu vedesti
da tutti i pesi del mondo costretto.
  Quelli che vedi qui furon modesti
a riconoscer sé da la bontate
che li avea fatti a tanto intender presti:
  per che le viste lor furo essaltate
con grazia illuminante e con lor merto,
si c'hanno ferma e piena volontate;
  e non voglio che dubbi, ma sia certo,
che ricever la grazia è meritorio
secondo che l'affetto l'è aperto.[49]

Now it is usual in relation to the first of these passages, the '"Spene",
diss' io, "è uno attender certo / de la gloria futura' passage, to invoke as
Dante's 'control' in the *Paradiso* Peter Lombard's formula in the third book
of the *Sentences* (dist. xxvi) to the effect that 'hope is a sure expectation
of future happiness stemming from the grace of God and from preceding
merits' ('Est enim [spes] certa expectatio futurae beatitudinis, veniens
ex Dei gratia et ex meritis praecedentibus'), a text which provides him
with everything he needs for his own position in the *Commedia*, for his
own 'parallel' association of grace and merit as the ground of lively
expectation. But simply to note the text as a possible source for Dante
in *Paradiso* XXV is to pass over what from a theological point of view
actually matters about it, for Peter Lombard's formula subsists in two
versions, a shorter and a longer version, the longer version, tending by
way of *caritas* as a prior and infused virtue of the spirit to privilege grace
over merit as the basis of hope, reading as follows: 'est autem spes virtus

---

[49] Then, sooner than one might count to twenty, a part of the angels disturbed the
substrate of your elements. The rest remained and with such great delight began this
art which you behold that they never cease from circling. The origin of the fall was the
accursed pride of him whom you have seen constrained by all the weight of the universe.
Those whom you see here were modest to recognize their being as from the goodness
which had made them apt for intelligence so great; wherefore their vision was exalted with
illuminating grace and with their merit, so that they have their will full and established.
And I would not have you doubt, but be assured that to receive grace is meritorious in
proportion as the affection is open to it. On Dantean angelology, with reference to Peter
Lombard, P. Boitani, 'Creazione e cadute di *Paradiso* XXIX', *L'Alighieri* 43, n.s. 19 (2002),
87-103 (and as 'Canto XXIX' in G. Güntert and M. Picone (eds), *Lectura Dantis Turicensis.*
Paradiso (Florence: Cesati, 2002), pp. 441-55); A. Mellone, 'Il canto XXIX del *Paradiso*
(una lezione di angelologia)', in *Saggi e letture dantesche* (Angri: Editrice Gaia, 2005), pp.
157-74 (originally in *Nuove Letture Dantesche* 7 (Florence: Le Monnier, 1974), pp. 193-213).

qua spiritualia et aeterna bona sperantur, id est cum fiducia expectantur. Est enim certa expectatio futurae beatitudinis, veniens ex Dei gratia et ex meritis praecedentibus vel ipsam spem, quam natura praeit caritas; vel rem speratam, id est beatitudinem aeternam.'[50] Now where and in what form Dante encountered Peter Lombard's text, either in the original or else in one or other of the abbreviated forms such as those conveyed by Thomas,[51] we shall probably never know; but given for the sake of the argument that he *was* in possession of the original, then his opting, not for the ur-text, but for the edited version is significant, for his opting for the edited version is all of a piece with his own sense of the issue here, with his understanding of grace and nature, not as consequential, but as complementary to the point of co-immanent within the deep structure of the moral and ontological instant. Throughout, then, the pattern is the same, Dante, whenever he reflects on this issue as among the most delicate

---

[50] hope is the virtue by which spiritual and eternal goods are hoped for, by virtue of which, that is to say, they are confidently expected. For hope is a sure expectation of future happiness, coming from the grace of God and from merits preceding either hope as such, itself preceded in the nature of things by charity, or the thing hoped for, that is to say eternal life.

[51] Among Thomas's citations of Peter Lombard's text, the following reproduce it in its short form: *Scriptum* 2, d. 43, q. 1, a. 5 obj. 4 ('Sed spes praesupponit merita: est enim spes certa expectatio futurae beatitudinis ex meritis et gratia proveniens'); *ST* IIa IIae.17.1 obj. 2 ('"Sed spes est ex gratia et meritis proveniens"; ut Magister dicit, XXVI dist. III Lib. Sent.'); IIa IIae. 18.4 obj. 2 ('spes ex gratia et meritis provenit, ut supra dictum est'). *ST* IIa IIae.17.8 obj. 3 has 'Magister dicit, XXVI dist. III Lib. Sent., quod "spes ex meritis provenit, quae praecedunt non solum rem speratam, sed etiam spem, quam natura praeit caritas". Caritas ergo est prior spe.' None has the 'praecedentibus' ('praecedentibus meritis') of the original. Exemplary in respect of Thomas's by and large negative attitude to the text is *ST* IIa IIae.17.1 ad 2, where although hope is said to follow upon merit in respect of this or that object hoped for, hope in itself must be regarded as an infused virtue of the spirit and as thus referable to grace as to its first cause: 'spes dicitur ex meritis provenire quantum ad ipsam rem expectatam, prout aliquis sperat se beatitudinem adepturum ex gratia et meritis. Vel quantum ad actum spei formatae. Ipse autem habitus spei, per quam aliquis expectat beatitudinem, non causatur ex meritis, sed pure ex gratia.' J. -G. Bougerol, *La Théologie de l'espérance aux XIIe et XIIIe siècles*, 2 vols (Paris: Etudes augustiniennes, 1985), vol. 1, pp. 97-99. Otherwise on Peter Lombard and the *Sentences* (in addition to the general histories of medieval thought), M. L. Colish, *Peter Lombard*, 2 vols (Leiden and New York: Brill, 1994); J. -G. Bougerol, 'The Church Fathers and the *Sentences* of Peter Lombard', in I. Backus (ed.), *The Reception of the Church Fathers in the West from the Carolingians to the Maurists*, 2 vols (Leiden and New York: Brill, 1997; also Boston: Brill Academic Publishers, 2001), vol. 1, pp. 113-64 (with 'The Church Fathers and *auctoritates* in Scholastic Theology to Bonaventure' in the same volume at pp. 289-336). On Dante and Peter Lombard, M. Papio, ad voc. 'Peter Lombard' in R. Lansing (ed.), *Dante Encyclopaedia* (London: Garland, 2000), pp. 682-83, with bibliography. Also, M. Da Carbonara, *Dante e Pier Lombardo; Sent, lib. IV, distt. 43-49* (Città di Castello: Lapi, 1897).

of theological issues, professing a commitment, less to the ascendancy of grace under the aspect of causality, than – in direct consequence of God's purpose in the moment both of creation and of man's fresh co-adequation in Christ – to a co-presencing of divine and human intentionality in the moment of seeing, understanding and choosing.

4. In a remarkable moment of the *Paradiso* (VII.58-60), a moment prefacing his account of why God chose to proceed in precisely the way he did in Christ on Calvary, Dante points to the indispensability of 'maturity in the flame of love', of an adult understanding of what love is and of how love works, as the key to it all:

> Questo decreto, frate, sta sepulto
> a li occhi di ciascuno il cui ingegno
> ne la fiamma d'amor non è adulto.[52]

And it is at this point, at the point of maturity in the flame of love, that movement as a way of seeing and understanding God's way of relating with man in his fallenness is overtaken by something more sublime, namely by a sense of God's commitment, despite all, to confirming him once more in his equality to the task in hand, this – this *letting it be* in the fullness of that being – being what love is and what love means. Short of this, Dante felt, there can be no making sense of the Christ event as a matter, not now of God's deigning to move man despite himself to his proper end and happiness, but of the kind of love-creativity whereby, irrespective of those forces making in human experience for something closer to the diabolic than to the divine, the individual is restored to something like his pristine integrity. Movement, in short, gives way to magnanimity as a means of seeing and understanding the question of morality and merit, magnanimity having the sense here, not of modifying human nature in favour of something which, of itself, it neither is or ever could be, but of confirming it in its proper possibility.

---

[52] This decree, brother, is buried from the eyes of everyone whose understanding is not matured within love's flame.

Chapter 2
Faith and Facticity

> E io: "Per filosofici argomenti
> e per autorità che quinci scende
> cotale amor convien che in me si 'mprenti:
>   ché 'l bene, in quanto ben, come
> s'intende,
> così accende amore, e tanto maggio
> quanto più di bontate in sé comprende.
>   Dunque a l'essenza ov' è tanto
> avvantaggio,
> che ciascun ben che fuor di lei si trova
> altro non è ch'un lume di suo raggio,
>   più che in altra convien che si mova
> la mente, amando, di ciascun che cerne
> il vero in che si fonda questa prova".
>
> (*Par.* XXVI.25-36)[1]

1. Faith as a condition of salvation in Dante and Aquinas: Aquinas, explicit faith and implicit faith. 2. Dante and the power of the encounter to regeneration and redemption – divine vulnerability and a reconfiguration of soteriological emphases.

The virtuous pagans, or rather the reprobation of the virtuous pagans, is a constant source of concern for Dante in the *Commedia*, and his encounter with the eagle in the great justice cantos of the *Paradiso* does little to allay this concern; for the eagle, for all its sense of the inscrutability of God's ways in the area of election (the 'Or tu chi se' che vuo' sedere a scranna' sequence beginning at XIX.79), and

---

[1] And I: "By philosophic arguments and by authority that descends from here, such love must needs imprint itself on me; for the good, inasmuch as it is good, kindles love in proportion as it is understood, and so much the more the more of good it contains in itself. Therefore, to that essence wherein is such supremacy that whatsoever good be found outside of it is naught save a beam of its own radiance, more than to any other must the mind be moved, in love, of whoever discerns the truth on which this proof is founded."

indeed of God's willingness, not only to honour the intercession of
the saints vis-à-vis the righteous of antiquity (the case of Trajan), but
even to grace them in their own right (the case of Rhipeus), confirms
also the status of explicit faith in the Christ as a necessary condition
of salvation.[2] In fact, Dante's position here – again turning on the
notion of explicit faith as a condition of homecoming – is already clear
from the fourth canto of the *Inferno* and from the seventh canto of the
Purgatorio, where it is a question of the noble pagans as excluded on
the basis (*a*) of their lacking baptism as the 'portal of faith' (the 's'elli
hanno mercedi, / non basta, perché non ebber battesmo, / ch'è porta
della fede che tu credi' of *Inf*. IV.34-36),[3] and (*b*) of their negative
unbelief (the 'Io son Virgilio; e per null' altro rio / lo ciel perdei che
per non aver fé' of *Purg*. VII.7-8),[4] a notion taken up with if anything
heightened pathos in the 'Matto è chi spera' passage of *Purg*. III.34-45:

> "Matto è chi spera che nostra ragione
> possa trascorrer la infinita via
> che tiene una sustanza in tre persone.
> State contenti, umana gente, al *quia*;

[2] Aquinas (on the terminology), *De ver*. 14.11, resp.: 'implicitum proprie dicitur esse
illud in quo quasi in uno multa continentur; explicitum autem in quo unumquodque
ipsorum in se consideratur. Et transferuntur haec nomina a corporalibus ad spiritualia.
Unde quando aliqua multa, virtute continentur in aliquo uno, dicuntur esse in illo
implicite, sicut conclusiones in principiis. Explicite autem in aliquo continetur quod in
eo actu existit; unde ille qui cognoscit aliqua principia universalia, habet implicitam
cognitionem de omnibus conclusionibus particularibus; qui autem conclusiones actu
considerat, dicitur ea explicite cognoscere. Unde et explicite dicimur aliqua credere
quando eis actu cogitatis adhaeremus; implicite vero quando adhaeremus quibusdam,
in quibus sicut in universalibus ista continentur; sicut qui credit fidem Ecclesiae veram
esse, in hoc quasi implicite credit singula quae sub fide Ecclesiae continentur.' T.
Penelhum, 'The Analysis of Faith in St. Thomas Aquinas', *Religious Studies* 13, 2 (1977),
133-54; A. Plantinga, 'Reason and Belief in God', in A. Plantinga and N. Wolterstorff
(eds), *Faith and Rationality* (Notre Dame, Ind.: University of Notre Dame Press, 1983),
pp. 16-93.

[3] but if they have merit, that does not suffice, for they did not have baptism, which is the
portal of the faith you hold. 'Parte' for 'porta' in the majority of MSS, but see Petrocchi
(ed.), vol. 1, pp. 170-71 on patristic and canonistic usage, and *Par*. XXV. 7-12 with its
account of 'entering' by way of baptism upon a life of faith: 'con altra voce omai, con altro
vello / ritornerò poeta, e in sul fonte / del mio battesmo prenderò 'l cappello; / però che
ne la fede, che fa conte / l'anime a Dio, quivi intra' io, e poi / Pietro per lei sì mi girò la
fronte.' On Dante and the sacraments generally, P. Armour, *The Door of Purgatory. A Study
of Multiple Symbolism in Dante's Purgatorio* (Oxford: Clarendon Press, 1983), especially pp.
1-15, and, more recently, F. Bucci, 'Memorie battesimali tra *Inferno* e *Purgatorio* alla luce
di tre figure veterotestamentarie', *La Cultura. Rivista trimestrale di filosofia letteratura e storia*
43 (2005), 2, 217-55.

[4] I am Virgil, and for no other fault did I lose heaven than for not having faith.

> ché, se potuto aveste veder tutto,
> mestier non era parturir Maria;
>   e disïar vedeste sanza frutto
> tai che sarebbe lor disio quetato,
> ch'etternalmente è dato lor per lutto:
>   io dico d'Aristotile e di Plato
> e di molt' altri"; e qui chinò la fronte,
> e più non disse, e rimase turbato.[5]

From the outset, then, the idea is secure, but it is in the justice cantos of the *Paradiso* that Dante's commitment to an explicit profession of the Christ as the condition of standing at last in God's presence moves unequivocally into view. Having raised, then, the case of the good man on the banks of the Indus innocent through no fault of his own of Christ and clergy but condemned even so to an eternity of separation and sadness, the Eagle of righteousness proceeds by way of the firmest possible indication that no one comes to the Father but by way of the Son, by way of the Christ either as to come or else as already present among us. True, not all those who *do* come to the Father by way of the Son will be welcomed into his company, for many among those who cry 'Lord! Lord!' do so to their shame.[6] But that, for the moment, is not what matters, Dante's main contention being that salvation can only ever be by way of the cross and of the degradation of the cross:

> Poi si quetaro quei lucenti incendi
> de lo Spirito Santo ancor nel segno
> che fé i Romani al mondo reverendi,
>   esso ricominciò: "A questo regno
> non salì mai chi non credette 'n Cristo,
> né pria né poi ch'el si chiavasse al legno.
>   Ma vedi: molti gridan "Cristo, Cristo!",
> che saranno in giudicio assai men *prope*
> a lui, che tal che non conosce Cristo;
>   e tai Cristian dannerà l'Etïòpe,

[5] "Foolish is he who hopes that our reason may compass the infinite course taken by the one substance in three persons. Be content, human race, with the *quia*; for if you had been able to see everything, no need was there for Mary to give birth; and you have seen desiring fruitlessly men such that their desire would have been satisfied which is given them for eternal grief: I speak of Aristotle and of Plato and of many others." And here he bent his brow and said no more, and remained troubled.

[6] Matt. 7: 21: 'Non omnis qui dicit mihi: "Domine, Domine" intrabit in regnum cœlorum', with, for the 'Ethiopean' moment of *Paradiso* XIX (ll. 109-11), Matt. 8: 11-12: 'dico autem vobis quod multi ab oriente et occidente venient, et recumbent cum Abraham et Isaac et Iacob in regno cœlorum; filii autem regni eicientur in tenebras exteriores ...'

quando si partiranno i due collegi,
l'uno in etterno ricco e l'altro inòpe".

(*Par.* XIX.100-11)[7]

In fact, the 'assai men *prope*' moment of line 107 opens up both a fresh set of problems and a fresh set of possibilities in the area of soteriological concern, the notion of those without knowledge of the Christ as even so standing more immediately in his presence than those naming the name straightaway inviting another look at the whole issue of election – an invitation by no means lost on Dante as his argument unfolds. For the moment, however, the case is open and shut. Other than for those who, like Trajan and Rhipeus among the pagans, were delivered miraculously from their paganism (the 'D'i corpi suoi non uscir, come credi, / Gentili, ma Cristiani, in ferma fede / quel d'i passuri e quel d'i passi piedi' of *Par.* XX.103-105),[8] or for those who, like the patriarchs in the celestial rose, were believers in Christ to come (the 'Da questa parte onde 'l fiore è maturo / di tutte le sue foglie, sono assisi / quei che credettero in Cristo venturo' of XXXII.22-24),[9] there can be no salvation, Christ and Christ alone being the door of the tabernacle, the sole way into God's presence and the blessedness thereof.[10]

Thomas's too, when it comes to the fundamentals of Christian belief and profession (to, for example, the threefold nature of the Godhead or the divinity of the Christ), is a commitment to the notion of explicit faith as a principle of salvation. In the *Summa theologiae* the matter arises in the

---

[7] After those glowing flames of the Holy Spirit became quiet, still in the sign which the Romans made reverend to the world, it began again: "To this realm none ever rose who believed not in Christ, either before or after he was nailed to the tree. But behold, many cry Christ, Christ, who, at the judgement, shall be far less near to him than he who knows not Christ; and the Ethiop will condemn such Christians when the two companies shall be separated, the one forever rich, and the other poor."

[8] They came forth from their bodies not as you think, Gentiles, but Christians, with firm faith, the one in the feet that were to suffer, the other in the feet that had suffered. V. Horia, 'L'Empereur Trajan personnage de la *Divine Comédie*', *Journal of American Romance Academy of Arts and Sciences* 8-9 (1986), 94-97; G. Whately, 'The Uses of Hagiography: the Legend of Pope Gregory and the Emperor Trajan in the Middle Ages', *Viator* 15 (1984), 25-63. Also, N. Vickers, 'Seeing is Believing: Gregory, Trajan and Dante's Art', *Dante Studies* 101 (1983), 67-86.

[9] On this side, wherein the flower is mature in all its petals, are seated those who believed in Christ yet to come.

[10] *Mon.* II.vii.4-6: 'quod nemo, quantumcunque moralibus et intellectualibus virtutibus et secundum habitum et secundum operationem perfectus, absque fide salvari potest, dato quod nunquam aliquid de Cristo audiverit ... Hostium tabernaculi Christum figurat, qui est hostium conclavis ecterni, ut ex evangelio elici potest.'

course of the faith articles at the beginning of the *Secunda secundae*, where
in reply to the question as to whether a man is bound to believe anything
explicitly ('utrum homo teneatur ad credendum aliquid explicite'), he
affirms that whereas the contingencies of the scriptural narrative need
not compel in conscience, the leading propositions of the faith are binding
for the purposes of salvation:

> Determinatio igitur virtuosi actus ad proprium et per se obiectum
> virtutis est sub necessitate praecepti, sicut et ipse virtutis actus. Sed
> determinatio actus virtuosi ad ea quae accidentaliter vel secundario
> se habent ad proprium et per se virtutis obiectum non cadit sub
> necessitate praecepti nisi pro loco et tempore. Dicendum est ergo
> quod fidei obiectum per se est id per quod homo beatus efficitur, ut
> supra dictum est. Per accidens autem vel secundario se habent ad
> obiectum fidei omnia quae in Scriptura divinitus tradita continentur,
> sicut quod Abraham habuit duos filios, quod David fuit filius Isai, et
> alia huiusmodi. Quantum ergo ad prima credibilia, quae sunt articuli
> fidei, tenetur homo explicite credere, sicut et tenetur habere fidem.

$$\text{(ST IIa IIae.2.5 resp.)}^{11}$$

Careful as it is to distinguish between the primary and the secondary
substance of the Christian profession, the passage nonetheless settles on
the notion of explicit faith regarding those things pertaining to it as of
the essence. And what applies in Article 5 relative to the contingencies of
Scripture applies also in Article 7, where it is a question of the incarnation,
and in Article 8, where it is a question of the Trinity, each of which requires
consent in conscience as a condition of man's coming home to God as the
beginning and end of his journeying.[12] True, there is in both these articles

---

[11] Accordingly, just as a virtuous act is required for the fulfilment of a precept, so is
it necessary that the virtuous act should terminate in its proper and direct object: but,
on the other hand, the fulfilment of the precept does not require that a virtuous act
should terminate in those things which have an accidental or secondary relation to the
proper and direct object of that virtue, except in certain places and at certain times. We
must, therefore, say that the direct object of faith is that whereby man is made one of the
blessed, as stated above [qu. 1, art. 8]; while the indirect and secondary object comprises
all things delivered by God to us in Holy Writ, for instance that Abraham had two sons,
that David was the son of Jesse, and so forth. Therefore, as regards the primary points or
articles of faith, man is bound to believe them, just as he is bound to have faith.

[12] *ST* IIa IIae.2.7 and 8 resp.: 'illud proprie et per se pertinet ad obiectum fidei per quod
homo beatitudinem consequitur. Via autem hominibus veniendi ad beatitudinem est
mysterium incarnationis et passionis Christi, dicitur enim Act. IV, "non est aliud nomen
datum hominibus in quo oportet nos salvos fieri". Et ideo mysterium incarnationis
Christi aliqualiter oportuit omni tempore esse creditum apud omnes ... mysterium Christi
explicite credi non potest sine fide Trinitatis, quia in mysterio Christi hoc continetur quod

a concession, or at any rate something close to it, when, speaking of the way in which Christ's passion was anticipated by the Jews in certain of their sacrifices, Thomas notes that, while for the leaders of the people (the *superiores* or *maiores*) an act of explicit faith in the Christ as yet to come was obligatory, for the ordinary followers of the Law (the *inferiores* or *minores*) implicit faith was enough.[13] Since the coming of Christ, however, superiors and inferiors alike stand in need of explicit faith as the ground of their salvation, Thomas's central contention to the effect that for man as man to be fully and unambiguously is to be explicitly in Christ therefore surviving intact.

To this extent, then, Aquinas's position on the need for explicit faith as a condition of salvation coincides with Dante's; for if each is of the opinion that all those born into the καιρός and living under the New Law are dependent on a formal profession of faith as the basis of their eternal happiness, each makes provision for those born before the καιρός and living under the Old Law, theirs too, albeit by way of anticipation, being a profession of the Messiah. True, Aquinas nuances the argument by introducing into it a distinction between (under the Old Law) Jewish inferiority and superiority, Dante contenting himself with a sense of the status of the patriarchs as believers in the Christ *avant la lettre*; but that notwithstanding, it is in both cases a question of imminent deliverance. Differences begin to open up, however, in respect of those born before the καιρός and living beyond the pale, for where Dante seems wedded to the notion of paganism as entailing an eternity, if not of suffering, then certainly of sighing, Thomas, by contrast, appears to extend the notion of implicit faith, or something close to it, to all those in the pagan world ignorant of the Christ but alert in some other way to God's salvific purpose for man. The key passage here comes in his reply to Objection 3 in the IIa

---

filius Dei carnem assumpserit, quod per gratiam spiritus sancti mundum renovaverit, et iterum quod de spiritu sancto conceptus fuerit.'

[13] Ibid. 7 resp. and 8 resp.: 'Post peccatum autem fuit explicite creditum mysterium Christi non solum quantum ad incarnationem, sed etiam quantum ad passionem et resurrectionem, quibus humanum genus a peccato et morte liberatur. Aliter enim non praefigurassent Christi passionem quibusdam sacrificiis et ante legem et sub lege. Quorum quidem sacrificiorum significatum explicite maiores cognoscebant, minores autem sub velamine illorum sacrificiorum, credentes ea divinitus esse disposita de Christo venturo, quodammodo habebant velatam cognitionem ... Et ideo eo modo quo mysterium Christi ante Christum fuit quidem explicite creditum a maioribus, implicite autem et quasi obumbrate a minoribus, ita etiam et mysterium Trinitatis. Et ideo etiam post tempus gratiae divulgatae tenentur omnes ad explicite credendum mysterium Trinitatis. Et omnes qui renascuntur in Christo hoc adipiscuntur per invocationem Trinitatis, secundum illud Matth. ult., "euntes, docete omnes gentes, baptizantes eos in nomine patris et filii et spiritus sancti".'

IIae.2.7 article mentioned above, an objection turning on the testimony of
the Areopagite relative to those living both before Christ and outside the
Law but nonetheless ministered to by the angels: 'multi gentilium salutem
adepti sunt per ministerium Angelorum, ut Dionysius dicit, IX cap. Cael.
Hier. Sed gentiles non habuerunt fidem de Christo nec explicitam nec
implicitam, ut videtur, quia nulla eis revelatio facta est. Ergo videtur quod
credere explicite Christi mysterium non fuerit omnibus necessarium ad
salutem',[14] to which Aquinas is ready with a twofold reply. First, then, he
rejects the claim that all pagans living before Christ were ignorant of him,
oracles and historians alike testifying to the truth about to be revealed:

> Ad tertium dicendum quod multis gentilium facta fuit revelatio
> de Christo, ut patet per ea quae praedixerunt ... Sibylla etiam
> praenuntiavit quaedam de Christo, ut Augustinus dicit. Invenitur
> etiam in historiis Romanorum, quod tempore Constantini Augusti et
> Irenae matris eius inventum fuit quoddam sepulcrum in quo iacebat
> homo auream laminam habens in pectore in qua scriptum erat,
> 'Christus nascetur ex virgine et credo in eum. O sol, sub Irenae et
> Constantini temporibus iterum me videbis'.[15]

Secondly, and more significantly from our present point of view, he
notes the possibility of salvation for those who, if not party to the full
revelation of the Christ, nonetheless knew and believed in him by way of a
general sense of the providential and thus in some sense salvific purposes
of God:

> Si qui tamen salvati fuerunt quibus revelatio non fuit facta, non
> fuerunt salvati absque fide mediatoris. Quia etsi non habuerunt fidem
> explicitam, habuerunt tamen fidem implicitam in divina providentia,
> credentes Deum esse liberatorem hominum secundum modos sibi

[14] further, many gentiles obtained salvation through the ministry of the angels, as
Dionysius states (*Coel. Hier.* ix). Now it would seem that the gentiles had neither explicit
nor implicit faith in Christ, since they received no revelation. Therefore, it appears that
it was not necessary for the salvation of all to believe explicitly in the mystery of Christ.

[15] To the third objection we may say that many of the gentiles received revelations of
Christ, as is clear from their predictions ... The Sibyl too foretold certain things about
Christ, as Augustine states [*Cont. Faust.* xiii.15]. Moreover, we read in the history of
the Romans that at the time of Constantine Augustus and his mother Irene a tomb was
discovered wherein lay a man on whose breast was a golden plate with the inscription
'Christ shall be born of a virgin, and in him I believe. O Sun, during the lifetime of
Irene and Constantine, you shall see me again'. See also, as far as the Sybilline oracle
is concerned, *De ver.* 14.11 ad 5, ult.: 'Probabile tamen est multis etiam gentilibus ante
Christi adventum mysterium redemptionis nostrae fuisse divinitus revelatum, sicut patet
ex sibyllinis vaticiniis.'

placitos et secundum quod aliquibus veritatem cognoscentibus ipse
revelasset ...[16]

True, the structure of the period is hypothetical ('Si qui tamen salvati
fuerunt ...'), but given for the sake of the argument that some souls before
Christ, other than the Jewish patriarchs, *were* saved, then this, Thomas
maintains, would not have been without faith in a mediator. As in the case
of the *minores* among the Jews, they would have been saved by implicit
faith in the Christ to come, or at least in some sort of mechanism designed
at God's good pleasure ('secundum modos sibi placitos') to bring them
home to their maker. The Jewish case has, in other words, been extended
to cover all those before Christ living in anticipation of God's wishing
to treat them well. In fact, and for the purposes of registering Thomas's
consistency at this point, it is worth noting that what we have here in
the *Secunda secundae* is but a reiteration of positions reached in the earlier
De veritate, where he had already enquired as to whether explicit faith is
in all circumstances a necessity, and where he had already (*a*) drawn a
distinction as far as the old Jews were concerned between the learned
in the law (for whom explicit faith in the Messiah is of the essence) and
the unlearned in the law (for whom implicit faith is enough), and (*b*)
accommodated the gentiles at least in so far as they too were committed
to a sense of the providentiality of it all, of God's intending to honour
them. On the one hand, then, these lines on the question of superiors and
inferiors among the Jews of the old dispensation:

> Sed ante peccatum et post, omni tempore necessarium fuit a
> maioribus explicitam fidem de Trinitate habere; non autem a
> minoribus post peccatum usque ad tempus gratiae; ante peccatum
> enim forte talis distinctio non fuisset, ut quidam per alios erudirentur
> de fide. Et similiter etiam post peccatum usque ad tempus gratiae
> maiores tenebantur habere fidem de redemptore explicite; minores
> vero implicite, vel in fide patriarcharum et prophetarum, vel in
> divina providentia.
>
> (*De ver.* 14.11 resp.)[17]

---

[16] If, however, some were saved without receiving any revelation, they were not saved
without faith in a mediator, for, though they did not believe in him explicitly, they did,
nevertheless, have implicit faith through believing in divine providence, since they
believed that God would deliver mankind in whatever way was pleasing to him, and
according to the revelation of the Spirit to those who knew the truth ...

[17] Before and after the fall, the leaders in every age had to have explicit faith in the
Trinity. Between the fall and the age of grace, however, the ordinary people did not have
to have such explicit belief. Perhaps before the fall there was not such a distinction of
persons that some had to be taught the faith by others. Likewise, between the fall and
the age of grace, the leading men had to have explicit faith in the Redeemer, and the

while on the other hand, this passage relative to the gentiles living before the time of Christ, souls wise, certainly, in the worldly way of being wise, but, like the Jewish minors, justified on the basis, not of this, but of an as yet intuitive sense of God's will to salvation:

> gentiles non ponebantur ut instructores divinae fidei. Unde, quantumcumque essent sapientes sapientia saeculari, inter minores computandi sunt: et ideo sufficiebat eis habere fidem de redemptore implicite, vel in fide legis et prophetarum, vel etiam in ipsa divina providentia.
>
> (*De ver.* 14.11 ad 5)[18]

From the *De veritate* to the *Secunda secundae*, there are, it is true, differences of emphasis and expression, and it is worth noting also that some of Thomas's most significant qualifications in respect of pagan or gentile salvation occur, not in the main body of his discourse, but in replies to objections or counter-theses – a situation always to be borne in mind when balancing one aspect of his argument with another. But for all that, his is a generous view of the matter, a readiness to look as favourably as may be at the plight of those living before and beyond the law. Given the contingencies of world history, he believes, the notion of explicit faith as a condition of ultimate homecoming has as a matter of necessity, or, rather, of charity, to be tempered by a sense of the efficacy of implicit faith as that whereby even those formally bereft of the Christ may be accommodated within the soteriological scheme.

2. Why, then, given the availability to him of such a versatile notion as that of implicit faith did Dante, troubled as he was by the plight of the pagan spirits, choose not to make use of it?

The answer to this lies in his commitment to the indispensability of the revelatory instant *in its own right* as a channel of grace. Where, in other words, Thomas is inclined to insist, not only on the event itself, but on a simultaneous movement of grace as the ground of its salvific efficacy, Dante, typically, will settle instead for the power of the event to persuade *from out of its eventuality*, from out of the substance itself of the encounter, a position straightaway making for the exclusion of all those not party to

ordinary people only implicit faith. This was contained either in their belief in the faith of the patriarchs and prophets or in their belief in divine providence.

[18] the gentiles were not established as teachers of divine faith. Hence, no matter how well versed they were in secular wisdom, they should be counted as ordinary people [*minores*]. Therefore, it was enough for them to have implicit faith in the Redeemer, either as part of their belief in the faith of the law and the prophets, or as part of their belief in divine providence itself.

it; on the one hand, then, as bearing on the twofold extrinsic and intrinsic causality of faith, on the coincidence of the event itself and of an inwardly operative movement of grace as the ground of consent, this from the threshold of the *Secunda secundae*:

> Respondeo dicendum quod ad fidem duo requiruntur. Quorum unum est ut homini credibilia proponantur, quod requiritur ad hoc quod homo aliquid explicite credat. Aliud autem quod ad fidem requiritur est assensus credentis ad ea quae proponuntur. Quantum igitur ad primum horum, necesse est quod fides sit a Deo. Ea enim quae sunt fidei excedunt rationem humanam, unde non cadunt in contemplatione hominis nisi Deo revelante. Sed quibusdam quidem revelantur immediate a Deo, sicut sunt revelata apostolis et prophetis, quibusdam autem proponuntur a Deo mittente fidei praedicatores, secundum illud Rom. X, 'quomodo praedicabunt nisi mittantur?' Quantum vero ad secundum, scilicet ad assensum hominis in ea quae sunt fidei, potest considerari duplex causa. Una quidem exterius inducens, sicut miraculum visum, vel persuasio hominis inducentis ad fidem. Quorum neutrum est sufficiens causa, videntium enim unum et idem miraculum, et audientium eandem praedicationem, quidam credunt et quidam non credunt. Et ideo oportet ponere aliam causam interiorem, quae movet hominem interius ad assentiendum his quae sunt fidei. Hanc autem causam Pelagiani ponebant solum liberum arbitrium hominis, et propter hoc dicebant quod initium fidei est ex nobis, inquantum scilicet ex nobis est quod parati sumus ad assentiendum his quae sunt fidei; sed consummatio fidei est a Deo, per quem nobis proponuntur ea quae credere debemus. Sed hoc est falsum. Quia cum homo, assentiendo his quae sunt fidei, elevetur supra naturam suam, oportet quod hoc insit ei ex supernaturali principio interius movente, quod est Deus. Et ideo fides quantum ad assensum, qui est principalis actus fidei, est a Deo interius movente per gratiam.

> (*ST* IIa IIae.6.1 resp.)[19]

[19] I answer that, two things are requisite for faith. First, that the things which are of faith should be proposed to man, this being necessary in order that man believe anything explicitly. The second thing requisite for faith is the assent of the believer to the things which are proposed to him. Accordingly, as regards the first of these, faith must needs be from God. Because those things which are of faith surpass human reason, hence they do not come to man's knowledge unless God reveal them. To some, indeed, they are revealed by God immediately, as those things which were revealed to the apostles and prophets, while to some they are proposed by God in sending preachers of the faith, according to Romans 10:15: "How shall they preach, unless they be sent?" As regards the second, namely man's assent to the things which are of faith, we may observe a twofold cause, one of external inducement, such as seeing a miracle, or being persuaded by someone

while on the other, and as bearing now on the demonstrative power of the word – of the word, to be sure, as irradiated by the Spirit, but nonetheless of the word in and for itself – to impress unaided, this from the *Paradiso* at XXIV.91-96:

> "La larga ploia
> de lo Spirito Santo, ch'è diffusa
> in su le vecchie e 'n su le nuove cuoia,
>   è silogismo che la m'ha conchiusa
> acutamente sì, che 'nverso d'ella
> ogne dimostrazion mi pare ottusa".[20]

– a notion at once reiterated and indeed reinforced by the addition of proofs physical and metaphysical as similarly apt *from out of themselves*, from out of their status as testimony to the truth they themselves ray forth, to confirm the soul in a mood of acquiescence:

> E io rispondo: Io credo in uno Dio
> solo ed etterno, che tutto 'l ciel move,

to embrace the faith: neither of which is a sufficient cause, since of those who see the same miracle, or who hear the same sermon, some believe, and some do not. Hence we must assert another internal cause, which moves man inwardly to assent to matters of faith. The Pelagians held that this cause was nothing other than man's free-will, and consequently they said that the beginning of faith is from ourselves, inasmuch as, to wit, it is in our power to be ready to assent to things which are of faith, but that the consummation of faith is from God, who proposes to us the things we have to believe. But this is false, for, since man, by assenting to matters of faith, is raised above his nature, this must needs accrue to him from some supernatural principle moving him inwardly; and this is God. Therefore faith, as regards the assent which is the chief act of faith, is from God moving man inwardly by grace.   H. Bouillard, *Conversion et grâce chez s. Thomas d'Aquin: étude historique* (Paris: Aubier, 1944); R. Garrigou-Lagrange, O.P., *Grace: Commentary on the* Summa Theologica *of St Thomas, Ia IIae, 109-14* (London: B. Herder, 1957); C. Ernst, O.P. (ed. and comm.), *Summa theologiae*, vol. 30 (*The Gospel of Grace. Ia 2ae. 106-114*) (London: Blackfriars, 1972); B. J. F. Lonergan, S.J., *Grace and Freedom. Operative Grace in the Thought of St Thomas Aquinas*, ed. F. E. Crowe and R. M. Doran (Toronto: University of Toronto Press, 2000; originally 1971; in respect of which see also his 'St Thomas's Thought on *Gratia Opereans*', *Theological Studies* 2 (1941), 3, 289-324; 3 (1942), 1, 69-88; 3, 375-402 and 4, 533-78). For Augustine, J. Patout Burns, *The Development of Augustine's Doctrine of Operative Grace* (Paris: Etudes Augustiniennes, 1980); J. Wetzel, *Augustine and the Limits of Virtue* (Cambridge: Cambridge University Press, 1992); B. Studer, *The Grace of Christ and the Grace of God in Augustine of Hippo: Christocentrism or Theocentrism?*, trans. M. J. O'Connell (Collegeville, Minn.: The Liturgical Press, 1997). In general, R. W. Gleason, S.J., *Grace* (London and New York: Sheed and Ward, 1962); N. P. Williams, *The Grace of God* (London: Hodder and Stoughton, 1966, originally 1930).

[20] The plenteous rain of the Holy Spirit which is poured over the old and over the new parchments is a syllogism that has proved it to me so acutely that, in comparison with this, every demonstration seems obtuse to me.

non moto, con amore e con disio;
  e a tal creder non ho io pur prove
fisice e metafisice, ma dalmi
anche la verità che quinci piove
  per Moïsè, per profeti e per salmi,
per l'Evangelio e per voi che scriveste
poi che l'ardente Spirto vi fé almi.

(ibid. ll. 130-38)[21]

And what applies in Canto XXIV by way of the pristine power of
the text to persuasion, applies also in the following cantos, where it is a
question, not of faith, but of hope and, as the greatest of these things, of
love as formed dispositions of the spirit. Here as before, Dante proceeds
by way (a) of the *quid est*, of saying what the virtue in question consists of,
and (b) of the *quo est*, of explaining how he himself came to be in possession
of it. If, then, hope, considered in itself, is but the sure expectation of
future glory as resting upon grace and upon antecedent merit, and if love,
again considered in itself, is but the connatural movement of the mind
towards the good as present in the forum of consciousness, each only ever
follows on from the positive encounter, from the evidence afforded either
by the text or by existence itself as but the text writ large; so, for example,
on the word as eloquent in respect of the mighty acts of God and tending
as such to engender in the attentive spirit a mood of lively expectation and
glowing ardour, these lines from Cantos XXV and XXVI:

"Spene", diss' io, "è uno attender certo
de la gloria futura, il qual produce
grazia divina e precedente merto.
  Da molte stelle mi vien questa luce;

[21] And I reply: I believe in one God, sole and eternal, who, unmoved, moves all heaven
with love and with desire; and for this belief I have, not only proofs physical and
metaphysical, but it is given me also in the truth that rains down hence through Moses
and the prophets and the psalms, through the gospel and through you who wrote after
the fiery Spirit had made you holy.   I. Borzi, 'L'apoteosi della fede (*Par.* XXIV)', in *Verso
l'ultima salute. Saggi danteschi* (Milan: Rusconi, 1985), pp. 177-209 (subsequently in S.
Zennaro (ed.), *Paradiso. Letture degli anni 1979-81* (Rome: Bonacci, 1989), pp. 643-66); F.
Di Gregorio, 'Il canto XXIV del *Paradiso*. La fede tra *ousia* e letteratura', in *L'Alighieri.
Rassegna bibliografica dantesca* 30, n.s., 1 (1989), 15-44 (and in *Violenza e carità* (San Severo:
Gerni,1995), pp. 31-54); B. Porcelli, '*Par.* XXIV e la sequenza degli esami sulle virtù
teologali', in *Nuovi studi su Dante e Boccaccio con analisi della 'Nencia'* (Pisa and Rome: Istituti
editoriali e poligrafici internazionali, 1997), pp. 41-55 (and in V. Masiello (ed.), *Studi di
filologia e letteratura italiana in onore di Gianvito Resta* (Rome: Salerno, 2000), pp. 203-21); A.
Battistini, 'Fede e bellezza. Il tessuto metaforico del canto XXIV del *Paradiso*', *L'Alighieri.
Rassegna dantesca* 45, n.s. 24 (2004), 79-92.

ma quei la distillò nel mio cor pria
che fu sommo cantor del sommo duce.
   'Sperino in te', ne la sua tëodia
dice, 'color che sanno il nome tuo':
e chi nol sa, s'elli ha la fede mia?
   Tu mi stillasti, con lo stillar suo,
ne la pistola poi; sì ch'io son pieno,
e in altrui vostra pioggia repluo"

...

   Quella medesma voce che paura
tolta m'avea del sùbito abbarbaglio,
di ragionare ancor mi mise in cura;
   e disse: "Certo a più angusto vaglio
ti conviene schiarar: dicer convienti
chi drizzò l'arco tuo a tal berzaglio".
   E io: "Per filosofici argomenti
e per autorità che quinci scende
cotale amor convien che in me si 'mprenti:
   ché 'l bene, in quanto ben, come s'intende,
così accende amore, e tanto maggio
quanto più di bontate in sé comprende.
   Dunque a l'essenza ov' è tanto avvantaggio,
che ciascun ben che fuor di lei si trova
altro non è ch'un lume di suo raggio,
   più che in altra convien che si mova
la mente, amando, di ciascun che cerne
il vero in che si fonda questa prova.
   Tal vero a l'intelletto mïo sterne
colui che mi dimostra il primo amore
di tutte le sustanze sempiterne.
   Sternel la voce del verace autore,
che dice a Moïsè, di sé parlando:
'Io ti farò vedere ogne valore'.
   Sternilmi tu ancora, incominciando
l'alto preconio che grida l'arcano
di qui là giù sovra ogne altro bando".

(*Par.* XXV.67-78 and XXVI.19-45)[22]

---

[22] "Hope", I said, "is a sure expectation of future glory, which divine grace produces, and preceding merit. From many stars this light comes to me, but he first distilled it in my heart who was the supreme singer of the supreme leader. 'Let them hope in you who know your name', he says in his divine song; and who knows it not, if he have my faith? You afterwards in your epistle did distil it in me, together with his distilling, so that I am full and pour again your shower on others" ... The same voice that had delivered me from

while on the life and death of the Christ in particular, not to mention the
sheer exhilaration of existence in general (the 'essere del mondo e l'esser
mio' of line 58), as apt upon reflection to confirm the soul in the way of
right loving, these lines again from Canto XXVI:

> E io udi': "Per intelletto umano
> e per autoritadi a lui concorde
> d'i tuoi amori a Dio guarda il sovrano.
> Ma dì ancor se tu senti altre corde
> tirarti verso lui, sì che tu suone
> con quanti denti questo amor ti morde".
> Non fu latente la santa intenzione
> de l'aguglia di Cristo, anzi m'accorsi
> dove volea menar mia professione.
> Però ricominciai: "Tutti quei morsi
> che posson far lo cor volgere a Dio,
> a la mia caritate son concorsi:
> ché l'essere del mondo e l'esser mio,
> la morte ch'el sostenne perch' io viva,
> e quel che spera ogne fedel com' io,
> con la predetta conoscenza viva,
> tratto m'hanno del mar de l'amor torto,
> e del diritto m'han posto a la riva.

my fear at the sudden dazzlement gave me concern to speak again; and it said, "Assuredly
you must sift with a finer sieve: you must tell who directed your bow to such a target".
And I: "By philosophic arguments, and by authority that descends from here, such love
must needs imprint itself on me; for the good, inasmuch as it is good, kindles love in
proportion as it is understood, and so much the more the more of good it contains in itself.
Therefore, to that essence wherein is such supremacy that whatsoever good be found
outside of it is naught else save a beam of its own radiance, more than to any other must
the mind be moved, in love, of whoever discerns the truth on which this proof is founded.
Such a truth he makes plain to my intelligence who demonstrates to me the first love of all
the eternal substances. The voice of the veracious author makes it plain where, speaking
of himself, he says to Moses, 'I will make you see all goodness'. You also set it forth to
me in the beginning of your sublime proclamation, which more than any other heralding,
declares below the mystery of this place on high." A. Tartaro, 'Certezze e speranza
nel XXV del *Paradiso*', *L'Alighieri. Rassegna bibliografica dantesca* 24 (1983), 1, 3-15 (also,
idem, 'Il canto XXV del *Paradiso*', in S. Zennaro (ed.), *Paradiso. Letture degli anni 1979-'81
tenute nella Casa di Dante* (Rome: Bonacci, 1989), pp. 667-83); E. Pasquini, 'Il canto della
speranza (*Pd* XXV)', in M. De Nichilo et al. (eds), *Confini dell'Umanesimo letterario. Studi in
onore di Francesco Tateo*, 3 vols (Rome: Roma nel Rinascimento, 2003), vol. 3, pp. 1039-47;
V. Capelli, 'Lettura del canto XXV del *Paradiso*. La speranza di Dante', in *Letture dantesche
tenute nella pieve di Polenta e nella basilica di S. Mercuriale in Forlì (1996-2005)* (Genoa and
Milan: Marietti, 2006), pp. 269-83. Also, J. Moltmann, 'Speranza cristiana: messianica
o trascendentale? Un dibattito teologico con Gioacchino da Fiore e Tommaso d'Aquino',
Asprenas 30 (1983), 23-46.

Le fronde onde s'infronda tutto l'orto
de l'ortolano etterno, am' io cotanto
quanto da lui a lor di bene è porto".
    Sì com' io tacqui, un dolcissimo canto
risonò per lo cielo, e la mia donna
dicea con li altri: "Santo, santo, santo!".

(Par. XXVI.46-69)[23]

Everywhere, then, the pattern is the same, for everywhere it is a question of Dante's trusting to the power of the event itself to impress as the means of divine purposefulness. But the price is high, for to settle on the power of the event itself to impress is to settle for the exclusion of those who, through no fault of their own, are a stranger to the event, and it is in this context that Dante begins to experiment with a revised scheme, with an alternative way of seeing and setting up the question of election. As if constrained by the innermost logic of it all (which for Dante is always the innermost *affective* logic of it all), old inclinations give way to a fresh configuration of thought, to a sense after all of God's willingness (*a*) to hear the prayer of those most anxious in respect of the predicament of the virtuous pagan, and (*b*) to grace the pagan spirit with a view to bringing it home at last to the high consistory of paradise. This at any rate – this twofold preoccupation with the susceptibility of the Godhead at the point of intercession and with the boundlessness of his grace with respect even to those innocent of Christ and clergy – is the substance of his discourse in the soteriological cantos *par excellence* of the *Commedia*, Cantos XIX and XX of the *Paradiso*, cantos which start out with the apparent injustice of things as they stand, with the apparent *un*righteousness of reprobating the merely unfortunate:

Assai t'è mo aperta la latebra
che t'ascondeva la giustizia viva,
di che facei question cotanto crebra;

<hr>

[23] And I heard: "On the ground of human reason and of the authorities concordant with it, the highest of all your loves looks to God; but tell me also if you feel other cords draw you toward him, so that you declare with how many teeth this love grips you." The holy intention of the Eagle of Christ was not hidden, indeed it was plain to me whither he would direct my profession. Therefore I began again: "All those things whose bite can make the heart turn to God have wrought together in my love; for the being of the world and my own being, the death that he sustained that I might live, and that which every believer hopes, as do I, with the living assurance of which I spoke, have drawn me from the sea of perverse love and placed me on the shore of right love. The leaves wherewith all the garden of the eternal gardener is enleaved I love in measure of the good borne unto them from him." As soon as I was silent a most sweet song resounded through the heaven, and my lady sang with the rest, "Holy, Holy, Holy!"

ché tu dicevi: "Un uom nasce a la riva
de l'Indo, e quivi non è chi ragioni
di Cristo né chi legga né chi scriva;
    e tutti suoi voleri e atti buoni
sono, quanto ragione umana vede,
sanza peccato in vita o in sermoni.
    Muore non battezzato e sanza fede:
ov' è questa giustizia che 'l condanna?
ov' è la colpa sua, se ei non crede?"

(*Par.* XIX.67-78)[24]

Thus the question everywhere lurking just beneath the surface
of Dante's particular species of bi-culturalism, the question of his
'simultaneous attachment both to Christianity and to paganism',[25] rises
up now to confront him in all its power not only to confound but, in its
apparent injustice, to scandalize the pious spirit. First, then, comes the
admonitory moment of the argument, the warning off of those taking it
upon themselves to question the substance of divine justice:

Or tu chi se', che vuo' sedere a scranna,
per giudicar di lungi mille miglia
con la veduta corta d'una spanna?
    Certo a colui che meco s'assottiglia,
se la Scrittura sovra voi non fosse,
da dubitar sarebbe a maraviglia.
    Oh terreni animali! oh menti grosse!
La prima volontà, ch'è da sé buona,
da sé, ch'è sommo ben, mai non si mosse.
    Cotanto è giusto quanto a lei consuona:
nullo creato bene a sé la tira,
ma essa, radïando, lui cagiona.

(*Par.* XIX.79-90)[26]

[24] Now is laid well open to you the hiding place which concealed from you the living
justice concerning which you have made question so incessantly. For you said: "A man
is born on the banks of the Indus, and none is there to speak, or read, or write of Christ,
and all his wishes and acts are good, so far as human reason sees, without sin in life or
in speech. He dies unbaptized, and without faith. Where is this justice which condemns
him? Where is his sin if he does not believe?"

[25] K. Foster, O.P., 'The Two Dantes (I): Limbo and Implicit Faith', in *The Two Dantes and
Other Studies* (London: Darton, Longman and Todd, 1977), p. 156.

[26] Now who are you who would sit upon the seat to judge at a thousand miles away with
the short sight that carries but a span? Assuredly, for him who subtilizes with me, if the
Scriptures were not set over you, there would be marvelous occasion for questioning.

But this, as Dante knows full well, is no answer at all, admonition being one thing but affirmation quite another. The answer proper – spectacular for its fashioning from one of Christ's harder sayings in the gospel (the 'a diebus autem Joannis Baptistae usque nunc, regnum cœlorum vim patitur, et violenti rapiunt illud' of Matthew 11:12)[27] a statement of superlative graciousness – comes in the next canto, Canto XX, beginning at line 94; for to contemplate the Godhead in its essential nature, Dante insists, is to contemplate it in terms, not of its *impassivity*, but of its *vulnerability*, of its readiness to give way to love in the elementary integrity of love, giving way, in God, being the sign, not of his defeat, but of his victory, of the victory of love over lovelessness:

> *Regnum celorum* vïolenza pate
> da caldo amore e da viva speranza,
> che vince la divina volontate:
>   non a guisa che l'omo a l'om sobranza,
> ma vince lei perché vuole esser vinta,
> e, vinta, vince con sua beninanza.[28]

O earthly animals! O gross minds! The primal will, which of itself is good, has never moved from itself, which is the supreme good. All is just that accords with it; no created good draws it to itself, but it, raying forth, is the cause of it. Cf. *Mon.* II.ii.4-5: 'Ex hiis iam liquet quod ius, cum sit bonum, per prius in mente Dei est; et, cum omne quod in mente Dei est sit Deus, iuxta illud "Quod factum est in ipso vita erat", et Deus maxime se ipsum velit, sequitur quod ius a Deo, prout in eo est, sit volitum. Et cum voluntas et volitum in Deo sit idem, sequitur ulterius quod divina voluntas sit ipsum ius. Et iterum ex hoc sequitur quod ius in rebus nichil est aliud quam similitudo divine voluntatis; unde fit quod quicquid divine voluntati non consonat, ipsum ius esse non possit, et quicquid divine voluntati est consonum, ius ipsum sit.'

[27] ever since the coming of John the Baptist the kingdom of Heaven has been subjected to violence and violent men are seizing it (*NEB*). Cf. Luke 16:16: 'Lex et prophetae, usque ad Joannem: ex eo regnum Dei evangelizatur, et omnis in illud vim facit.'

[28] *Regnum celorum* suffers violence from fervent love and from living hope which vanquishes the divine will; not as man overcomes man, but vanquishes it because it wills to be vanquished, and, vanquished, vanquishes with its own benignity.   G. Cannavò, *Regnum celorum vïolenza pate. Dante e la salvezza dell'umanità. Letture Dantesche Giubilari, Vicenza, ottobre 1999 - giugno 2000* (Montella (Avellino): Accademia Vivarium Novum, 2002), with, at pp. 193-203, A. M. Chiavacci Leonardi, 'La salvezza degli infedeli: il canto XX del *Paradiso*' (subsequently in *Le bianche stole. Saggi sul Paradiso di Dante* (Florence: Sismel, 2009), pp. 97-112). Also, F. Ruffini, 'Dante e il problema della salvezza degli infedeli', *Studi danteschi* 14 (1930), 79-92; B. Quilici, *Il destino dell'infedele virtuoso nel pensiero di Dante* (Florence: Ariani, 1936); T. O'H. Hahn, 'I "gentili" e "un uom nasce a la riva / de l'Indo" (*Par.* XIX, vv.70 sqq.)', *L'Alighieri. Rassegna bibliografica dantesca* 18 (1977), 2, 3-8; R. Morghen, 'Dante tra l'"umano" e la storia della salvezza', in *L'Alighieri. Rassegna bibliografica dantesca* 21 (1980), 1, 18-30; N. Iliescu, 'Will Virgil be saved?', *Mediaevalia* 12 (1986), 93-114 and as 'Sarà salvo Virgilio?' in C. Franco and L. Morgan (eds), *Dante. Summa medievalis. Proceedings of the Symposium of the Center for Italian Studies, SUNY Stony*

Now here, clearly, we have to be careful, for there can be no question of stepping outside grace as the encompassing, as the first and final cause of every salvific inflexion of the spirit in man. On the contrary, as Dante goes on to make plain in this canto, it is by grace and grace alone that the individual is brought home to the fold:

> D'i corpi suoi non uscir, come credi,
> Gentili, ma Cristiani, in ferma fede
> quel d'i passuri e quel d'i passi piedi.
> Ché l'una de lo 'nferno, u' non si riede
> già mai a buon voler, tornò a l'ossa;

Brook, (Stony Brook, N.Y.: Forum Italicum, 1995), pp. 112-33; M. Allan, 'Does Dante hope for Vergil's Salvation?', *Modern Language Notes* 104 (1989), 193-205; M. Picone, 'La "viva speranza" di Dante e il problema della salvezza dei pagani virtuosi. Una lettura di *Paradiso* 20', *Quaderni di Italianistica* 10 (1989), 1-2, 251-68; idem, '*Auctoritas* classica e salvezza cristiana: una lettura tipologica di *Purgatorio* XXII', in *Studi in memoria di Giorgio Varanini* (Pisa: Giardini, 1992), vol. I (*Dal Duecento al Quattrocento*), pp. 379-95; T. Barolini, 'Q: Does Dante hope for Vergil's Salvation?', *Modern Language Notes* 105 (1990), 1, 138-44 and 147-49 (and in *Dante and the Origins of Italian Literary Culture* (New York: Fordham University Press, 2006), pp. 151-57); B. D. Schildgen, 'Dante and the Indus', *Dante Studies* 111 (1993), 177-93; eadem, 'Dante's Utopian Political Vision, the Roman Empire, and the Salvation of Pagans', *Annali d'Italianistica* 19 (2001), 51-69; G. Muresu, 'Le "vie" della redenzione (*Paradiso* VII)', *Rassegna della letteratura italiana*, ser. 8, 98 (1994), 1-2, 5-19; N. Cacciaglia, '"Per fede e per opere" (una lettura del tema della salvezza nella *Divina Commedia*)', in *Critica Letteraria* 30 (2002), 2-3, 265-74 (also in *Annali dell'Università per Stranieri di Perugia* 29 (2002), 123-131); B. Martinelli, 'Canto XIX', in G. Güntert and M. Picone (eds), *Lectura Dantis Turicensis. Paradiso* (Florence: Cesati, 2002), pp. 281-305 (revised with the title 'La fede in Cristo. Dante e il problema della salvezza (*Paradiso* XIX)', *Rivista di Letteratura Italiana* 20 (2002), 2, 11-39, and in *Dante. L'"altro viaggio"* (Pisa: Giardini, 2007), pp. 289-319); G. Inglese, 'Il destino dei non credenti. Lettura di *Paradiso* XIX', La Cultura. Rivista trimestrale di filosofia letteratura e storia 42 (2004), 2, 315-29; A. Lanza, 'Giustizia divina e salvezza dei 'senza fede', in *Dante eterodosso* (Bergamo: Moretti Honegger, 2004), pp. 113-24; C. O'Connell Baur, *Dante's Hermeneutics of Salvation. Passages to Freedom in the Divine Comedy* (Toronto, Buffalo and London: University of Toronto Press, 2007). More generally, S. Harent, 'Infidèles, Salut des', in P. Moraux et al. (eds), *Dictionnaire de Théologie Catholique*, 15 vols (Paris: Letouzey et Ané, 1909-46), vol. 7, ii, cols 1276-1930; L. Capéran, *Le Problème du salut des infidèles*, 2 vols, revised edn (Toulouse: Grand Séminaire, 1934); T. P. Dunning 'Langland and the Salvation of the Heathen', Medium Aevum 12 (1943), 45-54; M. Frezza, *Il problema della salvezza dei pagani (da Abelardo al Seicento)* (Naples: Fiorentino, 1962); R. V. Turner, '"Descendit ad Inferos". Medieval Views on Christ's descent into Hell and the Salvation of the Ancient Just', *Journal of the History of Ideas* 27 (1966), 173-94; C. L. Vitto, *The Virtuous Pagan in Middle English Literature, Transactions of the American Philosophical Society* 79, part 5 (Philadelphia: The American Philosophical Society, 1989); N. Watson, 'Visions of Inclusion. Universal Salvation and Vernacular Theology in Pre-Reformation England', *Journal of Medieval and Early Modern Studies* 27 (1997), 145-88. On the cases of Trajan and Rhipeus, G. Whately, 'The Uses of Hagiography: the Legend of Pope Gregory and the Emperor Trajan in the Middle Ages' (note 8 above).

e ciò di viva spene fu mercede:
di viva spene, che mise la possa
ne' prieghi fatti a Dio per suscitarla,
sì che potesse sua voglia esser mossa.

L'anima glorïosa onde si parla,
tornata ne la carne, in che fu poco,
credette in lui che potëa aiutarla;

e credendo s'accese in tanto foco
di vero amor, ch'a la morte seconda
fu degna di venire a questo gioco.

L'altra, per grazia che da sì profonda
fontana stilla, che mai creatura
non pinse l'occhio infino a la prima onda,

tutto suo amor là giù pose a drittura:
per che, di grazia in grazia, Dio li aperse
l'occhio a la nostra redenzion futura;

ond' ei credette in quella, e non sofferse
da indi il puzzo più del paganesmo;
e riprendiene le genti perverse.

(*Par.* XX.103-26)[29]

But that neither is nor can be the end of the matter, for grace, properly understood, is a question, not only of facilitation, but of recognition, of welcoming home the one graced as itself a matter of grace, at which point, given the unspeakable substance of divine goodness and the unspeakable extent of divine loving, neither of them susceptible to contemplation 'within the short span of a man's hand', the way is open for a bringing home, not simply of those knowing the law, but of those knowing not the law but having it nonetheless inscribed on their heart.[30] In fashioning,

---

[29] They came forth from their bodies not as you think, gentiles, but Christians, with firm faith, the one in the feet that were to suffer, the other in the feet that had suffered. For the one came back to his bones from hell, where none ever returns to right will; and this was the reward of living hope, of living hope that gave power to the prayers made to God to raise him up, that it might be possible for his will to be moved. The glorious soul I tell of, having returned to the flesh for a short time, believed in him that was able to help him; and, believing, was kindled to such a fire of true love that on his second death he was worthy to come to this rejoicing. The other, through grace that wells from a fountain so deep that never did creature thrust eye down to its first wave, set all his love below on righteousness; wherefore, from grace to grace, God opened his eye to our future redemption, so that he believed in it, and therefore endured not the stench of paganism, and reproved the perverse peoples for it.

[30] Romans 2:11-15: 'Non est enim personarum acceptio apud Deum. Quicumque enim sine lege peccaverunt, sine lege et peribunt; et quicumque in lege peccaverunt, per legem iudicabuntur. Non enim auditores legis iusti sunt apud Deum, sed factores legis

in other words, from one of Christ's harder sayings an essay in divine vulnerability, in God's being defeated because he wishes to be defeated, Dante, just for a moment, delivers himself to something quite other than the exclusivities of classical soteriological consciousness, to a sense of how it is that, espying his son from afar, the Father rushes out to meet him, falling as he does so upon his neck and kissing him.[31] The moment, in short, is stupendous, for this, like all great theology, is theology busy about its own undoing, its dismantling of the leading emphasis in favour of something still more sublime.

iustificabuntur. Cum enim gentes, quae legem non habent, naturaliter ea quae legis sunt faciunt, eiusmodi legem non habentes, ipsi sibi sunt lex; qui ostendunt opus legis scriptum in cordibus suis, testimonium reddente illis conscientia ipsorum, et inter se invicem cogitationum accusantium aut etiam defendentium.'

[31] In respect of the hastening motif, the 'così corre ad amore' passage of *Purg.* XV.64-72: 'Ed elli a me: "Però che tu rificchi / la mente pur a le cose terrene, / di vera luce tenebre dispicchi. / Quello infinito e ineffabil bene / che là sù è, così corre ad amore / com' a lucido corpo raggio vene. / Tanto si dà quanto trova d'ardore; / sì che, quantunque carità si stende, / cresce sovr' essa l'etterno valore".'

Chapter 3
Desire and Destiny

> ed ènne dolce così fatto scemo,
> perché il ben nostro in questo ben s'affina,
> che quel che vole Dio, e noi volemo.
>
> (*Par.* XX.136-38)[1]

1. Introduction: the aetiology of desire. 2. Aquinas, *desiderium naturale* and a moment's uncertainty. 3. Dante and the coincidence of being and desiring in man. 4. Dante and predestination: a preliminary statement. 5. Aquinas and destiny under the aspect of transmission. 6. Dante and destiny under the aspect of emergence.

For both Dante and Aquinas the end of the moral and religious life lies in a direct vision of God, in a *visio Dei* apt to satisfy every kind of moral and intellectual yearning; so, for example, as far as Thomas is concerned, this passage – probably familiar to Dante – from the *Contra gentiles* on man's knowing God as the final cause of all he is and of all he has it in him to be and to become:

> Cum autem omnes creaturae, etiam intellectu carentes, ordinentur in Deum sicut in finem ultimum; ad hunc autem finem pertingunt omnia inquantum de similitudine eius aliquid participant: intellectuales creaturae aliquo speciliori modo ad ipsum pertingunt, scilicet per propriam operationem intelligendo ipsum. Unde oportet quod hoc sit finis intellectualis creaturae, scilicet intelligere Deum.
>
> (*ScG* III.xxv.1)[2]

---

[1] and to us such defect is sweet, because our good in this good is refined, that what God wills we also will.

[2] Since all creatures, even those devoid of understanding, are ordered to God as to an ultimate end, all achieve this end to the extent that they participate somewhat in his likeness. Intellectual creatures attain it in a more special way, that is, through their proper operation of understanding him. Hence this must be the end of the intellectual creature, namely to understand God. (Translation here and throughout, A. C. Pegis, New York: Image Books, 1955-57).

while as far as Dante is concerned this from the *Convivio* (IV.xii.14) on the return of the soul to God as the author and archetype of its presence in the world:

> E però che Dio è principio de le nostre anime e fattore di quelle simili a sé (sì come è scritto: "Facciamo l'uomo ad imagine e similitudine nostra"), essa anima massimamente desidera di tornare a quello.[3]

But the question arises as to where this yearning for God as the beginning and end of all yearning comes from. Is it from God or is it from man? Is it something which God instills in man subsequently, over and beyond his normal pattern of seeing, understanding and desiring, or is it there from the outset, as part of the original and abiding economy of specifically human being under the conditions of time and space? Aquinas wavers, but in keeping with the forces of Augustinianism and Neo-Augustinianism decisive for the shape and substance of his mature spirituality he is, with the passage of time, more inclined to the former than to the latter, to the notion that it is God himself who, bringing man home to the light of glory through a movement of grace as at once healing, illuminating and elevating, starts the whole thing off by breathing into him, as and when he so chooses, a desire to be in, through, and for his maker. Dante, by contrast, while maintaining a sense of the need for grace as the condition of every salvifically significant movement of the spirit, wishes to confirm the nature and status of that yearning as a property of what man as man already is as a creature of perception, predilection and orderly appetition. His desire for God is not instilled at some point along the way. It is there from the outset as a principle of self-interpretation.

2. Aquinas, as regards the notion of *desiderium naturale* or of man's natural yearning for God, is, as we have noted, uncertain, at times appearing to endorse the co-extensivity of being and desiring in man while elsewhere tending to refer the soul's desire for God to a special movement of grace. In relation, then, to his sense of the co-extensivity of these things, we may begin by noting Question 12 of the *Pars prima* of the *Summa theologiae*, a question which, concerned as it is with how far the creature is able to know the creator as of the essence ('per essentiam'), settles on the idea that to witness an effect in the world is to be curious about its first cause, an idea leading on to that of a natural desire for God: 'Inest enim homini naturale desiderium cognoscendi causam, cum intuetur effectum; et ex

---

[3] And since God is the first cause of our souls, and creates them in his own likeness (for thus it is written in Scripture: "Let us make man in our own image and likeness"), the soul desires first and foremost to return to him. (Translations from the *Convivio* by Christopher Ryan, *The Banquet*, Saratoga, Calif.: Anma Libri, 1989).

hoc admiratio in hominibus consurgit. Si igitur intellectus rationalis creaturae pertingere non possit ad primam causam rerum, remanebit inane desiderium naturae' (art. 1, resp.).[4] True, the article in question bears less on the *origin* than on the *fulfilment* of man's desire to see God, but its point of departure is unequivocal, the registering of effects in human experience carrying with it a desire to know not only their proximate but their primary cause. And this, to move on to the *Prima secundae*, is Thomas's position at 3.8, where it is a question of man's proper happiness as man. Anxious, then, to confirm how it is that the happiness proper to man as man lies in a vision of the divine essence, he proceeds to a distinction between the *that it is* ('an est') and the *what it is* ('quid est') of the Godhead as present to the created intellect, the former at once giving way to the latter as an object of concern:

> Si ergo intellectus aliquis cognoscat essentiam alicuius effectus, per quam non possit cognosci essentia causae, ut scilicet sciatur de causa quid est, non dicitur intellectus attingere ad causam simpliciter, quamvis per effectum cognoscere possit de causa an sit. Et ideo remanet naturaliter homini desiderium, cum cognoscit effectum, et scit eum habere causam, ut etiam sciat de causa quid est. ... Nec ista inquisitio quiescit quousque perveniat ad cognoscendum essentiam causae. Si igitur intellectus humanus, cognoscens essentiam alicuius effectus creati, non cognoscat de Deo nisi an est, nondum perfectio eius attingit simpliciter ad causam primam, sed remanet ei adhuc naturale desiderium inquirendi causam. Unde nondum est perfecte beatus. Ad perfectam igitur beatitudinem requiritur quod intellectus pertingat ad ipsam essentiam primae causae. Et sic perfectionem suam habebit per unionem ad Deum sicut ad obiectum, in quo solo beatitudo hominis consistit, ut supra dictum est.

> (*ST* Ia IIae.3.8 resp.)[5]

[4] For there resides in man a natural desire to know the cause of any effect which he sees; and thence arises wonder. But if the intellect of the rational creature could not reach so far as to the first cause of things, natural desire would remain void. A. Finili, 'Natural desire', *Dominican Studies* 1 (1948), 313-59; 2 (1949), 1-15; and 5 (1952), 159-84 ('New light on natural desire?'); J. Laporta, 'Pour trouver le sens exact des termes *appetitus naturalis, desiderium naturale, amor naturalis* etc. chez Thomas D'Aquin', *Archives d'histoire doctrinale et littéraire du moyen âge* 40 (1973), 37-95; L. Feingold, *The Natural Desire to See God according to St Thomas Aquinas and his Interpreters*, 2nd edn (Naples Florida: Sapientia Press of Ave Maria Univerisity, 2010).

[5] If, therefore, an intellect knows the essence of some effect, whereby it is not possible to know the essence of the cause, i.e. to know of the cause 'what it is', that intellect cannot be said to reach that cause simply, although it may be able to gather from the effect the knowledge that there is a cause. Consequently, when man knows an effect, and knows that it has a cause, there naturally remains in him the desire to know about the cause, 'what it is' ... Nor does this inquiry cease until he arrives at a knowledge of the essence of

Man's, therefore, inasmuch as it is a relentless seeking out of causes, is a relentless seeking out of the first cause, a notion explored in the *Contra gentiles* by way of the gathering momentum of his desire for understanding as he approaches the object of that understanding. The closer a man comes to God in point of intellection, the more eagerly he tends towards him as his point of arrival:

> Amplius. Corpus, quod naturali appetitu tendit in suum ubi, tanto vehementius et velocius movetur, quanto magis appropinquat fini ... Quod igitur vehementius in aliquid tendit postea quam prius, non movetur ad infinitum, sed ad aliquid determinatum tendit. Hoc autem invenimus in desiderio sciendi: quanto enim aliquis plura scit, tanto maiori desiderio affectat scire. Tendit igitur desiderium naturale hominis in sciendo ad aliquem determinatum finem. Hoc autem non potest esse aliud quam nobilissimum scibile, quod Deus est. Est igitur cognitio divina finis ultimus hominis.
>
> (*ScG* III.xxv.13)[6]

So much, then, is clear. Man as man, Thomas maintains, seeks out both intellection and ultimate intellection, all of which can only ever culminate in the moment of his resting in God as the alpha and omega of all intellection.

Elsewhere, however, Thomas is not so sure, other passages tending to suggest a referral of man's desire to know God, not to nature, but to grace as to its point of departure; so, for example, *ST* Ia.62.2, an article which, though concerned with angels or separate substances, reaches out to cover all reasonable creatures. The question here, then, is whether any reasonable creature, human or angelic, can turn to God without the grace whereby such turning is a possibility, Thomas's solution, secure in

---

the cause. If, therefore, the human intellect, knowing the essence of some created effect, knows no more of God than 'that He is', the perfection of that intellect does not yet reach simply the first cause, but there remains in it the natural desire to seek the cause. Wherefore it is not yet perfectly happy. Consequently, for perfect happiness the intellect needs to reach the very essence of the first cause. And thus it will have its perfection through union with God as with that object, in which alone man's happiness consists, as stated above [qu. 1, art. 7; qu. 2, art. 8].

[6] Furthermore, a body tending towards its proper place by natural appetite is moved more forcibly and swiftly as it approaches its end ... So a thing that tends more forcibly later rather than earlier towards an objective, is not moved towards an indefinite objective, but tends towards some determinate thing. Now we find this situation in the desire to know. The more a person knows, the more he is moved by desire to know. Hence man's natural desire tends, in the process of knowing, towards some definite end. Now this can be none other than the most noble object of knowledge, which is God. Therefore, divine knowledge is the ultimate end of man.

its sense of grace as a condition, not simply of the fulfilment of willing, but of willing itself, running as follows:

> Respondeo dicendum quod angeli indiguerunt gratia ad hoc quod converterentur in Deum, prout est obiectum beatitudinis. Sicut enim superius dictum est, naturalis motus voluntatis est principium omnium eorum quae volumus. Naturalis autem inclinatio voluntatis est ad id quod est conveniens secundum naturam. Et ideo, si aliquid sit supra naturam, voluntas in id ferri non potest, nisi ab aliquo alio supernaturali principio adiuta. Sicut patet quod ignis habet naturalem inclinationem ad calefaciendum, et ad generandum ignem, sed generare carnem est supra naturalem virtutem ignis, unde ignis ad hoc nullam inclinationem habet, nisi secundum quod movetur ut instrumentum ab anima nutritiva. Ostensum est autem supra, cum de Dei cognitione ageretur, quod videre Deum per essentiam, in quo ultima beatitudo rationalis creaturae consistit, est supra naturam cuiuslibet intellectus creati. Unde nulla creatura rationalis potest habere motum voluntatis ordinatum ad illam beatitudinem, nisi mota a supernaturali agente. Et hoc dicimus auxilium gratiae. Et ideo dicendum est quod angelus in illam beatitudinem voluntate converti non potuit, nisi per auxilium gratiae.

(ST Ia.62.2 resp.)[7]

Grace, then, is doubly indispensable. It is indispensable as that whereby the soul is lifted to its supernatural end (an emphasis unnegotiable in Aquinas), and it is indispensable as that whereby the soul wills that end in the first place. Man as man, in other words, has no desire of his own to seek out God, such desire as he *does* have being the product of a special 'auxilium Dei' as its efficient cause. And this too is the position in the

---

[7] I answer that the angels stood in need of grace in order to turn to God, as the object of beatitude. For, as was observed above [qu. 60, art. 2], the natural movement of the will is the principle of all things that we will. But the will's natural inclination is directed towards what is in keeping with its nature. Therefore, if there is anything which is above nature, the will cannot be inclined towards it, unless helped by some other supernatural principle. Thus it is clear that fire has a natural tendency to give forth heat, and to generate fire; whereas to generate flesh is beyond the natural power of fire; consequently, fire has no tendency thereto, except in so far as it is moved instrumentally by the nutritive soul. Now it was shown above [qu. 12, arts 4 and 5], when we were treating of God's knowledge, that to see God in his essence, wherein the ultimate beatitude of the rational creature consists, is beyond the nature of every created intellect. Consequently, no rational creature can have the movement of the will directed towards such beatitude, except it be moved thereto by a supernatural agent. This is what we call the help of grace. Therefore it must be said that an angel could not of his own will be turned to such beatitude, except by the help of grace.

grace treatise of the *Prima secundae*, where again it is a question of the supernatural end exceeding not only man's capacity for knowing (for this goes without saying), but his capacity for desiring, desire, typically, not extending beyond the ordinarily accomplishable:

> Actus autem cuiuscumque rei non ordinatur divinitus ad aliquid excedens proportionem virtutis quae est principium actus, hoc enim est ex institutione divinae providentiae, ut nihil agat ultra suam virtutem. Vita autem aeterna est quoddam bonum excedens proportionem naturae creatae, quia etiam excedit cognitionem et desiderium eius, secundum illud I ad Cor. II, "nec oculus vidit, nec auris audivit, nec in cor hominis ascendit". Et inde est quod nulla natura creata est sufficiens principium actus meritorii vitae aeternae, nisi superaddatur aliquod supernaturale donum, quod gratia dicitur.

(*ST* Ia IIae.114.2 resp.)[8]

True, the question of desiring and of the limits of that desiring is touched upon here only in passing, Thomas's main concern in this question being whether or not man as man can, without grace, merit eternal life ('utrum aliquis sine gratia possit mereri vitam aeternam'). Even so, it *is* there and there explicitly, all of which has implications not least for the discipline of theology; for if there is no desire in man to see and to know God, then what use theology as a discipline of the spirit? Freefloating in respect of anything that actually matters to man as man, of anything genuinely present to him as a principle of self-interpretation, it cannot but subsist adiaphorously, somewhere on the edge of his experience as a creature of moral and ontological determination.

3. A preliminary statement of the position in Dante, of his sense of man as connaturally inclined towards communion with God as the beginning and end of his every striving on the planes of knowing and loving, occurs half way through the *Purgatorio* in the context of the great love discourses placed by Dante upon the lips of Virgil. Speaking of the overall structure of purgatory, and coming now to the middle and upper circles of the mountain (the circles of sloth, avarice, gluttony and lust), he, Virgil, notes

---

[8] Now no act of anything whatsoever is divinely ordained to anything exceeding the proportion of the powers which are the principles of its act; for it is a law of divine providence that nothing shall act beyond its powers. Now everlasting life is a good exceeding the proportion of created nature; since it exceeds its knowledge and desire, according to I Corinthians 2 [v. 9]: 'Eye hath not seen, nor ear heard, neither hath it entered into the heart of man.' And hence it is that no created nature is a sufficient principle of an act meritorious of eternal life, unless there is added a supernatural gift, which we call grace.

how it is that all men, if hazily, perceive a good in which the soul might
at last find rest, that good constituting henceforth the final cause of their
every moral endeavour:

> Ciascun confusamente un bene apprende
> nel qual si queti l'animo, e disira;
> per che di giugner lui ciascun contende.

(Purg. XVII.127-29)[9]

Everything, then, is present and correct, the intuitive moment of the
text registering the inkling of a good apt at last to still the soul in its
restlessness (the 'ciascun confusamente un bene apprende' of line 127), the
appetitive moment registering the turning-back of the soul upon this same
inkling in a spirit of yearning (the 'e desira' of line 128), and the conative
moment registering the notion of being as militant in respect of its proper
resolution (the 'per che di giugner lui ciascun contende' of line 129),[10] the
period as a whole thus giving expression to a sense of specifically human
being as projected being, as constrained from deep within itself to its
ecstatic finality. But it is above all the Paradiso, the canticle par excellence of
desiring in the Commedia, that testifies most completely to this sense of the
coincidence of being and yearning in man, of being, in man, as by nature a
matter of desiring. First, then, and as preliminary in respect of the notion
of yearning proper (for it is as yet a question merely of the instinctive
disposition of whatever is in the world to its own proper finality), comes
the 'cose tutte quante' passage on the threshold of the text:

> Le cose tutte quante
> hanno ordine tra loro, e questo è forma

[9] Each one apprehends vaguely a good wherein the mind may find rest, and this it
desires; wherefore each one strives to attain thereto. ScG III.xlviii.1: 'Si ergo humana
felicitas ultima non consistit in cognitione Dei qua communiter ab omnibus vel pluribus
cognoscitur secundum quandam aestimationem confusam, neque iterum in cognitione
Dei qua cognoscitur per viam demonstrationis in scientiis speculativis, neque in
cognitione Dei qua cognoscitur per fidem ...'; ST Ia.2.1 ad 1: 'cognoscere Deum esse in
aliquo communi, sub quadam confusione, est nobis naturaliter insertum, inquantum
scilicet Deus est hominis beatitudo, homo enim naturaliter desiderat beatitudinem, et
quod naturaliter desideratur ab homine, naturaliter cognoscitur ab eodem.'

[10] For 'giugnere' as privileged lexis in the area of properly human being and becoming,
Par. IV.124-32: 'Io veggio ben che già mai non si sazia / nostro intelletto, se 'l ver non
lo illustra / di fuor dal qual nessun vero si spazia. / Posasi in esso, come fera in lustra, /
tosto che giunto l'ha; e giugner puollo: / se non, ciascun disio sarebbe frustra. / Nasce per
quello, a guisa di rampollo, / a piè del vero il dubbio; ed è natura / ch'al sommo pinge noi di
collo in collo', and, in the final moments of the canticle, XXXIII.79-81: 'E' mi ricorda ch'io
fui più ardito / per questo a sostener, tanto ch'i' giunsi / l'aspetto mio col valore infinito.'

che l'universo a Dio fa simigliante.
  Qui veggion l'alte creature l'orma
de l'etterno valore, il qual è fine
al quale è fatta la toccata norma.
  Ne l'ordine ch'io dico sono accline
tutte nature, per diverse sorti,
più al principio loro e men vicine;
  onde si muovono a diversi porti
per lo gran mar de l'essere, e ciascuna
con istinto a lei dato che la porti

...

  Non dei più ammirar, se bene stimo,
lo tuo salir, se non come d'un rivo
se d'alto monte scende giuso ad imo.
  Maraviglia sarebbe in te se, privo
d'impedimento, giù ti fossi assiso,
com' a terra quïete in foco vivo.

(Par. I.103-114 and 136-41)[11]

The model, clearly, is at once Platonizing and Peripateticizing, a sense of the nearness and farness of things from their origin (the 'più al principio loro e men vicine' of line 111) being complemented within the passage as a whole by a sense of the operational integrity of those same things in their own right, and thus of the cosmos generally as no more than the sum total of its analogical perfections. And it is this Peripateticizing aspect of the model that, for the moment at least, prevails, Dante's in this sense being an essay in movement as a matter of *self*-movement, in the will to self-actualization everywhere manifest in creation and everywhere confirming it in its likeness to God as its author and architect (the 'che l'universo a Dio fa simigliante' of line 105). But disposition thus understood is, as we have said, merely preliminary to desiring, desiring bringing to disposition an element of knowingness, at which point instinct is taken up in something closer to intentionality, to a determinate movement of the spirit; hence, moving on from Canto I, the exquisite 'concreation' tercet of Canto II,

---

[11] All things have order among themselves, and this is the form that makes the universe like God. Herein the high creatures behold the imprint of the eternal worth, which is the end for which the aforesaid ordinance is made. In the world whereof I speak all natures are inclined by different lots, nearer and less near unto their principle; wherefore they move to different ports over the great sea of being, each with an instinct given it to bear it on ... You should not wonder more at your rising, if I deem aright, than at a stream that falls from a mountain top to the base. It would be a marvel if you, being freed from hindrance, had settled down below, even as stillness would be in living fire on earth.

irradiated now by a sense of being as present to itself under the aspect of yearning:

> La concreata e perpetüa sete
> del deïforme regno cen portava
> veloci quasi come 'l ciel vedete.

(Par. II.19-21)[12]

to which we must add the no less exquisite love-perpetuity tercet of Canto VII:

> ma vostra vita sanza mezzo spira
> la somma beninanza, e la innamora
> di sé sì che poi sempre la disira.

(Par. VII.142-44)[13]

and, as an essay in their own right in the bliss of spiritual 'approximation' or drawing nigh, these lines from the very beginning and the very end of the *Paradiso*:

> perché appressando sé al suo disire,
> nostro intelletto si profonda tanto,
> che dietro la memoria non può ire
>
> ...
>
> E io ch'al fine di tutt' i disii
> appropinquava, sì com' io dovea,
> l'ardor del desiderio in me finii.

(Par. I.7-9 and XXXIII.46-48)[14]

Everywhere, then, the pattern is the same, for everywhere it is a question of the restlessness of the soul until it rests in the One who *is* as of the essence, in God himself as the beginning and end of all yearning in the human spirit, yearning thus understood, however, pertaining to the soul, not superadditionally, but structurally, as part of what from the

---

[12] The concreate and perpetual thirst for the deiform realm bore us away, swift almost as you see the heavens.

[13] but your life the supreme beneficence breathes forth without intermediary, and so enamours it of itself that it desires it ever after.

[14] because, as it draws near to its desire, our intellect enters so deep that it cannot go back upon the track ... And I, who was drawing near to the end of all desires, raised to its utmost, even as I ought, the ardour of my longing. Similarly *Par.* XXXI.64-69: 'E "Ov' è ella?", sùbito diss' io. / Ond' elli: "A terminar lo tuo disiro / mosse Beatrice me del loco mio; / e se riguardi sù nel terzo giro / dal sommo grado, tu la rivedrai / nel trono che suoi merti le sortiro".'

moment of its inception it always was and always will be. In short, no desiring, no being, the former entering into the latter as a principle of its recognizability.[15]

4. Towards the end of the justice cantos of the *Paradiso* – cantos remarkable for their sense of the soteriological issue as a matter of God's willingness to grace and to bring home even those without Christ as the long-awaited redeemer – Dante apostrophizes predestination, stressing as he does so its inscrutability and, in a purely Dantean inflexion of the line, its sweetness, the intimate congeniality of the unknown as sustained by faith in God's good purposes:

> O predestinazion, quanto remota
> è la radice tua da quelli aspetti
> che la prima cagion non veggion tota!
>   E voi, mortali, tenetevi stretti
> a giudicar: ché noi, che Dio vedemo,
> non conosciamo ancor tutti li eletti;
>   ed ènne dolce così fatto scemo,
> perché il ben nostro in questo ben s'affina,
> che quel che vole Iddio, e noi volemo.

> (*Par.* XX.130-38)[16]

---

[15] F. Ferrucci, 'La dialettica del desiderio', in *Il poema del desiderio. Poetica e passione in Dante* (Milan: Leonardo, 1990), pp. 221-64 (revised in *Dante. Lo stupore e l'ordine* (Naples: Liguori, 2007), pp. 228-64); L. Pertile, '"La punta del disio": storia di una metafora dantesca', in *Lectura Dantis 7* (1990), 3-28 (revised in *La punta del disio. Semantica del desiderio nella 'Commedia'* (Florence: Cadmo, 2005), pp. 163-79); idem, '*Paradiso*; a Drama of Desire', in J. C. Barnes and J. Petrie (eds), *Word and Drama in Dante* (Dublin: Irish Academic Foundation, 1993), pp. 143-80 (with a revised version in A. A. Iannucci (ed.), *Dante. Contemporary Perspectives* (Toronto, Buffalo and London: University of Toronto Press, 1997), pp. 148-66 with the title 'A Desire of Paradise and a Paradise of Desire: Dante and Mysticism', and an Italian version entitled 'Desiderio di Paradiso' in *La punta del disio* cit., pp. 137-61); A. Brasioli, 'Il suono del desiderio', in *Dante. Lo sguardo, la realtà. Tre incontri su Dante* (Sottomarina: Il Leggio, 1995), pp. 63-96; P. A. Olson, 'Boethius's Wisdom and Dante's Architectonics of Desire', in *The Journey to Wisdom. Self-education in Patristic and Medieval Literature* (Lincoln, Neb. and London: University of Nebraska Press, 1995), pp. 147-71; A. M. Chiavacci Leonardi, 'Il *Paradiso* di Dante: l'ardore del desiderio', in *Letture classensi 27* (1998), pp. 101-12; D. Fasolini, '"E io ch'al fine di tutt'i disii appropinquava": un'interpretazione teologica del "desiderium" nel XXXIII canto del *Paradiso*', in *Forum Italicum. A Quarterly of Italian Studies 37* (2003), 2, 297-328; E. Lombardi, *The Syntax of Desire. Language and Love in Augustine, the Modistae, Dante* (Toronto, Buffalo and London: University of Toronto Press, 2007).

[16] O predestination, how remote is your root from the vision of those who see not the first cause entire! And you mortals, keep yourselves restrained in judging, for we, who see God, know not yet all the elect. And to us such defect is sweet, because our good in this good is refined, that what God wills we also will.

But inscrutability does not exhaust Dante's meditation at this point, for the notion of inscrutability where God's purposes are concerned issues for him in something more sublime; for it is a question now, not so much of the soul's being *sent on* to something qualitatively other and out of all proportion to anything we could possibly know or even imagine here and now, but rather of *emergence*, of its at last opening out upon its proper God-likeness or deiformity. Now here, clearly, we have to be careful, for emergence thus understood is also a matter of otherness, of the soul's tasting the as yet untasted as it comes into the immediate presence of God. But for all that, the two things are not the same, predestination, for Dante, being a matter, less of *consignment*, than of *confirmation*, of the soul's at last knowing itself in the properly ecstatic substance of its humanity, at which point, relieved of its power to terrify, it is present to the individual only under the aspect of predilection.

5. Thomas's sense of predestination as a sending on of the soul to an order of experience out of all proportion to anything we could possibly know or imagine here and now, and this, moreover, on a rigorously selective basis, is readily open to documentation from the text. Take, for example, this passage from the *Pars prima* of the *Summa theologiae* at 23.1 resp., a passage sensitive, certainly, to the notion of capacity (Thomas's 'capax vitae eternae') as a property of specifically human being, but above all to that of 'transmission', of making over the soul to something other than what it already is, as a way of developing the question of predestination:

> Finis autem ad quem res creatae ordinantur a Deo, est duplex. Unus, qui excedit proportionem naturae creatae et facultatem, et hic finis est vita aeterna, quae in divina visione consistit, quae est supra naturam cuiuslibet creaturae, ut supra habitum est. Alius autem finis est naturae creatae proportionatus, quem scilicet res creata potest attingere secundum virtutem suae naturae. Ad illud autem ad quod non potest aliquid virtute suae naturae pervenire, oportet quod ab alio transmittatur; sicut sagitta a sagittante mittitur ad signum. Unde, proprie loquendo, rationalis creatura, quae est capax vitae aeternae, perducitur in ipsam quasi a Deo transmissa. Cuius quidem transmissionis ratio in Deo praeexistit; sicut et in eo est ratio ordinis omnium in finem, quam diximus esse providentiam. Ratio autem alicuius fiendi in mente actoris existens, est quaedam praeexistentia rei fiendae in eo. Unde ratio praedictae transmissionis creaturae rationalis in finem vitae aeternae, praedestinatio nominatur, nam destinare est mittere.[17]

---

[17] The end towards which created things are directed by God is twofold, one of which exceeds all proportion and faculty of created nature; and this end is life eternal, that

Predestination then, for Thomas, is a matter (*a*) of God's reshaping or re-proportioning the individual in respect of the good awaiting him (the 'Unus, qui excedit proportionem naturae creatae' moment of the text), and (*b*) of this as a matter of prior determination in the recesses of the divine mind (its 'transmissionis ratio in Deo praeexistens' moment). God alone, as the archetypal archer ('sicut sagitta a sagittante mittitur ad signum'), decides and despatches, man, inasmuch as he enters into this process at all, entering into it by way of pure passivity, as ripe for onward conveyance in keeping with the primordial plan. But there is more, for Thomas's, in the *Pars prima*, is an account, not simply of the *what*, but of the *who* and of the *how many* of predestination, at which point, impressed by the near-bankruptcy of the human situation under its moral aspect, he is forced to conclude that few after all will be invited to the feast. Given the unpreparedness of the greater part of men for their own proper good, numbers, he thinks, will always be small:

> bonum proportionatum communi statui naturae, accidit ut in pluribus; et defectus ab hoc bono, ut in paucioribus. Sed bonum quod excedit communem statum naturae, invenitur ut in paucioribus; et defectus ab hoc bono, ut in pluribus. Sicut patet quod plures homines sunt qui habent sufficientem scientiam ad regimen vitae

consists in seeing God, which is above the nature of every creature, as shown above [qu. 12, art 4]. The other end, however, is proportionate to created nature, to which end created being can attain according to the power of its nature. Now if a thing cannot attain to something by the power of its nature, it must be directed thereto by another; thus, an arrow is directed by the archer towards a mark. Hence, properly speaking, a rational creature, capable of eternal life, is led towards it, directed, as it were, by God. The reason of that direction pre-exists in God; as in him is the type of the order of all things towards an end, which we proved above to be providence [qu. 22 passim]. Now the type in the mind of the doer of something to be done is a kind of pre-existence in him of the thing to be done. Hence the type of the aforesaid direction of a rational creature towards the end of life eternal is called predestination. For to destine is to direct or send. Further on the terminology, *Sent.* I.40.2.1 resp.: 'Utrumque autem ex nomine praedestinationis accipi potest, in quo conjungitur actus destinationis cum hac praepositione prae per compositionem advenientem. Destinare autem significat directionem alicujus in aliquid, sicut nuntii'; *De ver.* 6.1 resp.: 'destinatio, unde nomen praedestinationis accipitur, importat directionem alicuius in finem: unde aliquis dicitur nuntium destinare qui eum dirigit ad aliquid faciendum', etc. H. J. M. J. Goris, 'Divine Foreknowledge, Providence, Predestination and Human Freedom', in R. Van Nieuwenhove and J. P. Wawrykow (eds), *The Theology of Thomas Aquinas* (Notre Dame, Ind.: University of Notre Dame Press, 2005), pp. 99–122. Also, R. L. Friedman, 'The *Sentences* Commentary, 1250-1320: General Trends, the Impact of Religious Orders, and the Test Case of Predestination' and C. Schabel, 'Parisian Commentaries from Peter Auriol to Gregory of Rimini, and the Problem of Predestination', in G. R. Evans (ed.), *Mediaeval Commentaries on the Sentences of Peter Lombard: Current Research*, vol. 1 (Leiden: Brill: 2002), pp. 41-128 and 221–65 respectively.

suae, pauciores autem qui hac scientia carent, qui moriones vel stulti dicuntur, sed paucissimi sunt, respectu aliorum, qui attingunt ad habendam profundam scientiam intelligibilium rerum. Cum igitur beatitudo aeterna, in visione Dei consistens, excedat communem statum naturae, et praecipue secundum quod est gratia destituta per corruptionem originalis peccati, pauciores sunt qui salvantur.

(ST Ia.23.7 ad 3)[18]

It is, in fact, at this point, at the point of numbers, that Thomas appeals to what has been called the aesthetic strand in classical Christian and Augustinian soteriology, to the notion that, just as a builder settles from beforehand on the proportions of the project in hand, so also does God, determining as he does so the ratio of the reprobate to the elect:

Sicut aedificator excogitat determinatam mensuram domus, et etiam determinatum numerum mansionum quas vult facere in domo, et determinatum numerum mensurarum parietis vel tecti, non autem eligit determinatum numerum lapidum, sed accipit tot, quot sufficiunt ad explendam tantam mensuram parietis. Sic igitur considerandum est in Deo, respectu totius universitatis quae est eius effectus. Praeordinavit enim in qua mensura deberet esse totum universum, et quis numerus esset conveniens essentialibus partibus universi, quae scilicet habent aliquo modo ordinem ad perpetuitatem; quot scilicet sphaerae, quot stellae, quot elementa, quot species rerum. Individua vero corruptibilia non ordinantur ad bonum universi quasi principaliter, sed quasi secundario, inquantum in eis salvatur bonum speciei ... Unde certus est Deo numerus praedestinatorum, non solum per modum cognitionis, sed etiam per modum cuiusdam principalis praefinitionis.

(ST Ia.23.7 resp.)[19]

---

[18] the good that is proportionate to the common state of nature is to be found in the majority and is wanting in the minority. But the good that exceeds the common state of nature is to be found in the minority, and is wanting in the majority. Thus it is clear that the majority of men have a sufficient knowledge for the conduct of life, and those who have not this knowledge are said to be half-witted or foolish; but they who attain to a profound knowledge of things intelligible are a very small minority in respect to the rest. Since their eternal happiness, consisting in the vision of God, exceeds the common state of nature, and especially in so far as this is deprived of grace through the corruption of original sin, those who are saved are in the minority.

[19] For instance, a builder thinks out the definite measurements of a house, and also the definite number of rooms which he wishes to make in the house; and definite measurements of the walls and roof; he does not, however, select a definite number of stones, but accepts and uses just so many as are sufficient for the required measurements of the wall. So also must we consider concerning God in regard to the whole universe,

But whatever the exact proportion, actual numbers, as far as the elect are concerned, will, again, be small, for such is the depth and extent of man's corruption that few will ever be eligible even for consideration.

What, then, are we to say about Thomas and predestination? The first thing is that, whatever else we make of it, there can be no passing over either the affective or the free will element of the argument, over his sense (*a*) of God's loving and of his wishing to bring home to himself those in whom he delights as the first fruits of his handiwork, and (*b*) of, on the face of it any rate,' man's having some say in all this. As far, then, as the first of these things is concerned, the affective moment of the argument, we have these lines from the *Pars prima* at 23.4 resp. on the notion of God's 'wishing his subjects well' as creatures of moral accountability ('inquantum vult eis hoc bonum salutis aeternae') and thus of love as preceding election in the order of divine intentionality:

> praedestinatio, secundum rationem, praesupponit electionem; et electio dilectionem. Cuius ratio est, quia praedestinatio, ut dictum est, est pars providentiae. Providentia autem, sicut et prudentia, est ratio in intellectu existens, praeceptiva ordinationis aliquorum in finem, ut supra dictum est. Non autem praecipitur aliquid ordinandum in finem, nisi praeexistente voluntate finis. Unde praedestinatio aliquorum in salutem aeternam, praesupponit, secundum rationem, quod Deus illorum velit salutem. Ad quod

which is his effect. For he pre-ordained the measurements of the whole of the universe, and what number would befit the essential parts of that universe – that is to say, which have in some way been ordained in perpetuity; how many spheres, how many stars, how many elements, and how many species ... Whence the number of the predestined is certain to God; not only by way of knowledge, but also by way of a principle of pre-ordination. John Hick, with Harnack, in his *Evil and the God of Love* (London: Collins, 1966; 2nd edn, Basingtoke: Palgrave, 2007), pp. 88-89: 'What I am calling Augustine's aesthetic theme is his affirmation of faith that, seen in its totality from the ultimate standpoint of the Creator, the universe is wholly good; for even the evil within it is made to contribute to the complex perfection of the whole. As Harnack says, "Augustine never tires of realizing the beauty (pulchrum) and fitness (aptum) of creation, of regarding the universe as an ordered work of art, in which the gradations are as admirable as the contrasts. The individual and evil are lost to view in the notion of beauty ... Even hell, the damnation of sinners, is an act in the ordination of evils (ordinatio malorum), an indispensable part of the work of art" ... In similar vein we find Augustine writing, "All have their offices and limits laid down so as to ensure the beauty of the universe. That which we abhor in any part of it gives us the greatest pleasure when we consider the universe as a whole ... The very reason why some things are inferior is that though the parts may be imperfect the whole is perfect, whether its beauty is seen stationary or in movement ... The black colour in a picture may very well be beautiful if you take the picture as a whole" [*De ver. rel.* xl.76].' Hick traces the notion back into Plato (*Laws* x.903) via Epictetus and Marcus Aurelius.

pertinet electio et dilectio. Dilectio quidem, inquantum vult eis hoc
bonum salutis aeternae, nam diligere est velle alicui bonum, ut supra
dictum est. Electio autem, inquantum hoc bonum aliquibus prae
aliis vult, cum quosdam reprobet, ut supra dictum est. Electio tamen
et dilectio aliter ordinantur in nobis et in Deo, eo quod in nobis
voluntas diligendo non causat bonum; sed ex bono praeexistente
incitamur ad diligendum. Et ideo eligimus aliquem, quem diligamus,
et sic electio dilectionem praecedit in nobis. In Deo autem est e
converso. Nam voluntas eius, qua vult bonum alicui diligendo, est
causa quod illud bonum ab eo prae aliis habeatur. Et sic patet quod
dilectio praesupponitur electioni, secundum rationem; et electio
praedestinationi. Unde omnes praedestinati sunt electi et dilecti.[20]

while on the other hand, and as far now as the free will moment of the
argument is concerned, we have these from the same question of the
Summa theologiae at Article 6 on God's involvement of man in the shaping
of his own destiny:

praedestinatio   certissime   et   infallibiliter   consequitur   suum
effectum, nec tamen imponit necessitatem, ut scilicet effectus eius
ex necessitate proveniat. Dictum est enim supra quod praedestinatio
est pars providentiae. Sed non omnia quae providentiae subduntur,
necessaria sunt, sed quaedam contingenter eveniunt, secundum
conditionem causarum proximarum, quas ad tales effectus divina
providentia ordinavit. Et tamen providentiae ordo est infallibilis, ut
supra ostensum est. Sic igitur et ordo praedestinationis est certus;
et tamen libertas arbitrii non tollitur, ex qua contingenter provenit
praedestinationis effectus. Ad hoc etiam consideranda sunt quae

---

[20] predestination presupposes election in the order of reason, and election presupposes
love. The reason for this is that predestination, as stated above [art. 1], is a part of
providence. Now providence, as also prudence, is the plan existing in the intellect
directing the ordering of some things towards an end, as was proved above [qu. 22, art.
2]. But nothing is directed towards an end unless the will for that end already exists.
Whence the predestination of some to eternal salvation presupposes, in the order of
reason, that God wills their salvation, and to this belong both election and love: love,
inasmuch as he wills them this particular good of eternal salvation, since to love is to
wish well to anyone, as stated above [qu. 20, arts 2 and 3]; and election, inasmuch as he
wills this good to some in preference to others, since he reprobates some, as stated above
[art. 3]. Election and love, however, are differently ordered in God and in ourselves,
because in us the will in loving does not cause good, but we are incited to love by the
good which already exists; and therefore we choose someone to love, and so election in
us precedes love. In God, however, it is the reverse. For his will, by which in loving he
wishes good to someone, is the cause of that good possessed by some in preference to
others. Thus it is clear that love precedes election in the order of reason, and election
precedes predestination. Whence all the predestinate are objects of election and love.

supra dicta sunt de divina scientia et de divina voluntate, quae contingentiam a rebus non tollunt, licet certissima et infallibilia sint.[21]

But for all his acknowledgement both of love and of willing – of God's love and of man's willing – as entering into the question of predestination, it is clear that Thomas's is a proposal of this issue in terms less of *emergence*, of the soul's issuing at last into the unqualified truth of what it already has it in itself to be and to become, than of *election*, of God's determining from beforehand the shape and substance of eschatological selfhood; for it is clear from these same passages (*a*) that in contemplating the goodness apt to commend the individual as a creature of free moral determination, God is simply contemplating the goodness which he himself put there in the first place (the 'Nam voluntas eius, qua vult bonum alicui diligendo, est causa quod illud bonum ab eo prae aliis habeatur' moment of *ST* Ia.23.4 resp.), and (*b*) that free will as a property of personality is for Thomas nothing but the means of God's own infallible will (the 'licet certissima et infallibilia sint' moment of 23.6 resp.), at which point the unilateralism of it all – Thomas's commitment to the notion that what God does *for* us he does *without* us – moves fully and unambiguously into view.[22]

---

[21] predestination most certainly and infallibly takes effect; yet it does not impose any necessity, so that, namely, its effect should take place from necessity. For it was said above [art. 1], that predestination is a part of providence. But not all things subject to providence are necessary; some things happening from contingency, according to the nature of the proximate causes, which divine providence has ordained for such effects. Yet the order of providence is infallible, as was shown above [qu. 22, art. 4]. So also the order of predestination is certain; yet free will is not destroyed, whence the effect of predestination has its contingency. Moreover, all that has been said [qu. 14, art. 13; qu. 19, art. 4] about the divine knowledge and will must also be taken into consideration; since they do not destroy contingency in things, although they themselves are most certain and infallible.

[22] Once and for all, therefore, the 'totum sub effectu praedestinationis' passage of *ST* Ia.23.5 (resp.): 'Et sic impossibile est quod totus praedestinationis effectus in communi habeat aliquam causam ex parte nostra. Quia quidquid est in homine ordinans ipsum in salutem, comprehenditur totum sub effectu praedestinationis, etiam ipsa praeparatio ad gratiam, neque enim hoc fit nisi per auxilium divinum ...' See, for Thomas's own sense of the difficulty of all this – the difficulty of finding some way of reconciling human and divine intentionality within the economy of historical selfhood without seriously prejudicing either the one or the other in the freedom and totality of its proper operation – *De ver.* 6. 3 resp.: 'Sed ordo praedestinationis est certus non solum respectu universalis finis, sed etiam respectu particularis et determinati, quia ille qui est ordinatus per praedestinationem ad salutem, nunquam deficit a consecutione salutis. Nec tamen hoc modo est certus ordo praedestinationis respectu particularis finis, sicut erat ordo providentiae: quia in providentia ordo non erat certus respectu particularis finis, nisi quando causa proxima necessario producebat effectum suum; in praedestinatione autem invenitur certitudo respectu singularis finis; et tamen causa proxima, scilicet liberum arbitrium, non producit effectum illum nisi contingenter. Unde

6. Dante, when it comes to predestination, sees the issue in terms, not so much of despatching or sending on, but of something closer to an opening out of the spirit upon the kind of transhumanity (the 'trasumanar' of *Par.* I.70) proper to it as a creature called from beforehand to be in, through and for God. Now here too we have to be careful, for this commitment in Dante to predestination as a matter, less of *sending on* than of *emergence*, of knowing self in the now ecstatic truth of self, presupposes and at every point is informed by a sense of the mystery and of the grace-conditionality of it all; so, for example, as far as the first of these things is concerned, the 'ché noi, che Dio vedemo, / non conosciamo ancor tutti li eletti' passage of *Par.* XX.134-35 already noted, while as far as the second is concerned, these lines (82-84) from *Paradiso* XXXIII on the exhilaration, certainly, of ultimate intellection but, more than this, on grace as the whereabouts of every implementation of self in its deiformity:

> Oh abbondante grazia ond' io presunsi
> ficcar lo viso per la luce etterna,
> tanto che la veduta vi consunsi!²³

But for all the indispensability of grace to an ultimate act of intellection and to the blessedness thereof, predestination remains even so, for Dante,

---

difficile videtur concordare infallibilitatem praedestinationis cum arbitrii libertate [...] Quod hoc modo potest considerari. Invenimus enim ordinem infallibilem esse respectu alicuius dupliciter. Uno modo inquantum una causa singularis necessario inducit effectum suum ex ordine divinae providentiae; alio modo quando ex concursu multarum causarum contingentium, et deficere possibilium, pervenitur ad unum effectum; quarum unamquamque Deus ordinat ad consecutionem effectus loco eius quae defecit, vel ne altera deficiat; sicut videmus quod omnia singularia unius speciei sunt corruptibilia, et tamen per successionem unius ad alterum potest secundum naturam in eis salvari perpetuitas speciei, divina providentia taliter gubernante, quod non omnia deficiant uno deficiente: et hoc modo est in praedestinatione. Liberum enim arbitrium deficere potest a salute; tamen in eo quem Deus praedestinat, tot alia adminicula praeparat, quod vel non cadat, vel si cadit, quod resurgat, sicut exhortationes, suffragia orationum, gratiae donum, et omnia huiusmodi, quibus Deus adminiculatur homini ad salutem. Si ergo consideremus salutem respectu causae proximae, scilicet liberi arbitrii, non habet certitudinem, sed contingentiam; respectu autem causae primae, quae est praedestinatio, certitudinem habet.' It is likely that Dante himself contemplated Thomas on this issue in the *Contra gentiles* at III. lxxiii, a chapter variously significant in the *Purgatorio* and the *Paradiso* (the 'tolleretur etiam iustitia praemiantis et punientis, si non libere homo ageret bonum vel malum' of note 5 for *Purg.* XVI.70-72 and the 'in rebus autem inanimatis causarum contingentia ex imperfectione et defectu est: secundum enim suam naturam sunt determinata ad unum effectum, quem semper consequuntur nisi sit impedimentum vel ex debilitate virtutis, vel ex aliquo exteriori agente, vel ex materiae indispositione' of note 2 for *Par.* I.127-35).

²³ O abounding grace whereby I presumed to fix my look through the eternal light so far that all my sight was spent therein!

a matter less of conveying than of confirming, less of God's moving the soul on to the qualitatively other-than-self than of his admitting it to the kind of transhumanity present to it as the most immanent of its immanent possibilities. This at any rate, or something close to it, is Dante's meaning in passages such as the following from *Paradiso* XXIII (lines 40-45) and XXX (lines 55-60), passages which, turning as they do on the notions of dilation ('dilatarsi'), of amplification ('farsi più grande'), of 'issuing forth' ('uscir di sé') and of surmounting ('sormontar'), involve a sense, not so much of otherness, as of the soul's at last rejoicing in its proper power to ulteriority:

> Come foco di nube si diserra
> per dilatarsi sì che non vi cape,
> e fuor di sua natura in giù s'atterra,
>   la mente mia così, tra quelle dape
> fatta più grande, di sé stessa uscìo,
> e che si fesse rimembrar non sape
> ...
>
>   Non fur più tosto dentro a me venute
> queste parole brievi, ch'io compresi
> me sormontar di sopr' a mia virtute;
>   e di novella vista mi raccesi
> tale, che nulla luce è tanto mera,
> che li occhi miei non si fosser difesi
>   ...[24]

With this, then, we are once again in the presence, not simply of good theology, but of courageous theology: of good theology in that, alongside the Pentateuchal preoccupation with fallenness as a dominant feature of the human situation, Dante makes room too for the other – and if anything still more primordial – feature of the text, namely the notion that God made it and God saw that it was good; and of courageous theology in that, here as throughout, the received emphasis is interrogated afresh with a view to testing its equality to the truth its seeks to encompass. If, then, for Dante too grace enters into human experience as the indispensable ground of its ultimate resolution, grace being that whereby the individual is lifted to an order of understanding and blessedness beyond anything he himself

---

[24] Even as fire breaks from a cloud, because it dilates so that it has not room there, and contrary to its own nature, falls down to earth, so my mind, becoming greater amid those feasts, issued from itself, and of what it became had no remembrance ... No sooner had those brief words come within me than I comprehended that I was surmounting beyond my own power, and such new vision was kindled within me that there is no light so bright that my eyes could not have withstood it.

is able to think or imagine, it enters into that experience, not magically or metaphysically, but as that whereby what already *is* as a property of historical selfhood is confirmed at last in its actuality, in the triumph of its innermost reasons. To suppose otherwise – to deliver the Dante of the *Commedia* to the more darkling and indeed to the more drastic aspects of Augustinianism either in its original form or in its subsequent elaboration – is entirely to mistake the spirit of the theological enterprise as he himself understands it. It is to deliver him to something both infinitely other and infinitely less than what he himself understood to be the case.

Chapter 4
The Augustinian Dimension:
Narratives of Succession and Secession

> E perché meno ammiri la parola,
> guarda il calor del sol che si fa vino,
> giunto a l'omor che de la vita cola.
>
> *(Purg.* XXV.76-78)[1]

1. Introduction: patterns of affirmation and emancipation. 2. Aquinas, Augustine, and the tyranny of the *Sed contra*. 3. Augustinian and non-Augustinian itineraries in Dante: patterns of sameness (the psychology and pathology of dissimilitude) and patterns of otherness (nature, grace and the viability of the human project). 4. Conclusion: Dantean Augustinianism: continuity and discontinuity in the depths.

Never far beneath the surface both of Thomist and of Dantean spirituality is the figure of Augustine, massively present to the Aquinas of the grace questions of the *Summa theologiae*, but everywhere discernible too in both the macro- and the micro-structures of the *Commedia*. As far as Aquinas is concerned, or at least the Aquinas of the grace treatise of the *Prima secundae*, there is no need to labour the point. Simply to turn the pages of the text is to be impressed by the omnipresence of Augustine, alongside Scripture, as the decisive voice;[2] so, for example, this from 109.4: 'Sed contra est quod Augustinus dicit, in libro de haeresibus, hoc pertinere ad haeresim Pelagianorum, ut credant "sine gratia posse hominem facere omnia divina mandata"';[3] or this from 109.8: 'Sed contra est quod Augustinus dicit, in libro de Perfect. Iustit., "quisquis negat nos orare debere ne intremus in

---

[1] And that you may marvel less at my words, look at the sun's heat which is made wine when combined with the juice that flows from the vine.

[2] J. G. Geenen, 'Le fonti patristiche come "autorità" nella teologia di san Tommaso', *Sacra Doctrina* 77 (1975), 7-67; L. J. Elders, 'Les citations de saint Augustin dans la Somme Théologique de saint Thomas d'Aquin', *Doctor Communis* (1987), 40, 115-67.

[3] Augustine, by contrast, in his book on heresies [*De haeres.* lxxxviii.2], says that it is part of the Pelagian heresy that they believe that 'without grace man can fulfil all the divine commandments'.

tentationem (negat autem hoc qui contendit ad non peccandum gratiae
Dei adiutorium non esse homini necessarium, sed, sola lege accepta,
humanam sufficere voluntatem), ab auribus omnium removendum, et ore
omnium anathematizandum esse non dubito'";[4] or this from 110.3: '"Neque
etiam caritas, quia gratia praevenit caritatem", ut Augustinus dicit, in
libro de Praedest. sanctorum. Ergo gratia non est virtus'.[5] Throughout,
the pattern is the same, Augustine everywhere being on hand both to
assist and to insist when it comes to resolving issues in the complex area
of grace theology. But with Dante it is different, for indebted as he is to
Augustine as a guide to the content of the religious life, his even so is
a rethinking of the Augustinian component of his spirituality, a steady
commitment, if not to *un*learning, exactly, everything he had learnt from
Augustine in the areas especially of ethics, psychology and soteriology,
then to a fresh substantiation and contextualization of the leading idea.
Here, then, is a further way of seeing and setting up the question of Dante
and Aquinas and of marking the difference between them, Dante's, for all
his rejoicing in the presence of Augustine as a fellow traveller and breaker
of bread, being a wish to distance himself from the severer aspects of
Augustinian piety in favour of a fresh account of God's dealings with man
and of man's with God within the salvific economy of the whole.

2. Notable as a feature of the grace questions in the *Prima secundae* are
their responsiveness to the sterner aspects of Augustine's grace theology,
to those aspects of it which, though everywhere discernible in the great
bishop, were sharpened by his encounter with Pelagius and Pelagianism.
The basic question, turning as it does on what Augustine came to regard
as a threat to the efficacy and indispensability of God's salvific work in
the Christ, is familiar enough, his misgivings with respect to the place
of free will in the area of soteriology constraining him to an ever more
insistent sense of the primacy of the divine in respect of the human
initiative as the principle in man of his ultimate well-being.[6] And it was

---

[4] Augustine, on the other hand, in his book *On the Perfection of Human Righteousness*
[xxi.44], maintains that 'whoever denies that we ought to say the prayer "Lead us not into
temptation" (and they deny it who maintain that the help of God's grace is not necessary
to man for salvation, but that the gift of the law is enough for the human will) ought
without doubt to be removed beyond all hearing, and to be anathematized by the tongues
of all'.

[5] Nor is it charity, since as Augustine says in his book on the *Predestination of the Saints*
[*De dono persev.* xvi], grace precedes charity. Therefore grace is not virtue.

[6] J. Ferguson, *Pelagius. A Historical and Theological Study* (Cambridge: W. Heffer, 1956);
T. Bohlin, *Die Theologie des Pelagius und ihre Genesis*, trans. from the Swedish by H. Buch
(Uppsala: Lundequistska bokhandeln, 1957); S. Prete, *Pelagio e il pelagianesimo* (Brescia:
Morcelliana, 1961); R. F. Evans, *Pelagius, Inquiries and Reappraisals* (New York: Seabury

doubtless the presence to Aquinas of the Augustine of the anti-Pelagian period that accounts for his own darkening spirituality in this area, his own deepening sense of the difficulty of man's aspiring to, or indeed even of his wishing to aspire to, a knowledge of God short of the grace whereby such knowledge is a possibility in the first place. Take, for example, the case of *ST* Ia IIae.109.2 relative to whether or not a man can do well, or even wish to do well, in the absence of grace ('Utrum homo possit velle et facere bonum absque gratia'), where Thomas's answer tends always to be no; for though in his innocence, Aquinas maintains, man was able both to will and actually to do the kind of good proportionate to his nature, needing grace only for the accomplishment of his supernatural end, in his fallenness he can do neither:

> in statu naturae integrae, quantum ad sufficientiam operativae virtutis, poterat homo per sua naturalia velle et operari bonum suae naturae proportionatum, quale est bonum virtutis acquisitae, non autem bonum superexcedens, quale est bonum virtutis infusae. Sed in statu naturae corruptae etiam deficit homo ab hoc quod secundum suam naturam potest, ut non possit totum huiusmodi bonum implere per sua naturalia.
>
> (*ST* Ia IIae.109.2 resp.)[7]

Press, 1968); G. Greshake, *Gnade als konkrete Freiheit; eine Untersuchung zur Gnadenlehre des Pelagius* (Mainz: Matthias-Grünewald-Verlag, 1972); B. R. Rees, *Pelagius. A Reluctant Heretic* (Woodbridge, Suffolk and Wolfeboro, NH: Boydell Press, 1988); idem, *Pelagius. Life and Letters* (Rochester, NY: Boydell Press, 1998); W. L. Löhr, *Pelagius. Portrait of a Christian Teacher in Late Antiquity* (Aberdeen: School of Divinity, History and Philosophy, University of Aberdeen, 2007). On Augustine and Pelagius, P. Lehmann, 'The Anti-Pelagian Writings', in R. W. Battenhouse (ed.), *A Companion to the Study of St. Augustine* (New York: Oxford University Press, 1955), pp. 203-34; J. A. Mourant and W. J. Collinge (trans.), *Four Anti-Pelagian Writings* (Washington D.C.: Catholic University of America Press, 1992). On Augustine and grace, X. Léon-Dufour, 'Grâce et libre arbitre chez saint Augustin. À propos de: *Consentire vocationi Dei ... propriae voluntatis est*', *Recherches de Science Religieuse* 33 (1946), 129-63; J. Patout Burns, *The Development of Augustine's Doctrine of Operative Grace* (Paris: Études augustiniennes, 1980); C. Harrison, 'Delectatio Victrix: Grace and Freedom in Saint Augustine', *Studia patristica* 27 (1993), 298-302; D. R. Creswell, *St Augustine's Dilemma. Grace and Eternal Law in the Major Works of Augustine of Hippo* (New York: Peter Lang, 1997); B. Studer, *The Grace of Christ and the Grace of God in Augustine of Hippo: Christocentrism or Theocentrism?*, trans. M. J. O'Connell (Collegeville, Minn.: Liturgical Press, 1997); D. Ogliari, *Gratia et certamen. The Relationship between Grace and Free Will in the Discussion of Augustine with the so-called Semipelagians* (Leuven: Leuven University Press, 2003). More generally, R. W. Gleason, S.J., *Grace* (London and New York: Sheed and Ward, 1962); N. P. Williams, *The Grace of God* (London: Hodder and Stoughton, 1966; originally 1930).

[7] in the state of integrity, as regards the sufficiency of the operative power, man by his natural endowments could wish and do the good proportionate to his nature, such

True, even in his fallenness, Aquinas goes on, *some* things can be done
without the prior and continuing assistance of grace, for human nature
after Eden is not entirely corrupt, entirely incapacitated in respect of its
power to do well:

> Quia tamen natura humana per peccatum non est totaliter corrupta,
> ut scilicet toto bono naturae privetur; potest quidem etiam in statu
> naturae corruptae, per virtutem suae naturae aliquod bonum
> particulare agere, sicut aedificare domos, plantare vineas, et alia
> huiusmodi.

(ibid.)[8]

But this notwithstanding, the answer still has to be no, and this
because, well before Thomas gets into his stride in the body of the article,
Augustine, the anti-Pelagian Augustine of the *De correptione et gratia*, has
already finessed the argument, insisting from beforehand, from out of
the peremptoriness of the *Sed contra*, that 'without grace men can do
nothing good when they either think or wish or love or act' ('sine gratia
nullum prorsus, sive cogitando, sive volendo et amando, sive agendo,
faciunt homines bonum' [*De corrept. et gratia* ii.3]). That, then, is that,
the 'building houses and planting vineyards' element of the argument
serving in its exiguousness merely to underline the hopelessness of the

---

as the good of acquired virtue; but no surpassing good, as the good of infused virtue.
But in the state of corrupt nature man falls short even of what he can do by his own
nature, so that he is unable to fulfil it by his own natural powers. More explicit on
the notion of the impossibility of right willing, as distinct from right doing, in the state
of disobedience, the *ad primum* of this article: 'Ad primum ergo dicendum quod homo
est dominus suorum actuum, et volendi et non volendi, propter deliberationem rationis,
quae potest flecti ad unam partem vel ad aliam. Sed quod deliberet vel non deliberet,
si huius etiam sit dominus, oportet quod hoc sit per deliberationem praecedentem. Et
cum hoc non procedat in infinitum, oportet quod finaliter deveniatur ad hoc quod
liberum arbitrium hominis moveatur ab aliquo exteriori principio quod est supra mentem
humanam, scilicet a Deo; ut etiam philosophus probat in cap. de bona fortuna. Unde
mens hominis etiam sani non ita habet dominium sui actus quin indigeat moveri a Deo.
Et multo magis liberum arbitrium hominis infirmi post peccatum, quod impeditur a
bono per corruptionem naturae.'

[8] Yet because man is not altogether corrupted by sin, so as to be shorn of every natural
good, even in the state of corrupted nature he can, by virtue of his natural endowments,
work some particular good, such as building houses, planting vineyards, and the like. *De
ver.* 24.14 resp.: 'Illud autem bonum quod est naturae humanae proportionatum, potest
homo per liberum arbitrium explere; unde dicit Augustinus quod homo per liberum
arbitrium potest agros colere, domos aedificare, et alia plura bona facere sine gratia
operante. Quamvis autem huiusmodi bona homo possit facere sine gratia gratum faciente,
non tamen potest ea facere sine Deo; cum nulla res possit in naturalem operationem exire
nisi virtute divina, quia causa secunda non agit nisi per virtutem causae primae ...'

situation in which we now find ourselves. And what applies in Article 2
of Ia IIae.109 applies also in Article 4, where it is a question of whether,
without grace, man can abide by the law ('Utrum homo sine gratia per
sua naturalia legis praecepta implere possit'). Now here as before, there
is a part of Thomas anxious as far as may be to affirm man's proper
power to moral determination, his native capacity for doing good. Before
the Fall, then, and as far as the substance (as distinct from the spirit) of
the law is concerned, man as man could meet the obligations laid upon
him by God from out of his ordinary humanity. True, the situation did
not last, grace, after the Fall, being a condition of obedience and of the
righteousness thereof. But *before* the Fall man as man was equal to the
task in hand:

> ... implere mandata legis contingit dupliciter. Uno modo, quantum
> ad substantiam operum, prout scilicet homo operatur iusta et fortia,
> et alia virtutis opera. Et hoc modo homo in statu naturae integrae
> potuit omnia mandata legis implere, alioquin non potuisset in statu
> illo non peccare, cum nihil aliud sit peccare quam transgredi divina
> mandata. Sed in statu naturae corruptae non potest homo implere
> omnia mandata divina sine gratia sanante.

(ST Ia IIae.109.4 resp.)[9]

But the distinction between substance and spirit, between the *what* and
the *how* of man's obedience to God's commandment, is, in the event, all
important here; for the fulfilment of the law, in respect of the *spirit* of that
fulfilment, is a matter of charity, and charity is a matter of grace, grace,
therefore, as Augustine had long since maintained, being a condition of
right doing both before and after the catastrophe:

> Alio modo possunt impleri mandata legis non solum quantum ad
> substantiam operis, sed etiam quantum ad modum agendi, ut scilicet
> ex caritate fiant. Et sic neque in statu naturae integrae, neque in
> statu naturae corruptae, potest homo implere absque gratia legis
> mandata. Unde Augustinus, in libro de Corrept. et Grat., cum
> dixisset quod sine gratia nullum prorsus bonum homines faciunt,
> subdit, 'non solum ut, monstrante ipsa quid faciendum sit, sciant;
> verum etiam ut, praestante ipsa, faciant cum dilectione quod sciunt'.

---

[9] there are two ways of fulfilling the commandments of the law. The first regards the
substance of the works, as when a man does works of justice, fortitude, and of other virtues,
and in this way man in the state of perfect nature could fulfil all the commandments of
the law; otherwise he would not have been able to sin in that state, since to sin is nothing
other than to transgress the divine commandments. But in the state of corrupted nature
man cannot fulfil all the divine commandments without healing grace.

Indigent insuper in utroque statu auxilio Dei moventis ad mandata
implenda, ut dictum est.

(ibid.)[10]

Here too, then, Augustine carries the day, and this in a manner which,
as far as Thomas is concerned, can only have reinforced his perplexity; for
if by creation we mean the letting of a thing be in the fullness of that being,
which is as much as to say in the fullness of its proper functionality and
intelligibility, then to speak in this way of the need for grace before things
have actually got under way must in some sense be to reflect adversely on
the basic idea, on the notion of creation as in any sense equal to its own
inner reasons.

Similarly exemplary in respect of Augustine's power to determine
well-nigh single-handedly the course of the argument in the *Summa
theologiae* is the case of 109.8, where it is a question of how far, if at all,
man without grace can avoid sin ('Utrum homo sine gratia possit non
peccare'). Thomas, typically, wishes to draw a distinction, for though in
his fallenness man cannot avoid sinning venially (this being a matter of the
waywardness of his lower parts), he can hold out against mortal sin, since
reason, wherein mortal sin resides, if not necessarily more stable than the
concupiscent part of human nature, is at least more biddable, more open to
negotiation. Here, then, with a statement of the relatively robust character
of man's moral presence in the world, is where Thomas begins:

In statu autem naturae corruptae, indiget homo gratia habituali
sanante naturam, ad hoc quod omnino a peccato abstineat. Quae
quidem sanatio primo fit in praesenti vita secundum mentem, appetitu
carnali nondum totaliter reparato, unde apostolus, ad Rom. VII,
in persona hominis reparati, dicit, 'ego ipse mente servio legi Dei,
carne autem legi peccati'. In quo quidem statu potest homo abstinere
a peccato mortali quod in ratione consistit, ut supra habitum est.
Non autem potest homo abstinere ab omni peccato veniali, propter

[10] Secondly, the commandments of the law can be fulfilled, not merely as regards the
substance of the act, but also as regards the mode of acting, i.e. their being done out of
charity. And in this way, neither in the state of perfect nature, nor in the state of corrupt
nature can man fulfil the commandments of the law without grace. Hence, Augustine,
having in his book on *Rebuke and Grace* [ii.3, prin.] stated that 'without grace men can do
no good whatever', adds 'Not only do they know by its light what to do, but by its help
they do lovingly what they know'. Beyond this, in both states they need the help of God's
motion as mover in order to fulfil the commandments, as stated above [arts 2 and 3].
Augustine (loc. cit.) has 'Intellegenda est enim gratia Dei per Iesum Christum Dominum
nostrum, qua sola homines liberantur a malo, et sine qua nullum prorsus sive cogitando,
sive volendo et amando, sive agendo faciunt bonum: non solum ut monstrante ipsa quid
faciendum sit sciant, verum etiam ut praestante ipsa faciant cum dilectione quod sciunt'.

corruptionem inferioris appetitus sensualitatis, cuius motus singulos quidem ratio reprimere potest (et ex hoc habent rationem peccati et voluntarii), non autem omnes, quia dum uni resistere nititur, fortassis alius insurgit; et etiam quia ratio non semper potest esse pervigil ad huiusmodi motus vitandos.

(*ST* Ia IIa.109.8 resp.)[11]

To this extent, then, and even in the state of disobedience, there is scope for moral activity properly understood, and indeed for moral activity of a very high order, for the struggle against mortal sin is by definition a struggle for the very survival of the soul in its power to significant determination. But here as throughout in these grace questions of the *Summa theologiae*, Augustine is there to oversee and overturn the argument. Taking his cue, then, from a particularly ferocious passage in the *De perfectione iustitiae hominis* relative to the anathematization of anyone daring to set aside the 'Lead us not into temptation' clause of the Lord's Prayer and thus to deny that we stand in need of grace for our salvation, he straightaway sets about the business of demolition, affirming as he does so the status of reason as, after all, an unstable quantity and liable to stray unless restored by grace. On the one hand, then, the *sed contra*, more than ever ominous in respect of Thomas's preliminary liberalism at this point, his willingness in some measure to credit human nature in the moral viability of that nature:

Sed contra est quod Augustinus dicit, in libro de Perfect. Iustit., 'quisquis negat nos orare debere ne intremus in tentationem (negat autem hoc qui contendit ad non peccandum gratiae Dei adiutorium non esse homini necessarium, sed, sola lege accepta, humanam sufficere voluntatem), ab auribus omnium removendum, et ore omnium anathematizandum esse non dubito'.

(ibid. sed contra)[12]

---

[11] But in the state of corrupt nature man needs grace to heal his nature in order that he may entirely abstain from sin. And in the present life this healing is wrought in the mind – the carnal appetite being not yet restored. Hence the Apostle, in Romans 7 [v. 25], says in the person of one who is restored: 'I myself, with the mind, serve the law of God, but with the flesh, the law of sin.' And in this state man can abstain from all mortal sin, which takes its stand in his reason, as stated above [qu. 74, art. 5]; but man cannot abstain from all venial sin on account of the corruption of his lower appetite of sensuality. For man can, indeed, repress each of its movements (by reason of which they are deemed sinful and voluntary), but not all, because while he is resisting one, another may arise, and also because the reason is not always alert to avoid these movements.

[12] On the contrary, Augustine says in his book *On the Perfection of Man's Righteousness* [xxi.44, ult.]: 'Whoever denies that we ought to say the prayer "Lead us not into

while on the other Thomas's gradual coming round in the remaining part
of the response to the Augustinian point of view, to a sense that perhaps
after all reason is not entirely equal to the matter in hand, to – unassisted
by grace – holding at bay the ravages of mortal sin:

> Similiter etiam antequam hominis ratio, in qua est peccatum
> mortale, reparetur per gratiam iustificantem, potest singula peccata
> mortalia vitare, et secundum aliquod tempus, quia non est necesse
> quod continuo peccet in actu. Sed quod diu maneat absque peccato
> mortali, esse non potest. Unde et Gregorius dicit, super Ezech., quod
> 'peccatum quod mox per poenitentiam non deletur, suo pondere ad
> aliud trahit'. Et huius ratio est quia, sicut rationi subdi debet inferior
> appetitus, ita etiam ratio debet subdi Deo, et in ipso constituere
> finem suae voluntatis. Per finem autem oportet quod regulentur
> omnes actus humani, sicut per rationis iudicium regulari debent
> motus inferioris appetitus. Sicut ergo, inferiori appetitu non totaliter
> subiecto rationi, non potest esse quin contingant inordinati motus in
> appetitu sensitivo; ita etiam, ratione hominis non existente subiecta
> Deo, consequens est ut contingant multae inordinationes in ipsis
> actibus rationis. Cum enim homo non habet cor suum firmatum in
> Deo, ut pro nullo bono consequendo vel malo vitando ab eo separari
> vellet; occurrunt multa propter quae consequenda vel vitanda
> homo recedit a Deo contemnendo praecepta ipsius, et ita peccat
> mortaliter, praecipue quia in repentinis homo operatur secundum
> finem praeconceptum, et secundum habitum praeexistentem, ut
> philosophus dicit, in III Ethic.; quamvis ex praemeditatione rationis
> homo possit aliquid agere praeter ordinem finis praeconcepti, et
> praeter inclinationem habitus. Sed quia homo non potest semper esse
> in tali praemeditatione, non potest contingere ut diu permaneat quin
> operetur secundum consequentiam voluntatis deordinatae a Deo,
> nisi cito per gratiam ad debitum ordinem reparetur.
>
> (ibid., resp., ult.)[13]

temptation" (and they deny it who maintain that the help of God's grace is not necessary
to man for salvation, but that the gift of the law is enough for the human will) ought
without doubt to be removed beyond all hearing, and to be anathematized by the tongues
of all.'

[13] So, too, before man's reason, wherein is mortal sin, is restored by justifying grace, he
can avoid each mortal sin, and for a time, since it is not necessary that he should be always
actually sinning. But it cannot be that he remains for long without mortal sin; hence
Gregory, on Ezekiel [*Hom.* xi], says that 'a sin not at once taken away by repentance, by
its weight drags us down to other sins': and this because, as the lower appetite ought to
be subject to the reason, so should the reason be subject to God, and should place in him
the end of its will. Now it is by the end that all human acts ought to be regulated, even
as it is by the judgment of the reason that the movements of the lower appetite should be

Now the general position here, to the effect that both the desire and the ability to do well by self as a creature of moral and eschatological accountability must ultimately be referred to God as the beginning and end of all desiring and all doing in man, is unremarkable, Thomas, with Augustine, being among the most attentive of theologians to the threat posed to the faith, and thus to theology as but the reasonable articulation of the faith, by Pelagianism. But it is difficult not to sense here, over and beyond the virtue of attentiveness, something approaching a species of intimidation, and, in consequence of this, of secession, a making way for something, if not foreign to self exactly (for we are speaking of one and the same Christian profession), then somewhat against the grain, more properly Augustinian in spirit than Thomist. As always, the matter needs careful statement, for Thomas is no less attuned to the tragic substance of the human situation in its post-Edenic phase than Augustine, the severe logic of it all weighing as heavily upon him as upon anybody else. But Augustine is Augustine, and his tremendous presence in the area of grace theology – an area of theology shaped not only by current controversy

regulated. And thus, even as inordinate movements of the sensitive appetite cannot help occurring since the lower appetite is not subject to reason, so likewise, since man's reason is not entirely subject to God, the consequence is that many disorders occur in the reason. For when man's heart is not so fixed on God as to be unwilling to be parted from him for the sake of finding any good or avoiding any evil, many things happen for the achieving or avoiding of which a man strays from God and breaks his commandments, and thus sins mortally; especially since, when surprised, a man acts according to his preconceived end and his pre-existing habits, as the Philosopher says in the third book of the *Ethics* [III.viii; 1117a20-21], although with premeditation of his reason he may do something outside the order of his preconceived end and the inclination of his habit. But because a man cannot always have this premeditation, it cannot help occurring that he acts in accordance with his will turned aside from God, unless, by grace, he is quickly brought back to due order. *ScG* III.clx. 3-4: 'Ad hoc etiam operantur impetus corporalium passionum; et appetibilia secundum sensum; et plurimae occasiones male agendi; quibus de facili homo provocatur ad peccandum, nisi retrahatur per firmam inhaesionem ad ultimum finem, quam gratia facit. Unde apparet stulta Pelagianorum opinio, qui dicebant hominem in peccato existentem sine gratia posse vitare peccata. Cuius contrarium apparet ex hoc quod Psalmus petit "dum defecerit virtus mea, ne derelinquas me. Et dominus orare nos docet et ne nos inducas in tentationem, sed libera nos a malo"; *De ver*. 24.12 resp.: 'Et ideo post statum naturae corruptae non est in potestate liberi arbitrii omnia huiusmodi peccata vitare, quia eius actum effugiunt, quamvis possit impedire aliquem istorum motuum, si contra conetur. Non est autem possibile ut homo continue contra conetur ad huiusmodi motus vitandos, propter varias humanae mentis occupationes et quietem necessariam. Quod quidem contingit ex hoc quod inferiores vires non sunt totaliter rationi subiectae, sicut erant in statu innocentiae, quando homini huiusmodi peccata omnia et singula per liberum arbitrium vitare facillimum erat, eo quod nullus motus in inferioribus viribus insurgere poterat nisi secundum dictamen rationis. Ad hanc autem rectitudinem homo in praesenti per gratiam non reducitur communiter loquendo; sed hanc rectitudinem expectamus in statu gloriae.'

but by the content of his own troubled existence – leaves little room for manoeuvre, little scope for sidestepping the archetypal utterance.

Lest the reader be tempted to see in all this an element of exaggeration, it is worth noting the way in which, in consequence of the gradual ascendancy of the Augustinian over the Aristotelian component of his spirituality, the Thomas of the *Prima secundae* actually reverses positions in the earlier *Scriptum*. Take, for example, the question as to whether or not the soul is necessarily graced in consequence of doing what it can – 'facienti quod in se est' – in the light of conscience ('Utrum necessario detur gratia se praeparanti, vel facienti quod in se est', *ST* Ia IIae.112.3), at which point Paul, the Areopagite and Anselm as the 'objectors' each in his way suggests that God's response to those doing their best in the light of conscience will always be a positive one.[14] And this, in the *Scriptum*, is Thomas's position, his too being a commitment to the notion that just as form enters willingly into matter as well disposed, so grace enters willingly into the spirit as duly open to it, God's, therefore, always being an inclination to reply in kind, to do *his* best for those doing *their* best:

> Loquendo autem de necessitate quae est ex suppositione divini propositi, quo propter benevolentiam suae bonitatis voluit unicuique eam communicare secundum suam capacitatem, necessarium est quod cuilibet materiae praeparatae forma infundatur.
>
> (*Scriptum* 4, d. 17, q. 1, art. 2, qc. 3, resp.)[15]

– a passage presupposing on analogy with the preparedness of matter in respect of the form about to be infused the readiness of the beneficiary in respect of the benefactor. But by the time we reach the *Prima secundae*

---

[14] *ST* Ia IIae.112.3, objs. 1 and 2: 'Videtur quod ex necessitate detur gratia se praeparanti ad gratiam, vel facienti quod in se est. Quia super illud Rom. V, "iustificati ex fide pacem habeamus" etc., dicit Glossa, "Deus recipit eum qui ad se confugit, aliter esset in eo iniquitas". Sed impossibile est in Deo iniquitatem esse. Ergo impossibile est quod Deus non recipiat eum qui ad se confugit. Ex necessitate igitur gratiam assequitur ... Praeterea, Anselmus dicit, in libro de casu Diaboli, quod ista est causa quare Deus non concedit Diabolo gratiam, quia ipse non voluit accipere, nec paratus fuit. Sed remota causa, necesse est removeri effectum. Ergo si aliquis velit accipere gratiam, necesse est quod ei detur.' More especially, in view of what follows, Dionysius in obj. 3: 'Praeterea, bonum est communicativum sui; ut patet per Dionysium, in IV cap. de Div. Nom. Sed bonum gratiae est melius quam bonum naturae. Cum igitur forma naturalis ex necessitate adveniat materiae dispositae, videtur quod multo magis gratia ex necessitate detur praeparanti se ad gratiam.'

[15] Speaking, then, of the kind of necessity pertaining to the suppositum of divine willing, by which God wishes out of his benevolence and goodness to communicate that goodness to everything according to its capacity, it is necessary that form is infused into matter as properly prepared.

the situation is less sanguine, grace, inasmuch as it countenances nature, countenancing it only in the degree to which it is graced in the first place, such deserving as nature has, therefore, being no real deserving at all, but rather (as Thomas puts it) something closer to inevitability or infallability (*infallabilitas*), to a necessary working-out of God's prior purposes:

> praeparatio ad hominis gratiam est a Deo sicut a movente, a libero autem arbitrio sicut a moto. Potest igitur praeparatio dupliciter considerari. Uno quidem modo, secundum quod est a libero arbitrio. Et secundum hoc, nullam necessitatem habet ad gratiae consecutionem, quia donum gratiae excedit omnem praeparationem virtutis humanae. Alio modo potest considerari secundum quod est a Deo movente. Et tunc habet necessitatem ad id ad quod ordinatur a Deo, non quidem coactionis, sed infallibilitatis, quia intentio Dei deficere non potest; secundum quod et Augustinus dicit, in libro *de Praedest. Sanct.*, 'quod per beneficia Dei certissime liberantur quicumque liberantur'. Unde si ex intentione Dei moventis est quod homo cuius cor movet, gratiam consequatur, infallibiliter ipsam consequitur ...
>
> (*ST* Ia IIae.112.3 resp.)[16]

Thus free will as the power in man to moral determination has now no real part to play in this at all, for free will, properly understood, is nothing but the means of God's working out his own plan for man, his own fail-safe scheme in man's regard, Augustine once again standing by to confirm in this sense the unilateralism of it all, its more or less complete one-sidedness. The old, in short, has been eclipsed by the new, and, with it, by a darker and less differentiated discourse than Thomas, left to himself, would probably have wished to entertain. And that is not all, for what applies in Question 112 by way of revising erstwhile emphases applies also in Question 109 in relation to the adequacy or otherwise of habitual grace for the purposes of doing good and of avoiding evil. The expression 'habitual grace', Thomas says in the *Summa*, denotes the steady

---

[16] man's preparation for grace is from God, as mover, and from free will, as moved. Hence preparation may be looked at in two ways: first, as it is from free-will, and thus there is no necessity that it should obtain grace, since the gift of grace exceeds every preparation of human power. But it may be considered, secondly, as it is from God as mover, and thus it has a necessity – not indeed of coercion, but of infallibility – as regards what it is ordained to by God, since God's intention, according to the saying of Augustine in his book on the *Predestination of the Saints* [*De dono persev.* xiv.35, prin.] to the effect that 'by God's good gifts, whoever is liberated, is most certainly liberated', cannot fail. Hence if God intends, while moving, that the one whose heart he moves should attain to grace, he will infallibly attain to it ...

state of divine solicitude whereby the soul is healed from its infirmities and lifted by way of good works to an order of happiness exceeding the possibilities of nature pure and simple: 'Uno quidem modo, quantum ad aliquod habituale donum, per quod natura humana corrupta sanetur; et etiam sanata elevetur ad operandum opera meritoria vitae aeternae, quae excedunt proportionem naturae' (*ST* Ia IIae.109.9 resp.).[17] Over and above this, however, there is the occasional grace whereby the soul is moved to a particular undertaking: 'Alio modo indiget homo auxilio gratiae ut a Deo moveatur ad agendum' (ibid.),[18] habitual grace thus requiring within the economy of the whole any number of transient effluxes of divine assistance as the condition of its proper operation:

> Quantum igitur ad primum auxilii modum, homo in gratia existens non indiget alio auxilio gratiae quasi aliquo alio habitu infuso. Indiget tamen auxilio gratiae secundum alium modum, ut scilicet a Deo moveatur ad recte agendum. Et hoc propter duo. Primo quidem, ratione generali, propter hoc quod, sicut supra dictum est, nulla res creata potest in quemcumque actum prodire nisi virtute motionis divinae. Secundo, ratione speciali, propter conditionem status humanae naturae. Quae quidem licet per gratiam sanetur quantum ad mentem, remanet tamen in ea corruptio et infectio quantum ad carnem, per quam servit legi peccati, ut dicitur ad Rom. VII. Remanet etiam quaedam ignorantiae obscuritas in intellectu, secundum quam, ut etiam dicitur Rom. VIII, 'quid oremus sicut oportet, nescimus'. Propter varios enim rerum eventus, et quia etiam nosipsos non perfecte cognoscimus, non possumus ad plenum scire quid nobis expediat; secundum illud Sap. IX, 'cogitationes mortalium timidae, et incertae providentiae nostrae'. Et ideo necesse est nobis ut a Deo dirigamur et protegamur, qui omnia novit et omnia potest.
>
> (*ST* Ia IIae.109.9 resp.)[19]

---

[17] First, a habitual gift whereby corrupted nature is healed, and, after being healed, is lifted up so as to work deeds meritorious of everlasting life, which exceed the capability of nature.

[18] In another way, man needs the help of grace in order to be moved by God to act.

[19] Now with regard to the first kind of help, man does not need a further help of grace – for example, a further infused habit. Yet he needs the help of grace in another way, namely, in order to be moved by God to act righteously, and this for two reasons: first, for the general reason that no created thing can put forth any act, unless by virtue of divine motion. Secondly, for this special reason – the condition of the state of human nature. For although healed by grace as to the mind, yet it remains corrupted and poisoned in the flesh, whereby, as it says in Romans 7 [v. 25] it serves the law of sin. In the intellect, too, there remains the darkness of ignorance, whereby, as is said in Romans 8 [v. 26], 'We know not what we should pray for as we ought'; since on account of the various

Thus Thomas, in the *Prima secundae*, offers an account of grace under the aspect of reiteration, there being in his view no possibility of man's making good on the plane of right doing other than by way of a constant process of divine guiding and guarding ('ut a Deo dirigamur et protegamur'), a position notably more severe than that advanced in the *Scriptum*:

> Supra dictum est, quod quamvis homo non haberet unde proficere posset, habuit tamen unde posset stare. Ergo liberum arbitrium sufficiebat ad justitiam retinendam. Et dicendum, quod ab eadem causa est esse rei et conservatio ejus; unde sicut esse justitiae gratuitae non est nisi a Deo; ita etiam et conservatio ejus. Sed verum est quod homo habens gratiam non indiget alia gratia ad ejus conservationem, et propter hoc dicitur, quod homo potest per se stare.
>
> (*Scriptum* 2, d. 29, qu. 1, art. 5 *expositio textus*)[20]

turns of circumstances, and because we do not know ourselves perfectly, we cannot fully know what is for our good, according to Wisdom 9 [v. 14]: 'For the thoughts of mortal men are fearful and our counsels uncertain.' Hence we must be guided and guarded by God, who knows and can do all things. On grace as super-additionality, *ScG* III.cl.3 and 6: 'Oportet autem hanc gratiam aliquid in homine gratificato esse, quasi quandam formam et perfectionem ipsius. Quod enim in aliquem finem dirigitur, oportet quod habeat continuum ordinem in ipsum: nam movens continue mutat quousque mobile per motum finem sortiatur. Cum igitur auxilio divinae gratiae homo dirigatur in ultimum finem, ut ostensum est, oportet quod continue homo isto auxilio potiatur, quousque ad finem perveniat. Hoc autem non esset si praedictum auxilium participaret homo secundum aliquem motum aut passionem, et non secundum aliquam formam manentem, et quasi quiescentem in ipso: motus enim et passio talis non esset in homine nisi quando actu converteretur in finem; quod non continue ab homine agitur, ut praecipue patet in dormientibus. Est ergo gratia gratum faciens aliqua forma et perfectio in homine manens, etiam quando non operatur ... Oportet quod homo ad ultimum finem per proprias operationes perveniat. Unumquodque autem operatur secundum propriam formam. Oportet igitur, ad hoc quod homo perducatur in ultimum finem per proprias operationes, quod superaddatur ei aliqua forma, ex qua eius operationes efficaciam aliquam accipiant promerendi ultimum finem'; *ST* Ia IIae.110.2 resp. and ad 1: 'Multo igitur magis illis quos movet ad consequendum bonum supernaturale aeternum, infundit aliquas formas seu qualitates supernaturales, secundum quas suaviter et prompte ab ipso moveantur ad bonum aeternum consequendum. Et sic donum gratiae qualitas quaedam est ... ergo dicendum quod gratia, secundum quod est qualitas, dicitur agere in animam non per modum causae efficientis, sed per modum causae formalis, sicut albedo facit album, et iustitia iustum', etc.

[20] As was noted above, although man would not have what is required for his ultimate fruition, he nevertheless had what was necessary for his standing as man. Free will, therefore sufficed for the purposes of holding fast to righteousness. We have, moreover, to maintain that both the being of a thing and its preservation proceed from the same cause; therefore, just as the gift of justice in its essence is of none other than God, so also is its preservation. But it is true that a man in possession of grace requires no further grace for his preservation, and this is why we say that man is sufficient for his standing as man.

What, then, has happened here? What has happened is that a disposition once rich in its commitment to the possibility of man's 'self-standing' (the 'quod homo potest per se stare' of the passage just quoted) on the basis of his justification by grace has been overtaken by something distinctly strange, by a sense of grace as nothing other than a searching out of further grace as the ground and guarantee of its efficacy as a principle of well-doing:

> Sed contra est quod Augustinus dicit, in libro de natura et gratia, quod 'sicut oculus corporis plenissime sanus, nisi candore lucis adiutus, non potest cernere; sic et homo perfectissime etiam iustificatus, nisi aeterna luce iustitiae divinitus adiuvetur, recte non potest vivere'. Sed iustificatio fit per gratiam; secundum illud Rom. III: 'Iustificati gratis per gratiam ipsius'. Ergo etiam homo iam habens gratiam indiget alio auxilio gratiae ad hoc quod recte vivat.
>
> (*ST* Ia IIae.109.9 sed contra)[21]

Here too, then, Augustine is triumphant, the effect of his presence to Thomas being to empty the notion of free will as the means of reasonable self-determination in man of anything resembling genuine soteriological significance. Free will functions, certainly, but it functions within the context, and as the means, of divine rather than of human intentionality. Man, inasmuch as he is called upon to cooperate with God in the working out of the cosmic plan, is called upon to cooperate with him, not as one who moves, but as one who is moved, as one knowing himself only in the passivity – and thus only in the paradox – of his presence in the world as a creature of moral and ontological accountability.

3. Direct references in Dante to Augustine are few in number.[22] In the *Convivio* there are four, though given their imprecision, it may be a matter

---

[21] On the contrary, as Augustine says in his book on nature and grace [xxvi.29, ult.], 'as the eye of the body, though most healthy, cannot see unless it is helped by the brightness of light, so, neither can a man, even if confirmed in all righteousness, live well unless he be helped by the eternal light of justice'. But according to Romans 3 [v. 24], justification is by grace: 'Being justified freely by his grace.' Hence even a man who already possesses grace needs a further assistance of grace in order to live righteously.

[22] G. Boffito, *Dante, S. Agostino ed Egidio Colonna (Romano)* (Florence: Olschki, 1911); C. Calcaterra, 'Sant'Agostino nelle opere di Dante e del Petrarca', in *S. Agostino. Pubblicazione commemorativa del XV centenario della sua morte*, special supplement to *Rivista di filosofia neoscolastica* 23 (Milan: Vita e pensiero, 1931), pp. 422-99 (reprinted in *Nella selva di Dante* (Bologna: Cappelli, 1942); P. Chioccioni, *L'agostinismo nella Divina Commedia* (Florence: Olschki, 1952); F. X. Newman, 'St Augustine's Three Visions and the Structure of the *Commedia*', *Modern Language Notes* 82 (1967), 56-78 (subsequently in *Dante*, ed. H. Bloom (New York and Philadelphia: Chelsea House, 1986), pp. 65-81, and in R. Lansing

here merely of memory or of second-hand citation: I.ii.14, with its account of how from time to time an author has perforce to speak of himself for the purposes of benefitting his neighbour, an allusion possibly to *Conf.* X.iii.4 and/or X.iv. 6;[23] I.iv.9, on the stain of sin everywhere proper to

(ed.), *Dante: The Critical Complex*, 8 vols (New York: Routledge, 2003), vol. 6, pp. 146-68); G.Fallani, 'Dante e S. Agostino', in *L'esperienza teologica di Dante* (Lecce: Milella, 1976), pp. 185-203; G. Mazzotta, *Dante, Poet of the Desert. History and Allegory in the Divine Comedy* (Princeton NJ: Princeton University Press, 1979); J. Freccero, *Dante: The Poetics of Conversion*, ed. and intro. R. Jacoff (Cambridge, Mass.: Harvard University Press, 1986); C. A. Cioffi, 'St Augustine Revisited: on "Conversion" in the *Commedia*', *Lectura Dantis* 5 (1989), 68-80 (subsequently in R. Lansing (ed.), *Dante: The Critical Complex*, 8 vols (New York: Routledge, 2003), vol. 4, pp. 372-84); I. Opelt, 'Augustinus bei Dante', in A. Zumkeller (ed.), *Signum pietatis. Festgabe für Cornelius Petrus Mayer O.S.A. zum 60. Geburtstag* (Würzburg: Augustinus-Verlag, 1989), pp. 523-27; M. Nussbaum, 'Augustine and Dante on the Ascent of Love', in G. B. Matthews (ed.), *The Augustinian Tradition* (Los Angeles: University of California Press, 1998), pp. 61-90; P. S. Hawkins, 'Augustine, Dante, and the Dialectic of Ineffability', in *Dante's Testaments: Essays in Scriptural Imagination* (Stanford: Stanford University Press, 1999), pp. 213-28; originally in P. S. Hawkins and A. H. Schotter (eds), *Ineffability. Naming the Unnamable from Dante to Beckett* (New York: AMS Press, 1984), pp. 5-22, with, idem, 'Divide and Conquer: Augustine in the *Divine Comedy*' at pp. 197-212 (originally in *Publications of the Modern Language Association of America*, 106 (1991), 3, 471-82 and subsequently in R. Lansing (ed.), *Dante, The Critical Complex*, 8 vols (New York: Routledge, 2003), vol. 4, pp. 343-54); S. Sarteschi, 'Sant'Agostino in Dante e nell'età di Dante', in *Per correr miglior acque. Bilanci e prospettive degli studi danteschi alle soglie del nuovo millennio. Atti del Convegno internazionale di Verona-Ravenna 25-29 ottobre 1999*, 2 vols (Rome: Salerno Editrice, 2001), vol. 2, pp. 1075-97 (subsequently in *Per la 'Commedia' e non per essa soltanto* (Rome: Bulzoni, 2002), pp. 171-94); idem, 'Sant'Agostino in Dante', in F. Ela Consolino (ed.), *L'adorabile vescovo di Ippona. Atti del Convegno di Paola, 24-25 maggio 2000* (Soveria Mannelli: Rubettino, 2001), pp. 275-303; F. Tateo, 'Agostino fra Dante e Petrarca', in *Riscrittura come interpretazione. Dagli umanisti a Leopardi* (Rome and Bari: Laterza, 2001), pp. 3-33; idem, 'Percorsi agostiniani in Dante', *Deutsches Dante-Jahrbuch* 76 (2001), 43-56; R. Hollander, 'Dante's Reluctant Allegiance to St Augustine in the *Commedia*', *L'Alighieri* 49, n.s. 32 (2008), 5-15.

[23] *Conv.* I.ii.14: 'L'altra è quando, per ragionare di sé, grandissima utilitade ne segue altrui per via di dottrina; e questa ragione mosse Agostino ne le sue Confessioni a parlare di sé, ché per lo processo de la sua vita, lo quale fu di [non] buono in buono, e di buono in migliore, e di migliore in ottimo, ne diede essemplo e dottrina, la quale per sì vero testimonio ricevere non si potea.' *Conf.* X.iii.4: 'Et delectat bonos audire praeterita mala eorum, qui iam carent eis, nec ideo delectat, quia mala sunt, sed quia fuerunt et non sunt. Quo itaque fructu, Domine meus, cui quotidie confitetur conscientia mea spe misericordiae tuae securior quam innocentia sua, quo fructu, quaeso, etiam hominibus coram te confiteor per has litteras adhuc, quis ego sim, non quis fuerim?'; X.iv.6 (also for the 'Ma però che ciascuno uomo a ciascuno uomo naturalmente è amico, e ciascuno amico si duole del difetto di colui ch'elli ama, coloro che a così alta mensa sono cibati non sanza misericordia sono inver di quelli che in bestiale pastura veggiono erba e ghiande sen gire mangiando' sequence of *Conv.* I.i.8): 'Hic est fructus confessionum mearum, non qualis fuerim, sed qualis sim, ut hoc confitear non tantum coram te secreta exsultatione cum tremore, et secreto maerore cum spe, sed etiam in auribus credentium filiorum

man as man, a reference, maybe, to *Conf.* I.vii.11 (though not only is the
parallel inexact but the notion is everywhere in Augustine);[24] IV.ix.8, on
the righteous having no need of the written law, reminiscent, possibly,
of passages in the *De libero arbitrio* or else the *Enarrationes in Psalmos*;[25]
and IV.xxi.14 on the importance of reining in youthful passion in the
interests of properly human happiness, an echo, perhaps, of something
similar in the *Confessions* and in the *De ordine*.[26] In the *Monarchia* there are
two references to him in a single chapter (III.iv), one to the *De civitate
Dei* and the other to the *De doctrina christiana*, where on both occasions
it is a question of hermeneutics, of the extent to which the biblical text
may be properly understood to yield a mystical meaning.[27] Two further

hominum, sociorum gaudii mei et consortium mortalitatis meae, ciuium meorum et
mecum peregrinorum, praecedentium et consequentium et comitum viae meae.'

[24] *Conv.* I.iv.9: 'La terza si è l'umana impuritade, la quale si prende da la parte di colui ch'è
giudicato, e non è sanza familiaritade e conversazione alcuna. Ad evidenza di questa, è da
sapere che l'uomo è da più parti maculato, e, come dice Agostino, "nullo è sanza macula"'.
Conf. I.vii.11: 'Quis me commemorat peccatum infantiae meae, quoniam "nemo mundus
a peccato coram te, nec infans, cuius est unius diei vita super terram"' (after Job 14:4
and 15:14). E. Moore, *Studies in Dante. First Series: Scripture and Classical Authors in Dante*,
ed. and intro. C. Hardie (Oxford: Clarendon Press, 1969; originally 1896), pp. 291-92.

[25] *Conv.* IV.ix.8: 'Onde dice Augustino: "Se questa – cioè equitade – li uomini la
conoscessero, e conosciuta servassero, la ragione scritta non sarebbe mestiere"; e però è
scritto nel principio del Vecchio Digesto: "La ragione scritta è arte di bene e d'equitade".'
De lib. arb. I.xv.31: 'eos vero qui legi aeternae per bonam voluntatem haerent, temporalis
legis non indigere, satis, ut apparet, intellegis'; *En. in psalmos* 1 (v. 2): 'Deinde aliud est
lex quae scribitur, et imponitur servienti; aliud lex quae mente conspicitur, ab eo qui non
indiget litteris.'

[26] *Conv.* IV.xxi.14: 'E però vuole santo Augustino, e ancora Aristotile nel secondo de
l'Etica, che l'uomo s'ausi a ben fare e a rifrenare le sue passioni, acciò che questo tallo,
che detto è, per buona consuetudine induri, e rifermisi ne la sua rettitudine, sì che possa
fruttificare, e del suo frutto uscire la dolcezza de l'umana felicitade.' *Conf.* IX.viii.17:
'Hac ratione praecipiendi et auctoritate imperandi frenabat aviditatem tenerioris aetatis
et ipsam puellarum sitim formabat ad honestum modum, ut iam nec liberet quod non
deceret', *De ord.* II.viii.25: 'Haec igitur disciplina eis qui illam nosse desiderant, simul
geminum ordinem sequi iubet, cuius una pars vitae, altera eruditionis est. Adolescentibus
ergo studiosis eius ita vivendum est ut a venereis rebus, ab illecebris ventris et gutturis,
ab immodesto corporis cultu et ornatu, ab inanibus negotiis ludorum, a torpore somni
atque pigritiae, ab aemulatione, obtrectatione, invidentia, ab honorum potestatumque
ambitionibus, ab ipsius etiam laudis immodica cupiditate se abstineant.' M. Corti, *La
felicità mentale* (Turin: Einaudi, 1983), p. 112 with a possible source, citing Augustine,
from Albert the Great (*Super Eth.* II, lect. 2).

[27] *Mon.* III.iv.7-8: 'Propter primum dicit Augustinus in Civitate Dei: "Non omnia que
gesta narrantur etiam significare aliquid putanda sunt, sed propter illa que aliquid
significant etiam ea que nichil significant actexuntur. Solo vomere terra proscinditur;
sed ut hoc fieri possit, etiam cetera aratri membra sunt necessaria". Propter secundum
idem ait in Doctrina Cristiana, loquens de illo aliud in Scripturis sentire quam ille qui

passages, one in the *Monarchia* at III.iii.13 and one in the letter to the Italian cardinals, note the prominence of Augustine among the Fathers, the former commending him as a servant of the Holy Spirit and thus as nourishment for the pious soul, and the latter lamenting the neglect into which he has now fallen.[28] Also among the letters there is an invitation to read Augustine – the Augustine of the *De quantitate animae* – on the exaltation or apotheosis of the spirit as bearing on the *Paradiso* as itself an essay in spiritual ecstasis.[29] As for the *Commedia*, there are just two references to Augustine, one – by way, probably, of Orosius – indirect (the 'Ne l'altra piccioletta luce ride / quello avvocato de' tempi cristiani / del cui latino Augustin si provide' of *Par.* X.118-20),[30] and the other celebrating him, not, in fact, as a theologian, but, alongside Benedict and Francis, as a founder of one of the great orders (the 'sotto lui così cerner sortiro / Francesco, Benedetto e Augustino / e altri fin qua giù di giro in giro' of *Par.* XXXII.34-36).[31] But for all the apparently slight nature of his

scripsit eas dicit, quod "ita fallitur ac si quisquam deserens viam eo tamen per girum pergeret quo via illa perducit"; et subdit: "Demonstrandum est ut consuetudine deviandi etiam in transversum aut perversum ire cogatur".' *De civ. Dei* XVI.ii.3: 'Non sane omnia, quae gesta narrantur, aliquid etiam significare putanda sunt; sed propter illa, quae aliquid significant, etiam ea, quae nihil significant, attexuntur. Solo enim vomere terra proscinditur; sed ut hoc fieri possit, etiam cetera aratri membra sunt necessaria ...'; *De doct. christ.* I.xxxvi.41: 'ita fallitur, ac si quisquam errore deserens viam, eo tamen per agrum pergat quo etiam via illa perducit.'

[28] *Mon.* III.iii.13: 'Sunt etiam Scripture doctorum, Augustini et aliorum, quos a Spiritu Sancto adiutos qui dubitat, fructus eorum vel omnino non vidit vel, si vidit, minime degustavit', *Ep.* xi.16: 'Iacet Gregorius tuus in telis aranearum, iacet Ambrosius in neglectis clericorum latibulis, iacet Augustinus adiectus ...'

[29] *Ep.* xiii.80: 'Et ubi ista invidis non sufficiant, legant Richardum de Sancto Victore in libro De Contemplatione; legant Bernardum in libro De Consideratione; legant Augustinum in libro De Quantitate Anime, et non invidebunt.' Augustine (*De quant. anim.* xxxiii.76) as a possibility here: 'Iamvero in ipsa visione atque contemplatione veritatis, qui septimus atque ultimus animae gradus est; neque iam gradus, sed quaedam mansio, quo illis gradibus pervenitur; quae sint gaudia, quae perfructio summi et veri boni, cuius serenitatis atque aeternitatis afflatus, quid ego dicam? Dixerunt haec quantum dicenda esse iudicaverunt, magnae quaedam et incomparabiles animae, quas etiam vidisse ac videre ista credimus. Illud plane ego nunc audeo tibi dicere, nos si cursum quem nobis Deus imperat, et quem tenendum suscepimus, constantissime tenuerimus, perventuros per Virtutem Dei atque Sapientiam ad summam illam causam, vel summum auctorem, vel summum principium rerum omnium, vel si quo alio modo res tanta congruentius appellari potest ...'

[30] In the next little light smiles that defender of the Christian times, of whose discourse Augustine made use. C. Reissner, '*Paradiso* X.118-120: "quello avvocato de' tempi cristiani": Orosius oder Lactantius?', *Deutsches Dante-Jahrbuch* 47 (1972), 58-76.

[31] and beneath him, Francis and Benedict and Augustine and others were allotted, as far down as here, from circle to circle.

presence to Dante in the text, we should not be misled, for the statistics
by no means reflect the depth of their companionship as fellow travellers,
as engaged one with the other at the point both of cosmological and of
ontological – and more especially still of psycho-ontological – concern.
When, for example, in the *Convivio*, Dante seeks to confirm his sense of
the fundamentally affective structure of the universe, of the cosmos as no
more than the sum total of its love-impulses, there ready and waiting is
Augustine with the necessary conceptual and expressive apparatus, with
his own distinctive sense of the love-gravitation of everything that *is* in
the world and of how, ideally, the notion stands to be expressed. On the
one hand, then, the *Convivio* at III.iii.2-5:

> Onde è da sapere che ciascuna cosa, come detto è di sopra, per la
> ragione di sopra mostrata ha 'l suo speziale amore. Come le corpora
> simplici hanno amore naturato in sé a lo luogo proprio, e però la terra
> sempre discende al centro; lo fuoco ha [amore a] la circunferenza
> di sopra, lungo lo cielo de la luna, e però sempre sale a quello. Le
> corpora composte prima, sì come sono le minere, hanno amore a
> lo luogo dove la loro generazione è ordinata, e in quello crescono e
> acquistano vigore e potenza; onde vedemo la calamita sempre da la
> parte de la sua generazione ricevere vertù. Le piante, che sono prima
> animate, hanno amore a certo luogo più manifestamente, secondo
> che la complessione richiede; e però vedemo certe piante lungo
> l'acque quasi c[ontent]arsi, e certe sopra li gioghi de le montagne,
> e certe ne le piagge e dappiè monti: le quali se si transmutano, o
> muoiono del tutto o vivono quasi triste, disgiunte dal loro amico. Li
> animali bruti hanno più manifesto amore non solamente a li luoghi,
> ma l'uno l'altro vedemo amare. Li uomini hanno loro proprio amore
> a le perfette e oneste cose. E però che l'uomo, avvegna che una sola
> sustanza sia, tuttavia [la] forma, per la sua nobilitade, ha in sé e la
> natura [d'ognuna di] queste cose, tutti questi amori puote avere e
> tutti li ha.[32]

[32] It should be explained here that, as was said above, for the reason given there, every
being has a love specific to it. Just as simple bodies have an inborn love for the place
proper to them – so that earth always descends to the centre, while fire has an inborn love
for the circumference above us bordering the heaven of the Moon, and therefore always
rises upwards towards that – so primary compound bodies, such as minerals, have a
love for the place suited to their generation; in that place they grow, and from it they
derive their vigour and power. That is why, as we observe, the magnet always receives
power from the quarter in which it was generated. Plants, which are the primary form
of animate life, even more clearly have a love for certain places, in accordance with
what their constitution requires; and so we see that some plants rejoice, as it were, when
alongside water, others when on the ridges of mountains, others when on slopes and on
foothills; if they are transplanted, they either die completely or live a sad life, as it were,

while on the other, the *City of God* at XI.xxviii:

Si enim pecora essemus, carnalem vitam et quod secundum sensum
eius est amaremus idque esset sufficiens bonum nostrum et secundum
hoc, cum esset nobis bene, nihil aliud quaereremus. Item si arbores
essemus, nihil quidem sentiente motu amare possemus, verumtamen
id quasi appetere videremur, quo feracius essemus uberiusque
fructuosae. Si essemus lapides aut fluctus aut ventus aut flamma vel
quid huiusmodi, sine ullo quidem sensu atque vita, non tamen nobis
deesset quasi quidam nostrorum locorum atque ordinis appetitus.
Nam velut amores corporum momenta sunt ponderum, sive deorsum
gravitate sive sursum levitate nitantur. Ita enim corpus pondere,
sicut animus amore fertur, quocumque fertur.[33]

And when in *Convivio* IV Dante is seeking to define the limits of
specifically imperial authority (for strictly speaking the emperor's writ
runs only in the area of pure positive law), there once again is Augustine,
eager as ever to assist in shaping the argument. On the one hand, then,
these lines from the *Convivio* at IV.ix.12-15:

E cose sono dove l'arte è in strumento de la natura, e queste sono meno
arti; e in esso sono meno subietti li artefici a loro prencipe: sì com'è
dare lo seme a la terra (qui si vuole attendere la volontà dela natura); sì
come è uscire di porto (qui si vuole attendere la naturale disposizione

like beings separated from their friends. Brute animals not only more clearly still have a
love for particular places, but, as we observe, they also love one another. Human beings
have their specific love, for what is perfect and just. And since the human being, despite
the fact that his whole form constitutes a single substance in virtue of its nobility, has
a nature that embraces all these features, he can have all these loves, and indeed does
have them.

[33] If we were mere beasts we would love the life of sensuality and all that relates to it;
this would be our sufficient good, and when this was satisfied, we should seek nothing
further. If we were trees, we would not be able to love anything with any sensual
emotion, yet we would seem to have a kind of desire for increased fertility and more
abundant fruitfulness. If we were stones, waves, wind or flame, or anything of that
kind, lacking sense and life, we would still show something like desire for our own
place and order. For the specific gravity of a body is, in a manner, its love, whether
a body tends downwards by reason of its heaviness or strives upwards because of its
lightness. A material body is borne along by its weight in a particular direction, as a
soul is by its love. Cf. *Conf.* XIII.ix.10: 'Corpus pondere suo nititur ad locum suum.
Pondus non ad ima tantum est, sed ad locum suum. Ignis sursum tendit, deorsum lapis.
Ponderibus suis aguntur, loca sua petunt. Oleum infra aquam fusum super aquam
attollitur, aqua supra oleum fusa, infra oleum demergitur; ponderibus suis aguntur,
loca sua petunt. Minus ordinata inquieta sunt: ordinantur et quiescunt. Pondus meum
amor meus; eo feror, quocumque feror' (with the 'In bona voluntate pax nobis est'
immediately preceding for *Par.* III.85).

del tempo). E però vedemo in queste cose spesse volte contenzione tra li artefici, e domandare consiglio lo maggiore al minore. Altre cose sono che non sono de l'arte, e paiono avere con quella alcuna parentela, e quinci sono li uomini molte volte ingannati; e in queste li discenti a lo artefice, o vero maestro, subietti non sono, né credere a lui sono tenuti quanto è per l'arte: sì come pescare pare aver parentela col navicare, e conoscere la vertù de l'erbe pare aver parentela con l'agricultura; che non hanno insieme alcuna regola, con ciò sia cosa che 'l pescare sia sotto l'arte de la venagione e sotto suo comandare, e lo conoscere la vertù de l'erbe sia sotto la medicina o vero sotto più nobile dottrina. Queste cose simigliantemente che de l'altre arti sono ragionate, vedere si possono ne l'arte imperiale; ché regole sono in quella che sono pure arti, sì come sono le leggi de' matrimonii, de li servi, de le milizie, de li successori in dignitade, e di queste in tutto siamo a lo Imperadore subietti, sanza dubbio e sospetto alcuno. Altre leggi sono che sono quasi seguitatrici di natura, sì come constituire l'uomo d'etade sofficiente a ministrare, e di queste non semo in tutto subietti.[34]

while on the other, these from the *De doctrina christiana* at II.xxx.47:

Artium etiam ceterarum, quibus aliquid fabricatur, vel quod remaneat post operationem artificis ab illo effectum, sicut domus et scamnum et

[34] There are matters in which art functions merely as a means of nature. These are arts in a lesser sense, and in them the artisans are less subject to their leader. Instances of this are the sowing of seed in the ground (where the principal factor is the will of nature), and setting sail from port (where the principal factor is the kind of weather nature decrees). So in these matters we often see disputes arising among the artisans, and the superior asking advice of the inferior. There are other matters which do not, in fact, belong to a particular art, yet appear at first sight to pertain to it; when this situation occurs, many people fall into error. In such cases the apprentices are not subject to the master, and do not have any obligation to follow him, as they do when the art in question truly is involved. For instance, fishing appears at first sight to pertain to navigation, and knowing the qualities of herbs appears at first sight to pertain to agriculture. But in neither case are the two governed by the same rules, since fishing comes within the purview of the art of hunting and is subject to its laws, and knowing the qualities of herbs comes within the purview of medicine or of some even more noble branch of learning. The points made above with reference to the other arts hold good also with regard to the art of ruling as emperor. In this case, too, there are regulations which are arts to a high degree; such is the case with laws governing marriages, slavery, military service and the inheritance of titles. In all these we are, without the slightest doubt, subject to the emperor. There are other laws which are almost totally dictated by nature, such as that establishing the age at which a man is able to hold office, and in respect of these we are not entirely subject. J. Took, '"Diligite iustitiam qui iudicatis terram": Justice and the Just Ruler in Dante', in J. R. Woodhouse (ed.), *Dante and Governance* (Oxford: Clarendon Press, 1997), pp. 137-51 (on the extent of imperial jurisdiction in Dante's understanding of it).

vas aliquod atque alia huiuscemodi, vel quae ministerium quoddam
exhibent operanti Deo, sicut medicina et agricultura et gubernatio
...[35]

And when, similarly, in an exquisite moment of the *Purgatorio* Dante
wishes to explore the inclusivity of man's proper happiness as man, its
somehow increasing in proportion to the number of those party to it,
Augustine is yet again on hand to clarify the basic idea, his – and now
Dante's – sense of the exponential or ever expanding structure of it all.
On the one hand, then, this from the *Purgatorio* at XV.61-75:

> "Com' esser puote ch'un ben, distributo
> in più posseditor, faccia più ricchi
> di sé che se da pochi è posseduto?".
>   Ed elli a me: "Però che tu rificchi
> la mente pur a le cose terrene,
> di vera luce tenebre dispicchi.
>   Quello infinito e ineffabil bene
> che là sù è, così corre ad amore
> com' a lucido corpo raggio vene.
>   Tanto si dà quanto trova d'ardore;

[35] Among other arts there are some concerned with the manufacture of a product
which is a result of the labour of the artificer, like a house, a bench, a dish, or something
else of this kind. Others exhibit a kind of assistance to the work of God, like medicine,
agriculture, and navigation ... *De lib. arb.* I. viii.18: 'Illud est quod volo dicere: hoc
quidquid est, quo pecoribus homo praeponitur, sive mens, sive spiritus, sive utrumque
rectius appellatur (nam utrumque in divinis Libris invenimus), si dominetur atque
imperet caeteris quibuscumque homo constat, tunc esse hominem ordinatissimum.
Videmus enim habere nos non solum cum pecoribus, sed etiam cum arbustis et
stirpibus multa communia: namque alimentum corporis sumere, crescere, gignere,
vigere, arboribus quoque tributum videmus, quae infima quadam vita continentur;
videre autem atque audire, et olfactu, gustatu, tactu corporalia sentire posse bestias, et
acrius plerasque quam nos, cernimus et fatemur. Adde vires et valentiam firmitatemque
membrorum, et celeritates facillimosque corporis motus, quibus omnibus quasdam
earum superamus, quibusdam aequamur, a nonnullis etiam vincimur.' Also for this
passage, however, Aquinas, *In Eth.* I, lect. 1, n. 16: 'quaecumque autem sunt talium etc.,
ponit ordinem habituum adinvicem. Contingit enim unum habitum operativum, quem
vocat virtutem, sub alio esse. Sicut ars quae facit frena est sub arte equitandi, quia ille
qui debet equitare praecipit artifici qualiter faciat frenum. Et sic est architector, idest
principalis artifex respectu ipsius. Et eadem ratio est de aliis artibus, quae faciunt alia
instrumenta necessaria ad equitandum, puta sellas, vel aliquid huiusmodi. Equestris
autem ulterius ordinatur sub militari. Milites enim dicebantur antiquitus non solum
equites, sed quicumque pugnatores ad vincendum. Unde sub militari continetur non
solum equestris, sed omnis ars vel virtus ordinata ad bellicam operationem, sicut
sagittaria, fundibularia vel quaecumque alia huiusmodi. Et per eundem modum aliae
artes sub aliis.'

sì che, quantunque carità si stende,
cresce sovr' essa l'etterno valore.
    E quanta gente più là sù s'intende,
più v'è da bene amare, e più vi s'ama,
e come specchio l'uno a l'altro rende".[36]

while on the other, this from the *De civitate Dei* at XV.v:

Nullo enim modo fit minor accedente seu permanente consorte possessio bonitatis, immo possessio bonitas, quam tanto latius, quanto concordius individua sociorum possidet caritas. Non habebit denique istam possessionem, qui eam noluerit habere communem, et tanto eam reperiet ampliorem, quanto amplius ibi potuerit amare consortem.[37]

And when, finally, in a still more exquisite moment of the *Paradiso*, Dante wishes to confirm the mutual immanence of human and divine purposefulness in circumstances of consummate human being, and this as the basis of every kind of spiritual peace, then Augustine, in all the maturity of his at once episcopal and pastoral presence, is on hand to confirm him in the substance of his own intuition; on the one hand, then, Dante in the *Paradiso* at III.79-87:

Anzi è formale ad esto beato esse
tenersi dentro a la divina voglia,
per ch'una fansi nostre voglie stesse;
    sì che, come noi sem di soglia in soglia
per questo regno, a tutto il regno piace
com' a lo re che 'n suo voler ne 'nvoglia.
    E 'n la sua volontade è nostra pace,

---

[36] "How can it be that a good distributed can make more possessors richer with itself than if it is possessed by a few?" And he to me: "Because you still set your mind on earthly things, you gather darkness from true light. That infinite and ineffable good that is there above speeds to love as a ray of light comes to a bright body. So much it gives of itself as it finds of ardour, so that how far soever love extends, the more does the eternal goodness increase upon it; and the more souls there are that are enamoured there above, the more there are for loving well, and the more love is there, and like a mirror the one returns to the other."

[37] A man's possession of goodness is in no way diminished by the arrival, or the continuance, of a sharer in it; indeed, goodness is a possession enjoyed more widely by the united affection of partners in that possession, in proportion to the harmony that exists among them. In fact, anyone who refuses to enjoy this possession in partnership will not enjoy it at all; and he will find that he possesses it in ampler measure in proportion to his ability to love his partner in it.

ell' è quel mare al qual tutto si move
ciò ch'ella crïa o che natura face.[38]

while on the other, Augustine in the *Confessions* at XIII.ix.10:

In dono tuo requiescimus: ibi te fruimur. Requies nostra locus noster. Amor illuc attollit nos et spiritus tuus bonus exaltat humilitatem nostram de portis mortis. In bona voluntate pax nobis est.[39]

Everywhere, therefore, the pattern is the same, for everywhere the Augustinian text – be it the *Confessions*, the *De doctrina christiana* or the *De civitate Dei* – is present to Dante as a friend, companion and comforter in the moment of elucidation, of clarifying above all for his own peace of mind the leading idea.

But with what amounts in this sense to the cherished reminiscence at the level of ideas we are as yet in the foothills where Dante and Augustine are concerned, for it is above all as a phenomenologist – as one engaged at the point, not now of the *what it is* but of the *how it is* with being in its lostness and foundness – that the great bishop is present to Dante as a fellow traveller. Take for example the opening lines of the *Commedia*, a meditation, whatever else they are, upon the symptomatology of estrangement as a condition of the spirit, on the kind of disorientation, self-forgetfulness, recidivism, and, as underlying and informing all these things, despair whereby the soul in its dividedness knows itself in the near-dissolution of self:

Nel mezzo del cammin di nostra vita
mi ritrovai per una selva oscura,
ché la diritta via era smarrita.
    Ahi quanto a dir qual era è cosa dura
esta selva selvaggia e aspra e forte
che nel pensier rinova la paura!
    Tant' è amara che poco è più morte;
ma per trattar del ben ch'i' vi trovai,
dirò de l'altre cose ch'i' v'ho scorte.

---

[38] Indeed, it is of the essence of this blessed existence to keep itself within the divine will, whereby our wills are made one; so that our being thus from threshold to threshold throughout this realm is a joy to all the realm as to the king, who inwills us with his will; and in his will is our peace. It is that sea to which all moves, both what it creates and what nature makes.

[39] In your gift we rest, and there we enjoy you. Our rest is our place. Love raises us there and your good spirit lifts up our lowliness from the gates of death. In your good will is our peace.

Io non so ben ridir com' i' v'intrai,
tant' era pien di sonno a quel punto
che la verace via abbandonai

...

Ed ecco, quasi al cominciar de l'erta,
una lonza leggera e presta molto,
che di pel macolato era coverta;

e non mi si partia dinanzi al volto,
anzi 'mpediva tanto il mio cammino,
ch'i' fui per ritornar più volte vòlto.

Temp' era dal principio del mattino,
e 'l sol montava 'n sù con quelle stelle
ch'eran con lui quando l'amor divino

mosse di prima quelle cose belle;
sì ch'a bene sperar m'era cagione
di quella fiera a la gaetta pelle

l'ora del tempo e la dolce stagione;
ma non sì che paura non mi desse
la vista che m'apparve d'un leone.

Questi parea che contra me venisse
con la test' alta e con rabbiosa fame,
sì che parea che l'aere ne tremesse.

Ed una lupa, che di tutte brame
sembiava carca ne la sua magrezza,
e molte genti fé già viver grame,

questa mi porse tanto di gravezza
con la paura ch'uscia di sua vista,
ch'io perdei la speranza de l'altezza.

(*Inf.* I.1-12 and 31-54)[40]

---

[40] Midway in the journey of our life I found myself in a dark wood, for the straight way was lost. Ah, how hard it is to tell what that wood was, wild, rugged, harsh; the very thought of it renews my fear! It is so bitter that death is hardly more so. But, to treat of the good that I found in it, I will tell of the other things I saw there. I cannot rightly say how I entered it, I was so full of sleep at the moment I left the true way ... And behold, near the beginning of the steep, a leopard light-footed and very fleet, covered with a spotted hide! And it did not depart from before my eyes, but did so impede my way that more than once I turned round to go back. It was the beginning of the morning, and the sun was mounting with the stars that were with it when divine love first set those beautiful things in motion, so that the hour of the day and the sweet season gave me cause for good hope of that beast with the gay skin; yet not so much that I did not feel afraid at the sight of a lion that appeared to me and seemed to be coming at me, head high and raging with hunger, so that the air seemed to tremble at it; and a she-wolf, that in her leanness seemed laden with every craving and had already caused many to live in sorrow; she put such heaviness upon me with the fear that came from the sight of her that I lost hope of the height.

Here, certainly, Augustine is not far away, his too being an account of the substance and psychology of being in its *longe peregrinare* or far wandering,[41] its standing over against self at the point of fundamental willing; so, then, to take first the substance of being in its remotion, as captive to the forces of self-destruction operative from out of the depths, these lines from the *Confessions* at VII.xxi.27 for the iconography of this first canto of the *Inferno*: 'Et aliud est de silvestri cacumine videre patriam pacis et iter ad eam non invenire et frustra conari per invia circum obsidentibus et insidiantibus fugitivis desertoribus cum principe suo leone et dracone';[42] while in respect of the mood or felt-condition of being in its alienation from self and from God as the beginning and end of the soul's every significant inflexion of the spirit (these two things coinciding within the moral and ontological economy of the whole), this passage from Book II of the *Confessions* (x.18) on the directionless of self in its lostness for the 'ché la diritta via era smarrita' and the 'esta selva selvaggia e aspra e forte' of *Inf.* I.3 and 5:

Defluxi abs te ego et erravi, Deus meus, nimis devius ab stabilitate tua in adulescentia et factus sum mihi regio egestatis.[43]

[41] For the terminology of far-offness ('longe peregrinare') of the soul in its alienation, *De doct. christ.* I.iv.4: 'Quomodo ergo, si essemus peregrini, qui beate vivere nisi in patria non possemus, eaque peregrinatione utique miseri et miseriam finire cupientes in patriam redire vellemus, opus esset vel terrestribus vel marinis vehiculis, quibus utendum esset, ut ad patriam, qua fruendum erat, pervenire valeremus; quod si amoenitates itineris et ipsa gestatio vehiculorum nos delectaret, conversi ad fruendum his, quibus uti debuimus, nollemus cito viam finire et perversa suavitate implicati alienaremur a patria, cuius suavitas faceret beatos ...'; *Conf.* II.ii.2: 'Tacebas tunc, et ego ibam porro longe a te in plura et plura sterilia semina dolorum superba deiectione et inquieta lassitudine'; V.ii. 2: 'Eant et fugiant a te inquieti iniqui'; VII.x.16: 'et inveni longe me esse a te in regione dissimilitudinis'; *De vera rel.* liv.105: 'Qui enim magis amant ire quam redire aut pervenire, in longinquiora mittendi sunt, quoniam caro sunt et spiritus ambulans et non revertens [Ps. 78:39]', etc. Otherwise, Eph. 2:13: 'Nunc autem in Christo Jesu vos, qui aliquando eratis longe, facti esti prope in sanguine Christi' (with 'qui longe fuistis' at v. 17); Bernard, *Cant. cantic.* lvi.5 (*PL* 183, 1048-49); lxxxiii.1 (ibid. 1181D); lxxxiv.3 (ibid. 1185D), etc. Dante, in the *Paradiso* (VII.31-32), has 'u' la natura, che dal suo fattore / s'era allungata ...'. G. B. Ladner, 'Homo viator: Mediaeval Ideas on Alienation and Order', *Speculum* 42 (1967), 2, 233-59.

[42] It is one thing to descry the land of peace from a wooded hilltop, and, unable to find the way to it, struggle on through trackless wastes where traitors and runaways, constrained by their prince, who is lion and serpent in one, lie in wait to attack. Cf. the 'Continete vos ab immani feritate superbiae, ab inerti voluptate luxuriae et a fallaci nomine scientiae, ut sint bestiae mansuetae et pecora edomita et innoxii serpentes. Motus enim animae sunt isti in allegoria: sed fastus elationis et delectatio libidinis et venenum curiositatis motus sunt animae mortuae ...' of XIII.xxi.30.

[43] But I deserted you, my God. In my youth I wandered away, too far from your sustaining hand, and created of myself a barren waste.

or these from the first book (vi.7) on the nightmare of self-unintelligibility for the 'io non so ben ridir com' i' v'intrai' of *Inf.* I.10:

> Quid enim est quod volo dicere, domine, nisi quia nescio, unde venerim huc, in istam dico vitam mortalem an mortem vitalem?[44]

or these from Book VIII (v.12) on the half-waking/half-sleeping truth of being in its dividedness for the 'tant' era pien di sonno a quel punto' of *Inf.* I.11:

> Ita sarcina saeculi, velut somno assolet, dulciter premebar, et cogitationes, quibus meditabar in te, similes erant conatibus expergisci volentium, qui tamen superati soporis altitudine remerguntur.[45]

or these from Book VII (iii.5 and xvii.23) on the rhythm of retreat for the 'ch'i' fui per ritornar più volte vòlto' of *Inf.* I.36 and the 'mi ripigneva là dove 'l sol tace' of *Inf.* I.60:[46]

> Itaque aciem mentis de profundo educere conatus mergebar iterum et saepe conatus mergebar iterum atque iterum ... sed aciem figere non evalui et repercussa infirmitate redditus solitis non mecum ferebam nisi amantem memoriam et quasi olefacta desiderantem, quae comedere nondum possem.[47]

or this passage from Book VI (i.1) on despair as the innermost substance of all these things for the 'ch'io perdei la speranza de l'altezza' of I.54:

> Et ambulabam per tenebras et lubricum et quaerebam te foris a me et non inveniebam Deum cordis mei; et veneram in profundum maris et diffidebam et desperabam de inventione veri.[48]

---

[44] For what I would say, Lord, is that I do not know how I came into this dying life, or, should I say, living death?

[45] In fact I bore the burden of the world as contentedly as someone bears a heavy load of sleep. My thoughts, as I meditated on you, were like the efforts of a man who tries to wake but cannot and sinks back into the depths of slumber.

[46] [the leopard ... did so impede my way] that more than once I turned round to go back ... she pushed me back to where the sun is silent.

[47] I tried to raise my mental perceptions out of the abyss which engulfed them, but I sank into it once more ... But I had no strength to fix my gaze upon them. In my weakness I recoiled and fell back into my old ways, carrying with me nothing but the memory of something that I had loved and longed for, as though I had sensed the fragrance of the fare but was not yet able to eat it.

[48] Yet I was walking on a treacherous path in darkness. I was looking for you outside myself, and I did not find the God of my own heart. I had reached the depths of the ocean. I had lost all faith and was in despair of finding the truth.

Right from the outset, then, Augustine is there, not so much to authorize the text, as, by way of a kind of formed friendship, to encourage the spirit in a moment of shared intelligence, his, liminally or subliminally, being a presence as decisive as any for the shape and substance of the text in its precise conception and articulation.

But if, in the sense we have described, the *Confessions* remains for Dante a faithful guide to the psychology and pathology of being in its estrangement, there can be no question of his acquiescing in quite the kind of grace theology developed by Augustine in the anti-Pelagian moment of his meditation and decisive in turn for the substance and complexion of Thomas's meditation in the twilight pages of the *Prima secundae*. For if by this we have in mind Augustine's sense of man's being and becoming as a matter of continuous gracing from on high, herein alone lying the solution to his original and continuing disobedience, then Dante's, by contrast, is a sense (*a*) of the moral and ontological co-adequation of human nature by way of God's work in Christ on Calvary, and (*b*), and as freshly confirmed by this, of the co-inherence of divine and human willing at the core itself of existence, at which point the dark substance of late Augustinian spirituality gives way to something more radiant, to a sense of the renewed functionality of the human project in consequence of its closeness to the Father's heart. Taking first, then, the position in Augustine we may begin by noting these lines from the *De gratia et libero arbitrio* at vi.15, settled in their sense of human deserving as but a mode or manifestation of divine deserving, of God's own righteousness:

Sed cum dicunt pelagiani hanc esse solam non secundum merita nostra gratiam, qua homini peccata dimittuntur, illam vero quae datur in fine, id est, aeternam vitam, meritis nostris praecedentibus reddi, respondendum est eis. Si enim merita nostra sic intellegerent, ut etiam ipsa dona Dei esse cognoscerent, non esset reprobanda ista sententia; quoniam vero merita humana sic praedicant, ut ea ex semetipso habere hominem dicant, prorsus rectissime respondet Apostolus: "Quis enim te discernit? Quid autem habes quod non accepisti? Si autem et accepisti, quid gloriaris quasi non acceperis?" Prorsus talia cogitanti verissime dicitur: Dona sua coronat Deus, non merita tua, si tibi a te ipso, non ab illo sunt merita tua. Haec enim si talia sunt, mala sunt; quae non coronat Deus: si autem bona sunt, Dei dona sunt: quia, sicut dicit apostolus Iacobus: "Omne datum optimum, et omne donum perfectum desursum est, descendens a Patre luminum". Unde dicit et Ioannes praecursor Domini: "Non potest homo accipere quidquam, nisi fuerit ei datum de caelo" – utique de caelo, unde etiam venit Spiritus Sanctus, quando Iesus ascendit in altum, captivavit captivitatem, dedit dona hominibus. Si

ergo Dei dona sunt bona merita tua, non Deus coronat merita tua
tamquam merita tua, sed tamquam dona sua.[49]

or, as bearing on man's inability, not only to do well, but to do at all, these
from the *Contra duas epistolas Pelagianorum* at II.viii.18, uncompromising in
their statement of this as the leading idea:

Hoc enim nobis obiciendum putarunt, quod invito et reluctanti
homini Deum dicamus inspirare, non quanticumque boni, sed et
ipsius imperfecti cupiditatem. Fortassis ergo ipsi eo modo saltem
servant locum gratiae, ut sine illa putent hominem posse habere boni,
sed imperfecti cupiditatem, perfecti autem non facilius per illam
posse, sed nisi per illam omnino non posse. Verum et sic gratiam
Dei dicunt secundum merita nostra dari ... Si enim sine Dei gratia
per nos incipit cupiditas boni; ipsum coeptum erit meritum, cui
tamquam ex debito gratiae veniat adiutorium ac sic gratia Dei non
gratis donabitur, sed secundum meritum nostrum dabitur. Dominus
autem, ut responderet futuro Pelagio, non ait: "Sine me difficile
potestis aliquid facere", sed ait: "Sine me nihil potestis facere". Et ut
responderet futuris etiam istis in eadem ipsa evangelica sententia,
non ait: "Sine me nihil potestis *perficere*", sed *facere*. Nam si "perficere"
dixisset, possent isti dicere non ad incipiendum bonum, quod a nobis
est, sed ad perficiendum esse Dei adiutorium necessarium. Verum
audiant et Apostolum. Dominus enim cum ait: "Sine me nihil potestis
facere", hoc uno verbo initium finemque comprehendit.[50]

[49] When, however, the Pelagians say that the only grace which is not awarded according
to our merits is that whereby a man has his sins forgiven him, but that the final grace
which is bestowed upon us, even eternal life, is given in return for preceding merits, they
must not be allowed to go without an answer. If, indeed, they understand our merits
in such a sense as to acknowledge even them to be the gifts of God, then their opinion
would not deserve reprobation. But inasmuch as they preach up human merits to such an
extent as to declare that a man has them of his own self, then the apostle's reply becomes
an absolutely correct one: 'Who makes you to differ from one another? And what have
you that you have not received? Now if you did receive it, why do you glory as if you
had not received it?' [1 Cor. 4:7] To a man who holds such views, it is perfect truth to
say that it is his own gifts that God crowns, not your merits, although you hold these
as done by your own self, not by him. If, indeed, they are of such a character, they are
evil, and God does not crown them ; but if they are good, they are God's gifts, because,
as the Apostle James says, 'Every good gift and every perfect gift is from above, and
comes down from the Father of lights' [James 1:17]. In accordance with which John also,
the Lord's forerunner, declares: 'A man can receive nothing except it be given him from
heaven' [John 3:27] – from heaven, of course, for from thence came also the Holy Spirit,
when Jesus ascended up on high, led captivity captive, and gave gifts to men. Inasmuch,
then, as your merits are God's gifts, God does not crown your merits as such, but only
as his own gifts.

[50] For they have thought that it was to be objected to us that we say that God infuses
into man, unwilling and resisting, the desire, not of good, how great soever it be, but

All the main ingredients of Augustine's mature theology of grace are here, from the impressive array of proof-texts (John 3:27; 15:5; 1 Corinthians 4:7; James 1:17) through to the conclusion (a) that in acknowledging what man does for God, God is merely acknowledging what he himself does for man; (b) that man as man is properly speaking powerless to do well, for he has nothing which he has not received from another; and (c) that every kind of authentic movement of desiring and doing in man begins with God himself as its author and sustainer. Now to this, as the substance of Augustinian grace-theological wisdom as conveyed by Thomas in the mature phase of his meditation, Dante brings an alternative model, a sense (a) of man's having been created in a state of moral and ontological freedom (his leading intuition in the area of creation theology); (b) of his having been confirmed in that freedom by the work of Christ on the cross (his leading intuition in the area of atonement theology); and (c) of God's abiding with him in the recesses of personality, shaping and substantiating as he does so – but *with* man as distinct from *over against* him – in the critical moment of seeing, understanding and choosing (his leading intuition in the area of grace theology). First, then, as bearing on the original *let it be* in the freedom of that being, these lines (67-78) from *Paradiso* VII, consummate in their sense of freedom thus understood as the freedom fully and unambiguously *to be*, as the mark in man of his Godlikeness:

> Ciò che da lei sanza mezzo distilla
> non ha poi fine, perché non si move
> la sua imprenta quand' ella sigilla.
>   Ciò che da essa sanza mezzo piove
> libero è tutto, perché non soggiace
> a la virtute de le cose nove.

even of imperfect good. Possibly, then, they themselves are keeping open a place at least for grace, as thinking that man may have the desire of good without grace, but only of imperfect good; while in respect of the perfect good, it is not that he could enjoy such good more easily with grace, but that, short of grace, he could not enjoy it at all. Truly, they are saying here yet again that God's grace is given according to our merits ... for if without God's grace the desire of good begins with ourselves, merit itself will have begun with us, to which, as if by way of obligation, comes the assistance of grace; and thus God's grace will not be bestowed freely, but will be given according to our merit. But that he might furnish a reply to the future Pelagius, the Lord does not say 'Without me you can do anything only with difficulty' [John 15:5], but he says 'Without me you can do nothing'. And, that he might also furnish an answer to these future heretics, in that very same evangelical saying he does not say 'Without me you can *perfect* nothing', but '*do* nothing'. For if he had said 'perfect', they might say that God's aid is necessary, not for beginning good, which is of ourselves, but for perfecting it. But let us hear the apostle. For when the Lord says 'Without me you can do nothing', in this one word he comprehends both the beginning and the ending.

> Più l'è conforme, e però più le piace;
> ché l'ardor santo ch'ogne cosa raggia,
> ne la più somigliante è più vivace.
> Di tutte queste dote s'avvantaggia
> l'umana creatura, e s'una manca,
> di sua nobilità convien che caggia.[51]

– lines to which, as similarly secure in their sense of man's freedom for manoeuvre as the substance of his humanity, we should add these from *Purgatorio* XVI:

> Lo cielo i vostri movimenti inizia;
> non dico tutti, ma, posto ch'i' 'l dica,
> lume v'è dato a bene e a malizia,
> e libero voler; che, se fatica
> ne le prime battaglie col ciel dura,
> poi vince tutto, se ben si notrica.
> A maggior forza e a miglior natura
> liberi soggiacete; e quella cria
> la mente in voi, che 'l ciel non ha in sua cura.
>
> (*Purg.* XVI.73-81)[52]

and, as bearing on free will as, of all God's gifts to man, the one he most delights in, these from *Paradiso* V:

> Lo maggior don che Dio per sua larghezza
> fesse creando, e a la sua bontate
> più conformato, e quel ch'e' più apprezza,
> fu de la volontà la libertate;
> di che le creature intelligenti,
> e tutte e sole, fuoro e son dotate.
> Or ti parrà, se tu quinci argomenti,
> l'alto valor del voto, s'è sì fatto

---

[51] That which immediately derives from it thereafter has no end, because when it seals, its imprint may never be removed. That which rains down from it immediately is wholly free, because it is not subject to the power of new things. It is the most conformed to it and therefore pleases it the most; for the holy ardour, which irradiates everything, is most living in what is most like itself. With all these gifts the human creature is advantaged, and if one fails, it needs must fall from its nobility.

[52] The heavens initiate your movements – I do not say all of them, but given for the moment that that is what I am saying, a light is given you to know good and evil, and free will, which if it endure fatigue in its first battles with the heavens, afterwards, if it is well nurtured, it conquers completely. You lie subject, in your freedom, to a greater power and to a better nature, and that creates the mind in you which the heavens have not in their charge.

che Dio consenta quando tu consenti;
   ché, nel fermar tra Dio e l'omo il patto,
vittima fassi di questo tesoro,
tal quale io dico; e fassi col suo atto.

(Par. V.19-30)[53]

But that is not all, for the freedom proper to man in the moment of
his creation is the freedom confirmed afresh by God through his work
in Christ on the cross, a work designed in response to the catastrophe of
Eden to enable him to participate in his own resurrection. This, then, is
his point of arrival in *Paradiso* VII as the atonement canto *par excellence* of
the *Commedia*, a canto which, alert to the judicial moment of the Christ
event, to the notion of a price to be paid in the wake of Eden, settles
even so on a sense of God's wishing to involve man in his own making
good. Straightaway, then, the object pronoun (the 'rilevar*vi*' of line 111)
gives way to the reflexive pronoun (the 'rilevar*si*' of line 116) as testimony
to the completeness and courage of Dante's meditation at this point, his
fashioning from the content of atonement theology in its classical form an
essay in spiritual re-potentiation:

---

[53] The greatest gift which God in his bounty bestowed in creating, and the most
conformed to his own goodness and that which he most prizes, was the freedom of the
will, with which the creatures who have intelligence, they all and they alone, were and
are endowed. Now, if you argue from this, the high worth of the vow will appear to you,
if it be such that God consents when you consent; for in establishing the compact between
God and man, this treasure becomes the sacrifice, such as I pronounce it, and that by
its own act. C. J. Ryan, 'Free Will in Theory and Practice: *Purgatorio* XVIII and Two
Characters in the *Inferno*', in D. Nolan (ed.), *Dante Soundings* (Dublin and Totowa, NJ:
Irish Academic Press, 1981), pp. 100-12 (see too, idem, 'Man's Free Will in the Works
of Siger of Brabant', *Medieval Studies* 45 (1983), 155-99); S. Harwood-Gordon, *A Study
of the Theology and Imagery of Dante's 'Divina Commedia'. Sensory Perception, Reason and Free
Will* (Lewiston: The Edwin Mellen Press, 1991); A. Bufano, 'Applicazione della dottrina
del libero arbitrio nella *Commedia*', in A. Paolella et al. (eds), 2 vols, *Miscellanea di studi
danteschi in memoria di Silvio Pasquazi* (Naples: Federico & Ardia, 1993), vol. 1, pp. 193-99;
C. Fordyce, 'Il problema di amore e libero arbitrio nella *Commedia* di Dante', *Romance
Review* 4 (1994), 1, 35-51; E. G. Miller, 'Free will', in *Sense Perception in Dante's Commedia*
(Lewiston: The Edwin Mellen Press, 1996), pp. 189-230; M. Roddewig, '*Purgatorio* XVI:
Zorn und Willensfreiheit', *Deutsches Dante-Jahrbuch* 74 (1999), 123-35; E. N. Girardi, 'Al
centro del *Purgatorio*: il tema del libero arbitrio', in A. Ghisalberti (ed.), *Il pensiero filosofico e
teologico di Dante Alighieri* (Milan: V&P Università, 2001), pp. 21-38; P. Falzone, 'Psicologia
dell'atto umano in Dante', in N. Bray and L. Sturlese (eds), *Filosofia in volgare nel Medioevo.
Atti del Convegno della Società Italiana per lo Studio del Pensiero Medievale, Lecce, 27-29 settembre
2002* (Louvain-La-Neuve: Fédération Internationale des Instituts d'Études Médiévales,
2003), pp. 331-66; F. Silvestrini, 'Libero arbitrio e libertà nella *Divina Commedia*', in G.
Carletti (ed.), *Prima di Machiavelli. Itinerari e linguaggi della politica tra il XIV e il XVI secolo.
Atti del Convegno di Teramo, 29-30 aprile 2004* (Pescara: Edizioni Scientifiche Abruzzesi,
2007), pp. 73-86; M. Sità, 'Il problema del libero arbitrio nella *Divina Commedia*', in *Dante
Füzetek. A Magyar Dantisztikai Társaság Folyóirata* 2 (2007), 2, 43-51.

Ma perché l'ovra tanto è più gradita
da l'operante, quanto più appresenta
de la bontà del core ond' ell' è uscita,
    la divina bontà che 'l mondo imprenta,
di proceder per tutte le sue vie,
a rilevarvi suso, fu contenta.
    Né tra l'ultima notte e 'l primo die
sì alto o sì magnifico processo,
o per l'una o per l'altra, fu o fie:
    ché più largo fu Dio a dar sé stesso
per far l'uom sufficiente a rilevarsi,
che s'elli avesse sol da sé dimesso;
    e tutti li altri modi erano scarsi
a la giustizia, se 'l Figliuol di Dio
non fosse umilïato ad incarnarsi.

(*Par.* VII.106-20)[54]

And it is this sense of God's work in Christ as a matter of his entering
into the human situation there to quicken it afresh in respect of its power
to make a difference which determines in Dante's mind the precise
nature of his presence to man in the moment of deciding and doing, in the
depths of the ontic instant; for it is a question now, not of referring that
deciding and doing to the divine initiative as the ground and guarantee of
their efficacy, but of an 'inwilling' of the human by the divine, where by
'inwilling' we mean, not repossessing or dispossessing, but – somewhat
after the manner of the hypostatic idea itself – indwelling, abiding with,
making its home with:

Frate, la nostra volontà quïeta
virtù di carità, che fa volerne
sol quel ch'avemo, e d'altro non ci asseta.
    Se disïassimo esser più superne,
foran discordi li nostri disiri
dal voler di colui che qui ne cerne;
    che vedrai non capere in questi giri,

---

[54] But because the deed is so much the more prized by the doer, the more it displays of
the goodness of the heart whence it issued, the divine goodness, which puts its imprint on
the world, was pleased to proceed by all its ways to raise you up again; nor between the
last night and the first day has there been or will there be so exalted and so magnificent
a procedure, either by one or the other; for God was more bounteous in giving himself
to make man sufficient to uplift himself again, than if he solely of himself had remitted;
and all other modes were scanty in respect to justice, if the Son of God had not humbled
himself to become incarnate.

s'essere in carità è qui *necesse*,
e se la sua natura ben rimiri.
    Anzi è formale ad esto beato *esse*
tenersi dentro a la divina voglia,
per ch'una fansi nostre voglie stesse;
    sì che, come noi sem di soglia in soglia
per questo regno, a tutto il regno piace
com' a lo re che 'n suo voler ne 'nvoglia.
    E 'n la sua volontade è nostra pace:
ell' è quel mare al qual tutto si move
ciò ch'ella crïa o che natura face.

(Par. III.70-87)[55]

God, in other words, far from merely looking on where the exiguousness of the human situation is concerned and operating at a remove from that situation, does what God always does in these circumstances, which is to enter into it there to resolve it from within, by way of what already *is* in consequence of the primordial *let it be*. It is in this sense, then, that, for all the presence of the great bishop to him in point both of world-historical and of self-interpretation in all the dire substance of these things, Dante feels able to delight in the viability of the human project. For all the presence of the great bishop to him in both these senses, there can be no question either of confusing them or, as far as Dante is concerned, of underestimating the completeness of his rethinking of the theological issue; for taking seriously as he does the incarnational idea as the basis for any genuine expression of the Christian mind, his, inevitably, was a rethinking of Augustinian positions in the area of grace theology, a recalibration of antique emphases in favour of a fresh act of rejoicing.

4. To live with Augustine is always to live with the complexity of Augustine, with his tremendous power both to detain and to deter the spirit in one and the same instant, and this, certainly, was Dante's experience of him, his too being a resting in the congeniality of the text and a flight from its leading contentions. On the one hand, then, there was his shared commitment to

---

[55] Brother, the power of love quiets our will and makes us wish only for that which we have and gives us no other thirst. Did we desire to be more aloft, our longings would be discordant with his will who assigns us here, which you will see is not possible in these circles if to exist in charity here is of necessity, and if you well consider what is love's nature. Indeed, it is of the essence of this blessed existence to keep itself within the divine will, whereby our wills are made one; so that our being thus from threshold to threshold throughout this realm is a joy to all the realm as to the king, who inwills us with his will; and in his will is our peace. It is that sea to which all moves, both what it creates and what nature makes.

the notion of the Godhead as apt to comprehend every kind of temporal
and spatial determination,[56] of paradise as a coming home of the spirit
to the perfect peace of the One who *is* as of the essence,[57] of the universe
as no more than the sum total of its love-impulses and of love itself as a
matter of spiritual gravitation,[58] of the rational soul in man as a matter of
God's inspiration or in-breathing of the body,[59] of language as a system of
signs,[60] and of Peripateticism as a high point in the history of philosophy;[61]
while on the other there was his misgiving relative to Augustine on, for
example, Rome and the iniquity thereof and on the stench of paganism

[56] *De civ. Dei.* VII.xxx: 'Haec autem facit atque agit unus verus Deus, sed sicut Deus,
id est ubique totus, nullis inclusus locis, nullis vinculis alligatus, in nullas partes sectilis,
ex nulla parte mutabilis, implens caelum et terram praesente potentia, non indigente
natura', etc., for the 'fuor d'ogne altro comprender' moment of *Par.* XXIX.17 (cf. *Conv.*
II.iii.11: 'Questo è lo soprano edificio del mondo, nel quale tutto lo mondo s'inchiude, e
di fuori dal quale nulla è; ed esso non è in luogo ma formato fu solo ne la prima Mente, la
quale li Greci dicono Protonoè').

[57] Ibid. XIX.xvii: 'Utitur ergo etiam caelestis civitas in hac sua peregrinatione
pace terrena et de rebus ad mortalem hominum naturam pertinentibus humanarum
voluntatum compositionem, quantum salva pietate ac religione conceditur, tuetur atque
appetit eamque terrenam pacem refert ad caelestem pacem, quae vere ita pax est, ut
rationalis dumtaxat creaturae sola pax habenda atque dicenda sit, ordinatissima scilicet
et concordissima societas fruendi Deo et invicem in Deo.'

[58] The 'corpus pondere suo nititur ad locum suum' moment of the *Confessions* at XIII.
ix.10 (note 34 above).

[59] *De civ. Dei.* XIII.xxiv.4: 'In hominis autem conditione obliviscimur, quemadmodum
loqui Scriptura consueverit, cum suo prorsus more locuta sit, quo insinuaret hominem
etiam rationali anima accepta, quam non sicut aliarum carnium aquis et terra
producentibus, sed Deo flante creatam voluit intelligi ...', for the 'spira / spirito novo'
sequence of *Purg.* XXV (ll. 61-75).

[60] *De doct. christ.* I.ii.2 and vi.6: 'Nemo enim utitur verbis nisi aliquid significandi gratia.
Ex quo intellegitur quid appellem signa: res eas videlicet quae ad significandum aliquid
adhibentur ... Et tamen Deus, cum de illo nihil digne dici possit, admisit humanae vocis
obsequium, et verbis nostris in laude sua gaudere nos voluit. Nam inde est et quod
dicitur Deus', for the 'aliquod rationale signum et sensuale' and the 'consequens est quod
primus loquens primo et ante omnia dixisset "Deus"' moments of *DVE* I.iii.2 and I.iv.4
respectively.

[61] *De civ. Dei.* VIII.xii: 'cum Aristoteles Platonis discipulus, vir excellentis ingenii et
eloquio Platoni quidem impar, sed multos facile superans, cum sectam Peripateticam
condidisset, quod deambulans disputare consueverat, plurimosque discipulos praeclara
fama excellens vivo adhuc praeceptore in suam haeresim congregasset ...', for the 'e
massimamente Aristotele' moment of *Conv.* IV.vi.15-16 (with its 'che tanto vale quanto
"deambulatori"' at 15 ult.). E. Moore, *Studies in Dante* (note 25 above), p. 294, notes the
repeated sensation of familiarity in turning the pages of the text: 'I must confess, in
conclusion, that I have not been able as yet to investigate the question of Dante's probable
acquaintance with the works of St Augustine nearly as fully as the subject seems to
deserve. I am continually coming on fresh points of resemblance.'

generally. But – and this now is the point – Dante's difficulty with Augustine, conspicuous as it is at the level of itemized intentionality, of this or that discrete inflexion of the spirit, reaches all the way down into the depths, into the unitemized because unitemizable substance of what fundamentally he, vis-à-vis Augustine, actually was and is; for his, over against Augustine's, was and is a commitment, less to the dereliction of the human project in consequence of Eden and of the Eden which lives on in the recalcitrant spirit of every man, but to the grace and beauty of that project as confirmed in the moment both of its original articulation and of its fresh affirmation in Christ and Christ's work on the cross. The agony of it all – meaning by this the hopelessness everywhere engendered by man's seeing the best but clinging to the worst – is there as a dominant structure of consciousness in each alike, and this indeed is where Dante comes closest to Augustine as the great genius of the religious life in our tradition. But there is in Dante more besides; for his, amid that agony but in a manner apt ultimately to transcend it, is a sense of the human project as forever indwelt by grace, as forever refreshed by grace, and, in direct consequence of these things, as forever invited to participate at first hand in its own resurrection.

Appendix A
Some Disputed Texts in the *Commedia*

1. *Purg.* XXII.55-99: Statius and the dynamics of conversion. 2. *Par.* IV.124-32: natural desire for the beatific vision. 3. *Par.* XXIX.64-66: 'Affetto' and the meriting of grace.

In the twenty-second canto of the *Purgatorio* Dante offers the following account of Statius's conversion to the faith and, as he himself understands it, the circumstances of its coming about:

> "Or quando tu cantasti le crude armi
> de la doppia trestizia di Giocasta",
> disse 'l cantor de' buccolici carmi,
>
> "per quello che Clïò teco lì tasta,
> non par che ti facesse ancor fedele
> la fede, sanza qual ben far non basta.
>
> Se così è, qual sole o quai candele
> ti stenebraron sì, che tu drizzasti
> poscia di retro al pescator le vele?".
>
> Ed elli a lui: "Tu prima m'invïasti
> verso Parnaso a ber ne le sue grotte,
> e prima appresso Dio m'alluminasti.
>
> Facesti come quei che va di notte,
> che porta il lume dietro e sé non giova,
> ma dopo sé fa le persone dotte,
>
> quando dicesti: 'Secol si rinova;
> torna giustizia e primo tempo umano,
> e progenïe scende da ciel nova'.
>
> Per te poeta fui, per te cristiano:
> ma perché veggi mei ciò ch'io disegno,
> a colorare stenderò la mano.
>
> Già era 'l mondo tutto quanto pregno
> de la vera credenza, seminata
> per li messaggi de l'etterno regno;
>
> e la parola tua sopra toccata
> si consonava a' nuovi predicanti;

ond' io a visitarli presi usata.

Vennermi poi parendo tanto santi,
che, quando Domizian li perseguette,
sanza mio lagrimar non fur lor pianti;

e mentre che di là per me si stette,
io li sovvenni, e i lor dritti costumi
fer dispregiare a me tutte altre sette.

E pria ch'io conducessi i Greci a' fiumi
di Tebe poetando, ebb' io battesmo;
ma per paura chiuso cristian fu'mi,

lungamente mostrando paganesmo;
e questa tepidezza il quarto cerchio
cerchiar mi fé più che 'l quarto centesmo.

Tu dunque, che levato hai il coperchio
che m'ascondeva quanto bene io dico,
mentre che del salire avem soverchio,

dimmi dov' è Terrenzio nostro antico,
Cecilio e Plauto e Varro, se lo sai:
dimmi se son dannati, e in qual vico".

(*Purg.* XXII.55-99)[1]

---

[1] "Now, when you sang of the cruel strife of Jocasta's twofold sorrow", said the singer of the Bucolic songs, "it does not appear, from that which Clio touches with you there, that the faith, without which good works suffice not, had yet made you faithful. If that's so, then what sun or what candles dispelled your darkness, so that thereafter you set your sails to follow the fisherman?" And he to him: "You it was who first sent we toward Parnassus to drink in its caves, and you who first did light me on to God. You were like one who goes by night and carries the light behind him and profits not himself, but makes those wise who follow him, when you said 'the ages are renewed; justice returns and the first age of man, and new progeny descends from heaven'. Through you I was a poet, through you a Christian; but that you may see better what I outline, I will set my hand to colour it. Already the whole world was big with the true faith, sown by the messengers of the eternal realm, and those words of yours I have just spoken were so in accord with the new preachers that I began to frequent them. They came then to seem to me so holy that when Domitian persecuted them, their wailing was not without my tears, and while I remained yonder I succoured them and their righteous lives made me scorn all other sects. And before I had led the Greeks to the rivers of Thebes in my verse, I received baptism; but, for fear, I was a secret Christian, long making show of paganism, and this lukewarmness made me circle round the fourth circle for more than four centuries. You, therefore, that did lift for me the covering that was hiding from me the great good I tell of, while we still have time to spare on the ascent, tell me, where is our ancient Terence, and Caecilius and Plautus and Varius, if you know; tell me if they are damned, and in which ward." On Dante's Statius, in addition to editions, commentaries and encyclopaedias generally, H. D. Baumble, 'Dante's Statius', *Cithara* 15 (1975), 1, 59-67; A. Pézard, 'Rencontres de Dante et de Stace', in *Dans le sillage de Dante* (Paris: Société d'Études Italiennes,1975), pp. 115-33; G. Padoan, 'Teseo "figura redemptoris" e il cristianesimo di Stazio', in *Il pio Enea, l'empio Ulisse* (Ravenna: Longo, 1977), pp. 125-150; P. Baldan, 'Stazio e le possibili

Now from the point of view of the relationship in human experience between the human and the divine initiative the passage needs careful handling, for neither the words 'qual sole' in Virgil's question regarding the origin of Statius's conversion (line 61), nor the words 'appresso Dio' in the latter's reply (line 66) should necessarily be understood to refer to a direct intervention of God designed to bring about that conversion. Neither, in other words, necessarily commits Dante to a sense of God's having had a hand personally in Statius's change of heart. In one sense, to be sure, he most definitely did, for there can be no prescinding within the economy of the whole from the idea of grace as the remote cause of all significant being and becoming in human experience. But, for all that, neither of these expressions should be invoked as evidence of a regular theology of prevenience, certainly, at any rate, if by this we mean prevenience at the expense of the cultural encounter as possessed of the power to spiritual renewal. To take first, then, the 'sole' moment of line 61, the notion that this must refer to God, and thus to God as the immediate cause in respect of each and every creative inflexion of the spirit, rests on the fact that 'sole' is one of Dante's leading metaphors for God both in and beyond the *Commedia*; so, for example, as far as the *Commedia* itself is concerned, the 'Non per far, ma per non fare ho perduto / a veder l'alto Sol che tu desiri'

"vere ragion che son nascose" della sua conversione. *Purg* XXII, 40-41', *Lettere Italiane* 38 (1986), 2, 149-165 (subsequently in *Ritorni su Dante* (Bergamo: Moretti e Vitali, 1991), pp. 105-20); G. Brugnoli, 'Statius christianus', *Italianistica* 17 (1988), 1, 9-15; M. Camilucci, *Stazio fra Dante e Virgilio* (Borgo alla Collina: Accademia Casentinese di Lettere, Arti, Scienze ed Economia, 1990); J. Küppers, 'Dante and Statius', *Deutsches Dante-Jahrbuch* 65 (1990), 77-106; R. Scrivano, 'Stazio personaggio, poeta e cristiano', *Quaderni d'Italianistica* 13 (1992), 2, 175-97 (subsequently, with the title 'Stazio compagno di viaggio; *Purg*. XXI, XXII, XXV', in idem, *Dante, Commedia. Le forme dell'oltretomba* (Rome: Nuova Cultura, 1997), pp. 65-103; W. Franke, 'Resurrected Tradition and Revealed Truth: Dante's Statius', *Quaderni di Italianistica* 15 (1994), 1-2, 7-34 (subsequently in *Dante's Interpretive Journey* (Chicago: The University of Chicago Press, 1996), pp. 191-232); R. L. Martinez, 'Dante and the Two Canons: Statius in Virgil's Footsteps (*Purgatorio* 21-30)', *Comparative Literature Studies* 32 (1995), 2, 151-75; idem, 'Lament and Lamentations in *Purgatorio* and the Case of Dante's Statius', *Dante Studies* 115 (1997), 45-88; A. Boccia, 'Appunti sulla presenza di Stazio nella *Divina Commedia*', *Annali dell'Istituto Italiano per gli Studi Storici* 18 (2001), 29-45; M. T. Lanza, 'A proposito di Dante e Stazio', *Esperienze Letterarie* 26 (2001), 3, 3-11; V. De Angelis, 'Lo Stazio di Dante; poesia e scuola', *Schede umanistiche* 16 (2002), 2, 29-69; C. Kallendorf and H. Kallendorf, '"Per te poeta fui, per te cristiano" (*Purg*. 22.73): Statius as Christian, from "Fact" to Fiction', *Deutsches Dante-Jahrbuch* 77 (2002), 61-72; A. Lanza, 'L'enigma Stazio (Canti XXI-XXII del *Purgatorio*)', in *Dante eterodosso. Una diversa lettura della 'Commedia'* (Bergamo: Moretti Honegger, 2004), pp. 153-69; E. Pasquini, 'Dante e il crocevia di Stazio', in F. Tateo and D. M. Pergorari (eds), *Contesti della 'Commedia'. Lectura Dantis Fridericiana 2002-2003* (Bari: Palomar, 2004), pp. 123-130; A. Teresa Hankey, 'Dante and Statius', in J. C. Barnes and J. Petrie (eds), *Dante and His Literary Precursors. Twelve Essays* (Dublin: Four Courts Press, 2007), pp. 37-50.

of *Purg.* VII.25-26, placed by Dante on the lips of Virgil;[2] the 'rivolta s'era al Sol che la rïempie' of *Par.* IX.8;[3] the 'Ringrazia, / ringrazia il Sol de li angeli' of *Par.* X.52-53;[4] the 'però che 'l sol che v'allumò e arse, / col caldo e con la luce' of *Par.* XV.76-77;[5] and the 'sì come 'l sol che l'accende sortille' of *Par.* XVIII.105,[6] while as far as the *Convivio* is concerned the following passage at III.xii.7-8:

> Nullo sensibile in tutto lo mondo è più degno di farsi essemplo di Dio che 'l sole. Lo quale di sensibile luce sé prima e poi tutte le corpora celestiali e le elementali allumina: così Dio prima sé con luce intellettuale allumina, e poi le [creature] celestiali e l'altre intelligibili. Lo sole tutte le cose col suo calore vivifica ... così Iddio tutte le cose vivifica in bontade ...[7]

Both in and beyond the *Commedia*, then, the sun is used to denote both the Godhead itself and the regenerative character of the Godhead, the light and life which he is in himself and which, in and through the outpouring of self in love, he imparts to others. But for all the power of the image in denoting the substance and operation of the Godhead, its interpretation in this sense in the *Purgatorio* passage is neither warranted nor necessary; for not only is the image a versatile one in the *Commedia*, having about it a number of different referents, but it straightaway commends itself, as far as *Purgatorio* XXII is concerned, as a means of seeing and celebrating, not so much God, as Virgil as the agent of Statius's conversion, this, therefore, rather than anything more exalted, furnishing its inner meaning. On the one hand, then, there is its polysemy or predication by turns of the pope

---

[2] Not for doing, but for not doing, have I lost sight of the high sun [that you desire and that was known by me too late].

[3] [And now that life of the holy light] had turned again to the sun which fills it, [as to the good which is sufficient to all things].

[4] Give thanks, give thanks to the sun of the angels [who of his grace has raised you to this visible one].

[5] because the sun which illumined you and warmed you [is of such equality in its heat and light that all comparisons fall short].

[6] [so thence there seemed to arise more than a thousand lights, and mount, some much, some little,] even as the sun which kindles them allotted them.

[7] No sense object in the entire universe is more worthy of acting as a symbol of God than the sun. It illuminates with sensible light first itself, then all the heavenly bodies and the bodies formed from the elements. God likewise illuminates with intellectual light first himself, then the heavenly creatures and the other intelligible creatures. The sun gives life to all things with its heat ... God likewise gives life to all things by his goodness ... (on the 'Non vede il sol, che tutto 'l mondo gira, / cosa tanto gentil' moment of the canzone *Amor che ne la mente mi ragiona* at ll. 19-20).

and the emperor (the 'Soleva Roma, che 'l buon mondo feo, / due soli aver' of *Purg.* XVI.106-107),[8] of Beatrice (the 'Quel sol che pria d'amor mi scaldò 'l petto' of *Par.*III. 1 and the 'così mi disse il sol de li occhi miei' of *Par.* XXX.75),[9] of the sage spirits collectively in the heaven of the sun (the 'Poi, sì cantando, quelli ardenti soli / si fuor girati intorno a noi tre volte' of *Par.* X.76-77),[10] of Francis (the 'nacque al mondo un sole' of *Par.* XI.50),[11] of Mary (the 'di colui ch'abbelliva di Maria / come del sole stella mattutina' of *Par.* XXXII.107-108),[12] and, again, of Virgil himself (the 'O sol che sani ogne vista turbata' of *Inf.* XI.91);[13] while on the other hand, there is the plain sense of the text, its referring, not to God, but to Virgil as the agent of enlightenment and renewal (the 'Facesti come quei che va di notte, / che porta il lume dietro e sé non giova, / ma dopo sé fa le persone dotte, / quando dicesti: "Secol si rinova; / torna giustizia e primo tempo umano, / e progenïe scende da ciel nova"' of lines 67-72 and the 'Tu dunque, che levato hai il coperchio / che m'ascondeva quanto bene io dico ...' of lines 94-96),[14] all of which suggests a commitment on Dante's part to the encounter itself – the dealings of one historical figure with another – as the means of Statius's emergence as a Christian spirit.

Turning now to the 'appresso Dio' component of the text (line 66), this, normally, is taken to mean 'after' in one or other of two senses: either in the sense of 'secondarily to God', in which case Statius is saying that next to God, and not far behind him, came Virgil as his leading inspiration in the area of religious understanding;[15] or else in the sense of 'following', in

---

[8] Rome, which made the world good, was wont to have two suns ...

[9] That sun which first had heated my breast with love ... so spoke the sun of my eyes to me ...

[10] When, so singing, those blazing suns had circled three times round about us ...

[11] a sun rose on the world ...

[12] [Thus did I again recur to the teaching of him] who drew beauty from Maria, as the morning star from the sun.

[13] O sun that heals every troubled vision ...

[14] You were like the one who goes by night and carries the light behind him and profits not himself, but makes those wise who follow him when you said, "the ages are renewed; justice returns and the first age of man, and a new progeny descends from heaven" ... You, therefore, that did lift for me the covering that was hiding me from the great good I tell of ...

[15] Pietrobono (Turin: Società editrice internazionale, 1982) ad loc.: '*prima*, tu primieramente, *appresso Dio*, dopo Dio, m'illuminasti'; Bosco and Reggio: 'Bisogna dunque ripiegare, per ragioni di lessico e di dottrina cristiana, su questa interpretazione: e tu per primo, dopo Dio, mi illuminasti. "Dopo Dio (*sole*) Stazio riconosce in Virgilio chi primo fra gli uomini lo illuminò (*candele*) rispetto alla fede" (Scartazzini-Vandelli)', etc. See, however, Chimenz (Turin: UTET, 1962) ad loc.: 'Appresso a Dio: presso, verso Dio, sulla strada che mi doveva portare a Dio: l'espressione è parallela a verso Parnaso.

the more recognizably biblical sense of Statius's taking up his cross and following Christ in consequence of all that Virgil had meant to him.[16] Both of these interpretations, especially the former, have something to commend them, particularly in so far as the term 'appresso' often has about it in Dante the sense of coming next, of following on closely.[17] There

Questo parallelismo sopprimono quei commentatori antichi e moderni che interpretano: "tu, dopo (*appresso*) Dio, m'illuminasti": interpretazione improbabile, anche perché tale concetto sarebbe meno aderente allo spirito dell'episodio, che vuol essere tutto un'esaltazione dei meriti di Virgilio, e inoltre, perché, se si ammette che la prima luce alla fede fosse venuta a Stazio da Dio, non avrebbe senso una successiva illuminazione umana. Del resto, nel racconto della sua conversione al cristianesimo Stazio non fa il minimo accenno a un'illuminazione divina, mentre diffusamente spiega le ragioni umane che alla conversione lo indussero; e sarebbe veramente strano che mentre professa ripetutamente la sua gratitudine a Virgilio, non avesse una parola di ringraziamento a Dio, se in questo momento pensasse a Dio come causa prima della sua conversione.' Among the ancients, the Ottimo Commento, ad loc., has: 'Tu, Vergilio, prima m'invitasti verso Parnasso, cioè verso la perfezione della poesia: e prima, dopo Idio, ch'è prima causa di tutte le cause, ed il quale è padre de' lumi, dal quale discende ogni dono perfetto, e ogni dono ottimo, mi illuminasti del lume della vera fede, del quale tu non eri illuminato.'

[16] Porena (Bologna: Zanichelli, 1946) ad loc.: '"Tu fosti primo ad avviarmi verso la poesia (simboleggiata dalle acque della fonte Castalia scaturente dalle grotte, cioè rocce, del monte Parnaso); e tu fosti primo a illuminarmi la strada che doveva farmi seguace di Dio". Altri spiega appresso a Dio come un inciso: "fosti primo, dopo Dio, a illuminarmi". Ma ne vien turbata la simmetria delle espressioni: "m'inviasti verso Parnaso", "m'illuminasti sulla via di Dio". E poi il primo incentivo venne da Virgilio, non da Dio'; Sapegno (Florence: La Nuova Italia, 1968) ad loc.: 'e *appresso Dio*, "a farmi seguace di Dio". Altri spiega invece: "dopo Dio, causa prima d'ogni bene, tu m'iniziasti alla fede"; ma questa precisazione e limitazione avrebbe uno strano sapore dottrinario, e riuscirebbe solo a rompere e a raffreddare l'eloquente rassegna che qui Stazio fa dei suoi debiti verso il maestro. A Virgilio solo egli riconosce ogni merito del suo progresso spirituale: l'iniziazione alla poesia, la liberazione dal vizio della prodigalità, il primo avvío alla vera fede. E si capisce che, in ultima analisi, a ciascuno di questi tre acquisti, e specialmente all'ultimo, ha presieduto un intervento piú o meno diretto della Grazia; ma la situazione qui esige che prenda risalto piuttosto la causa mediante, che non la causa prima'; Chiavacci Leonardi (Milan: Mondadori, 1991-97) ad loc.: '*e prima appresso Dio*: e ugualmente per primo mi illuminasti a seguire il vero Dio ... Virgilio è stato la luce (la *candela* del v. 61, il *lume* del v. 68) per cui Stazio ha trovato la via della fede. Tutto il contesto – che fa centro su Virgilio – porta così chiaramente a questa spiegazione del verso, da far inaccettabile l'altra proposta: "tu primo mi illuminasti, dopo Dio, causa prima di ogni bene", già avanzata dal Buti e ripresa da più di un moderno', etc.

[17] So, for example, the 'Come d'autunno si levan le foglie / l'una appresso de l'altra, fin che 'l ramo / vede a la terra tutte le sue spoglie ...' of *Inf*. III.112-14, or the 'Poi appresso convien che questa caggia / infra tre soli ...' of VI.67-68, or the 'tutti li altri che venieno appresso, / non sappiendo 'l perché, fenno altrettanto' of *Purg*. III.92-93, or the 'lo duca mio, e io appresso ...' of IV. 23, or the 'Ond' ella, appresso d'un pïo sospiro, / li occhi drizzò ver' me con quel sembiante / che madre fa sovra figlio delíro' of *Par*. I.100-102, or the 'Ond' io appresso: "O perpetüi fiori / de l'etterna letizia ..."' of XIX.22-23. Note, however, as closer to 'in respect of' or 'concerning' the '"Non ti maravigliar perch' io

are, however, grounds for misgiving, to the fore among them being once again the centrality of Virgil, rather than of God, to everything Statius has to say in this passage, a consideration suggesting something closer to 'in respect of' or 'as regards', or simply 'concerning', as Dante's meaning here. Pre-eminent, in other words, in matters of art, he was pre-eminent, too, in matters of religion, an interpretation confirmed by the unusual insistence of the line (the 'Tu *prima* m'invïasti / verso Parnaso ... / e *prima* appresso Dio m'alluminasti' of lines 64-66).[18] True, Statius, as a Christian convert, is anxious to register the specifically Christian component in all this, the heroism of the early Christian martyrs and its value as testimony to the faith; but none of this, as far as Dante is concerned, suggests a preoccupation with the dialectics of grace as the condition of new life. On the contrary, if there is a dialectic here, it is the dialectic of eventuality, of the cultural encounter as salvifically significant.

2. In the main body of our argument we insisted on Dante's sense of human nature as naturally desirous of God, and this on the basis of what the *Purgatorio* has to say relative to the connatural yearning of the spirit for the peace of perfect intellection (the 'Ciascun confusamente un bene apprende / nel qual si queti l'animo' passage of XVII.127-29)[19] and of what the *Paradiso* has to say concerning man's 'concreate thirst' for God and God's prior enamouring of the soul in this respect (the 'concreata e perpetüa sete' moment of *Par.* II.19-21 and the 'e la innamora / di sé' moment of *Par.* VII.142-44).[20] Notable too, however, as pointing in this

sorrida", / mi disse, "appresso il tuo püeril coto, / poi sopra 'l vero ancor lo piè non fida ..." of *Par.* III.25-27.

[18] You it was who first sent me towards Parnassus ... and you who first did light me on to God.

[19] Each one apprehends vaguely a good wherein the mind may find rest [and this it desires; wherefore each one strives to attain thereto].

[20] The concreate and perpetual thirst [for the deiform realm bore us away, swift almost as you see the heavens] ... [but your life the supreme beneficence breathes forth without intermediary,] and so enamours it of itself [that it desires it ever after]. For the *Convivio* – and irrespective of its concern at one point (III.xv.7-10, and again at IV.xiii.7-8) to delimit the extent of specifically human desiring – IV. xii. 14: 'E la ragione è questa: che lo sommo desiderio di ciascuna cosa, e prima da la natura dato, è lo ritornare a lo suo principio. E però che Dio è principio de le nostre anime e fattore di quelle simili a sé (sì come è scritto: "Facciamo l'uomo ad imagine e similitudine nostra"), essa anima massimamente desidera di tornare a quello.' Kenelm Foster, in his essay on 'Dante's Vision of God', in *The Two Dantes* (London: Darton, Longman and Todd, 1977), p. 82, has 'These ideas – if not explicitly in these terms – I find everywhere in Dante; and particularly in his thought about the relations between God and creatures. "The chief desire of anything", he says, "and the first given it by nature, is to return to its originating principle." Here is the assimilation of effect as such to cause as such. And

direction are these lines (124-32) from *Paradiso* IV, lines following on
from Beatrice's clarification in this same canto (*a*) of what it might mean
to speak of the soul's return to the stars at the point of death, and (*b*) of the
difference between conditional and unconditional consent on the plane of
properly human willing. Dante the character, however, is still perplexed,
or, rather, caught up, he says, in a new conundrum:

> Io veggio ben che già mai non si sazia
> nostro intelletto, se 'l ver non lo illustra
> di fuor dal qual nessun vero si spazia.
> Posasi in esso, come fera in lustra,
> tosto che giunto l'ha; e giugner puollo:
> se non, ciascun disio sarebbe *frustra*.
> Nasce per quello, a guisa di rampollo,
> a piè del vero il dubbio; ed è natura
> ch'al sommo pinge noi di collo in collo.[21]

Now a preliminary reading of these lines would suggest that what
Dante has in mind here is the beatific vision as the point of arrival in
respect of man's quest on the plane of understanding, of his coming home
by way of an intermediate to an ultimate act of intellection, and that,
chiming as it does with the passages noted above, would be a reasonable
way of looking at it. The problem, however, is that he does not say as
much. He implies it perhaps, but does not actually say it, his words
stricto sensu denoting nothing more than man's ordinary progression
from one epistemic instance to another. Dante, apparently alert to the
uncertainty he has generated at this point, seeks straightaway – on the
threshold of the next canto – to resolve it; proceeding as we do from
height to height on the plane of knowing, we shall at last, he says, come
into the eternal light as the beginning of all our loving and the end of
all our desiring:

where the causing is unmediated, the consequent trend to assimilation will be at its
strongest. Hence the rational soul of man, "breathed out" by God immediately ("sanza
mezzo"), not only resembles God *ab origine* more than anything in the physical world
(which comes into being through secondary causes) but it also must tend, of its nature,
to a certain direct and immediate assimilation to the divine nature; and this through its
proper and innate capacity for knowledge. Its nature tends to a God-assimilation by
direct knowledge of God; the immediacy of its origination from God being the measure
of the force of its essential impulse to return to him'.

[21] Well do I see that never can our intellect be wholly satisfied unless that truth shine on
it, beyond which no truth has range. Therein it rests, as a wild beast in his lair, so soon as
it has reached it; and reach it it can, else every desire would be in vain. Because of this,
questioning springs up like a shoot, at the foot of the truth; and this is nature which urges
us to the summit, from height to height.

> Io veggio ben sì come già resplende
> ne l'intelletto tuo l'etterna luce,
> che, vista, sola e sempre amore accende;
> e s'altra cosa vostro amor seduce,
> non è se non di quella alcun vestigio,
> mal conosciuto, che quivi traluce.

(Par.V. 7-12)[22]

Straightaway, then, perspectives are defined, ultimacy rather than proximity constituting the object of Dante's concern in this passage. Each successive movement of the mind as knowing, he suggests, is indeed a triumph, but a triumph only in so far as it anticipates something still greater than itself, an act of understanding apt at last to surpass all understanding.

3. In the *Paradiso* at XXIX.64-66 Dante has this to say on the merit accruing to the angels by way of an authentic or rightly-directed movement of love, a matter he says, not of opinion or hypothesis, but of certainty:

> e non voglio che dubbi, ma sia certo,
> che ricever la grazia è meritorio
> secondo che l'affetto l'è aperto.[23]

Commentators in search of authorization for this startling assertion are inclined to invoke Bonaventure in the *Breviloquium* at II.vii.2,[24] where

---

[22] Well do I note how in your intellect already is shining the eternal light which, seen, alone and always kindles love; and if aught else seduce your love, it is naught save some vestige of that light, ill-recognized, which therein shines through.

[23] and I would not have you doubt, but be assured that to receive grace is meritorious, in proportion as the affection is open to it.

[24] Bosco and Reggio (in their preface to *Paradiso* XXIX (Florence: Le Monnier, 1979), p. 474): 'Anche sul peccato le opinioni degli stessi maestri di Dante divergevano tra loro: incerti se gli angeli ricevettero la grazia santificante nel momento della loro creazione o in un secondo tempo: se la ebbero subito, pareva ad alcuni inammissibile che essi potessero peccare. Tommaso elimina con sottile ragionamento questa difficoltà, ma Dante non lo segue: inclina verso l'opinione bonaventuriana (Mellone) secondo la quale la grazia fu conferita solo agli angeli rimasti fedeli, che così avevano dimostrato il loro amore a Dio, e perciò la meritarono (64-66). Questione anch'essa tanto controversa che Beatrice rafforza la sua tesi con un'asserzione finale perentoria: "non voglio che dubbi, ma sia certo ...".' Thomas, in the *Pars prima* (Ia.62.3, resp.), notes that various positions have been taken up here, the better opinion, however, being that the angels were created in a state of sanctifying grace, and that, on this basis, they merited beatitude (ibid. 4). Dante's understanding, however, is that the merit accruing to the good angels by way of their humility and obedience merited a further measure of grace, a position he goes on to reinforce in the 'e non voglio che dubbi' tercet beginning at XXIX. 64. Typically, then,

we discover that man, though a mere creature and thus wanting both intellectually and morally, may even so, in the degree to which he is disposed towards him in love, approach God as the highest good, love, therefore, having about it the aspect of deserving:

> Ratio autem ad intelligentiam praedictorum haec est: quia, cum primum principium sit summe bonum, nihil facit, quod non sit bonum; quia a bono non procedit nisi bonum; quod tamen fit ab ipso hoc ipso minus est eo, et ideo non potest esse summum bonum. Fuit igitur Angelus a Deo conditus bonus quidem, sed non summus, perficiendum tamen, si affectu tenderet in summum.[25]

Given for the sake of the argument that Dante knew this passage, he would have approved of it, for love, as the ordinary inclination of whatever *is* in the world in keeping with its own inner rationale, is everywhere apt, he thinks, to commend the lover in the sight of God. But there is a problem here, for although the 'perficiendum tamen' clause in the passage just cited does indeed appear to suggest the contingency of grace upon merit (i.e. that in the degree to which the soul loves well it will be lifted to its proper perfection), this is not what Bonaventure meant, his being a sense of merit as flowing from grace rather than the other way round. Taking first, then, the case of the angels as he himself sees it, we read just prior to the passage quoted a moment ago these words:

> De apostasia daemonum hoc tenendum est, quod Deus angelos fecit bonos, medios tamen inter se, summum bonum, et commutabile bonum, quod est creatura; ita quod, si converterentur ad amandum quod est supra, ascenderent ad statum gratiae et gloriae; si vero ad bonum commutabile, quod est infra, hoc ipso ruerent in malum culpae et poenae.
>
> (*Brevil.* II.vii.1)[26]

---

though without prejudice to the grace dimension of the Thomist solution, the specifically moral component of the argument moves into the ascendant.

[25] The reason for these things and the way they are to be understood, therefore, are as follows: since the first principle is the highest good, it makes nothing other than what is good, for from goodness proceeds nothing but the good; but what it makes must be less than itself, and cannot therefore, on its own account, be the highest good. The angels, therefore, were made good, but not the highest good, though perfection might be theirs, however, if they inclined towards it in love.

[26] As far as the apostasy of the devils is concerned we must hold fast to the following, that God created the angels as good, as a good, however, ranged between himself as the supreme good and the creature as a changeable good; so that, should they turn to loving what is above them, they would rise to a state of grace and glory, whereas should they

Now the key term here is 'convertere' ('si converterentur ad amandum quod est supra'), a term which, though denoting a *turning towards* or *redirection* of the spirit, invariably has about it in Bonaventure the sense of a turning of the spirit *in grace*, as facilitated by grace; so, for example, from his commentary on the *Sentences*, and indeed from a passage having to do, precisely, with angels and with the 'turning' thereof, this passage from II, dist. 4, art. 1, qu. 2: 'sicut enim facile fuit diabolo averti, ita facile bonis Angelis converti; et sicut aversio fuit demeritoria, ita conversio facta est meritoria, statim apposita gratia'[27] – a passage in which the merit of turning is brought into the closest possible association with grace as its necessary condition. Free will, certainly, has a part to play in this, Bonaventure going so far as to speak of the process of conversion as initiated in free will, grace, therefore, entering into it by way, less of operation, than of co-operation:

> Rursus, quia per illam conversionem obtinuerunt gratiam, oportet ponere quod conversionem illam inchoaverit voluntas libera, sed consummaverit gratia; et ideo fuit ibi gratia *subsequens*, non *praeveniens*; gratia *cooperans*, non *operans*, ut dicit Magister in littera. Concedendum est ergo, quod illa Angelorum conversio, in qua confirmati sunt, non fuit sine gratiae auxilio.
>
> (ibid. II, dist. 5, art. 3, qu. 1)[28]

This, given again that Dante *did* know this passage, would have been music to his ears, his, soteriologically, being a sympathetic glance in the direction of the Franciscans, a sense of what man does for God having implications for what God does for man.[29] All the same, Dante's, if it *is* a

turn to the changeable good which is below them, by this very fact they would tumble into guilt and pain.

[27] just as it was easy for the devil to be *a*verted, so it was easy for the angels to be *con*verted; and just as aversion is unmeritorious, conversion, grace once being granted, is meritorious.

[28] Again, because through that conversion they obtained grace, it is necessary to maintain that free will initiated that conversion, but that grace consummated it; and that for this reason it was a question of subsequent rather than of prevenient grace, of co-operating rather than of operating grace, as the Master says in the text. It must be conceded, therefore, that the conversion of the angels, in which they were confirmed, was not without the help of grace.

[29] A. E. McGrath, *Iustitia Dei. A History of the Christian Doctrine of Justification (The Beginnings to the Reformation)* (Cambridge: Cambridge University Press, 1986), p. 111: 'The pastoral intention of the concept cannot be overlooked. Although man has no claim to justification on the basis of divine justice, he may look towards the divine generosity and kindliness for some recognition of his attempts to amend his life in accordance with the demands of the gospel. It may be pointed out that the concept of a disposition

glance in the direction of Franciscan soteriology, is a fashioning from it something rather more than Bonaventure would have allowed, namely a privileging of the volitional and conative aspect of the matter at the expense of the grace aspect, a position merely confirmed by the peremptoriness of it all (the 'e non voglio che dubbi, ma sia certo' of line 64).

towards justification which is meritorious *de congruo* is particularly associated with the Franciscan Order and the school of theology which came to be associated with it. The pastoral emphasis upon God's kindness towards sinful mankind finds its appropriate expression in the concept of congruous merit.' On the grace theology of Bonaventure and of high scholasticism generally, G. Bozitković O.F.M., *S. Bonaventurae doctrina de gratia et libero arbitrio* (Marienbad: Egerland, 1919); J. Auer, *Die Entwicklung der Gnadenlehre in der Hochscholastik*, 2 vols (Freiburg: Herder, 1951); B. Marthaler, *Original Justice and Sanctifying Grace in the Writings of Saint Bonaventure* (Rome: Miscellanea francescana, 1965). More generally on Bonaventure, E. Gilson, *The Philosophy of Bonaventure*, trans. I. Trethowan and F. J. Sheed (London: Sheed and Ward, 1940; see also, idem, 'La Conclusion de la *Divine Comédie* et la mystique franciscaine' in the *Revue d'histoire franciscaine* 1 (1924), 55-63); J. -G. Bougerol, *Introduction to the Works of Bonaventure*, trans. J. de Vinck (Paterson, N.J.: St Anthony Guild Press, 1964); S. Vanni Rovighi, *San Bonaventura* (Milan: Vita e Pensiero, 1974). On Dante and Bonaventure, and in addition to the *Enciclopedia dantesca* ad loc. (Rome: Istituto dell'Enciclopedia Italiana, 1970-78, vol. 1, pp. 669-73; S. Vanni Rovighi), L. Cicchitto, *Postille bonaventuriane-dantesche* (Rome: Miscellanea francescana, 1940); E. H. Cousins, 'Bonaventure and Dante: The Role of Christ in the Spiritual Journey', in L. J. Bowman (ed.), *Itinerarium, the Idea of Journey: a Collection of Papers given at the Fifteenth International Congress on Medieval Studies, Kalamazoo, Michigan, May 1980* (Salzburg: Institut für Anglistik und Amerikanistik, University of Salzburg, 1983), pp. 113-31; P. Di Vona, 'Dante filosofo e San Bonaventura', *Miscellanea francescana* 84 (1984), 1-2, pp. 3-19; F. Adorno, 'Dante (1265-1321), tra San Tommaso (1225/26-1274) e San Bonaventura (1221-1274)', in *Letture classensi* 32-34 (2005), pp. 13-22; P. Fedrigotti, 'Presenze tomiste e bonaventuriane nella concezione dantesca della beatitudine', in *Studi Danteschi* 72 (2007), 141-213 (with a revised version in *Esprimere l'inesprimibile. La concezione dantesca della beatitudine* (Bologna: Edizioni Studio Domenicano, 2009), pp. 23-60, 87-125 and 187-213).

Appendix B
Cruces in Aquinas

1. Divine intervention in the process of deliberation. 2. The fundamental option – but whose option?

Much of our discussion in these pages has turned on – as Aquinas sees it – the indispensability of grace to any kind of moral activity in man, to any kind of activity, that is to say, bearing on his ultimate well-being and thus on his ultimate happiness as man. Not only then, for Thomas, is man unable for long to avoid falling into sin without the aid of grace, but he requires also of God a preliminary orientation of the spirit if in any salvifically significant sense he is to make good as a creature of moral determination. More exactly, not only does he need grace for the purposes of doing good, but he needs it for the purposes of willing the good, his dependence on divine intentionality in the area of moral activity thus being total. And this, if only for the sake of strengthening a key aspect of our argument so far, is the point we need now to linger over; for there is an irony here, the irony implicit in a theology of grace so 'high' that, by way of diminishing the substance and scope of the moral life into which grace enters as a principle of renewal, both grace (as love) and nature (as beloved) are diminished to the point of disappearing, at which stage love itself as the deep ground of each alike slips out of sight.

As far, then, as Thomas is concerned, the argument gets under way in the *Prima secundae* at 109.2, the question here being whether or not man can do good without grace. The 'objection' or antithesis is in no doubt: man, being a creature of reasonable moral determination, needs no special gracing for the purposes either of doing well or of wishing to do well. In both respects he is perfectly able to manage by himself:

> Videtur quod homo possit velle et facere bonum absque gratia. Illud enim est in hominis potestate cuius ipse est dominus. Sed homo est dominus suorum actuum, et maxime eius quod est velle, ut supra

dictum est. Ergo homo potest velle et facere bonum per seipsum absque auxilio gratiae.

(*ST* Ia IIae.109.2 obj. 1)[1]

Predictably, however, this will not do, for deliberation, both in its cognitive and volitional aspect, is a process, and processes need to be started up, something that is dependent, not on man, but on God. Lest, then, we be obliged to settle for infinite regression, we must suppose that God is the principle of significant willing in man, that whereby he is moved to act in the first place:

Ad primum ergo dicendum quod homo est dominus suorum actuum, et volendi et non volendi, propter deliberationem rationis, quae potest flecti ad unam partem vel ad aliam. Sed quod deliberet vel non deliberet, si huius etiam sit dominus, oportet quod hoc sit per deliberationem praecedentem. Et cum hoc non procedat in infinitum, oportet quod finaliter deveniatur ad hoc quod liberum arbitrium hominis moveatur ab aliquo exteriori principio quod est supra mentem humanam, scilicet a Deo; ut etiam philosophus probat in cap. de bona fortuna. Unde mens hominis etiam sani non ita habet dominium sui actus quin indigeat moveri a Deo. Et multo magis liberum arbitrium hominis infirmi post peccatum, quod impeditur a bono per corruptionem naturae.

(ibid. ad 1)[2]

In fact, the referral of the deliberative moment of human activity to God as the remote cause of every significant movement of the spirit in man – in truth but an elementary feature of theological consciousness – is everywhere there in Aquinas. It is there on the threshold of the *Prima secundae*, where somewhat paradoxically the control text is the *Eudemian Ethics*:

---

[1] It would seem that man can wish and do good without grace. For that is in man's power, whereof he is master. Now man is master of his acts, and especially of his willing, as stated above. Hence man, of himself, can wish and do good without the help of grace.

[2] In reply to the first objection, then, man is master of his acts and of his willing or not willing, because of his deliberate reason, which can be bent to one side or another. And although he is master of his deliberating or not deliberating, yet this can only be by a previous deliberation; and since it cannot go on to infinity, we must come at length to this, that man's free will is moved by an extrinsic principle, which is above the human mind, to wit by God, as the Philosopher proves in the chapter on good fortune [*Ethic. Eudem.* viii]. Hence the mind of man still unweakened is not so much master of its act that it does not need to be moved by God; and much more the free will of man weakened by sin, whereby it is hindered from good by the corruption of nature.

secundum quod voluntas movetur ab obiecto, manifestum est
quod moveri potest ab aliquo exteriori. Sed eo modo quo movetur
quantum ad exercitium actus, adhuc necesse est ponere voluntatem
ab aliquo principio exteriori moveri. Omne enim quod quandoque
est agens in actu et quandoque in potentia, indiget moveri ab aliquo
movente. Manifestum est autem quod voluntas incipit velle aliquid,
cum hoc prius non vellet. Necesse est ergo quod ab aliquo moveatur
ad volendum. Et quidem, sicut dictum est, ipsa movet seipsam,
inquantum per hoc quod vult finem, reducit seipsam ad volendum
ea quae sunt ad finem. Hoc autem non potest facere nisi consilio
mediante, cum enim aliquis vult sanari, incipit cogitare quomodo hoc
consequi possit, et per talem cogitationem pervenit ad hoc quod potest
sanari per medicum, et hoc vult. Sed quia non semper sanitatem
actu voluit, necesse est quod inciperet velle sanari, aliquo movente.
Et si quidem ipsa moveret seipsam ad volendum, oportuisset quod
mediante consilio hoc ageret, ex aliqua voluntate praesupposita. Hoc
autem non est procedere in infinitum. Unde necesse est ponere quod
in primum motum voluntatis voluntas prodeat ex instinctu alicuius
exterioris moventis, ut Aristoteles concludit in quodam capitulo
Ethicae Eudemicae.

(*ST* Ia IIae.9.4 resp.)[3]

and it is there in the *De malo*, where Thomas is careful, however, to stress
the indeterminate nature of God's movement of the will. God, in other
words, does not move the will to this or that particular course of action,
but just moves the will, disposing it to any number of precise possibilities:

Relinquitur ergo, sicut concludit Aristoteles in cap. de bona fortuna,
quod id quod primo movet voluntatem et intellectum, sit aliquid

[3] as far as the will is moved by the object, it is evident that it can be moved by something
exterior. But in so far as it is moved in the exercise of its act, we must again hold it to be
moved by some exterior principle. For everything that is at one time an agent actually,
and at another time an agent in potentiality, needs to be moved by a mover. Now it
is evident that the will begins to will something, whereas previously it did not will it.
Therefore it must, of necessity, be moved by something to will it. And, indeed, it moves
itself, as stated above [art. 3], in so far as through willing the end it reduces itself to the
act of willing the means. Now it cannot do this without the aid of counsel: for when a
man wills to be healed, he begins to reflect how this can be attained, and through this
reflection he comes to the conclusion that he can be healed by a physician: and this he
wills. But since he did not always actually will to have health, he must, of necessity, have
begun, through something moving him, to will to be healed. And if the will moved itself
to will this, it must, of necessity, have done this with the aid of counsel following some
previous volition. But this process could not go on to infinity. Wherefore we must, of
necessity, suppose that the will advanced to its first movement in virtue of the instigation
of some exterior mover, as Aristotle concludes in a chapter of the *Eudemian Ethics*.

supra voluntatem et intellectum, scilicet Deus; qui cum omnia moveat secundum rationem mobilium, ut levia sursum et gravia deorsum, etiam voluntatem movet secundum eius conditionem, non ut ex necessitate, sed ut indeterminate se habentem ad multa. Patet ergo quod si consideretur motus voluntatis ex parte exercitii actus, non movetur ex necessitate.

(*De malo* 6 resp.)[4]

The concession, clearly, leaving as it does a certain room for manoeuvre at the practical level, is a significant one, but hardly sufficient to resolve what we referred to a moment ago as the irony of this, the irony implicit in a grace theology so high, so complete in its sense of the dysfunctionality of man, that there is nothing there to be graced, or rather – grace being nothing other than love by another name – nothing there to be loved. And it is this sense of the unloveability of what God himself has done

---

[4] It remains to say, therefore, as Aristotle concludes in the chapter on good fortune [in the *Eudemian Ethics*], that what first moves the intellect and the will is something superior to them, namely God. And since he moves every kind of thing according to the nature of the moveable thing, for example, light things upward and heavy things downward, he also moves the will according to its condition, as indeterminately disposed to many things, not in a necessary way. Therefore, if we should consider the movement of the will regarding the performance of an act, the will is evidently not moved in a necessary way. Cf. *In Rom.* ix, lect. 3: 'Voluntas autem hominis movetur a Deo ad bonum. Unde supra VIII, v. 14 dictum est: "qui spiritu Dei aguntur, hi sunt filii Dei." Et ideo hominis operatio interior non est homini principaliter, sed Deo attribuenda. Phil. II, 13: "Deus est qui operatur in nobis velle et perficere pro bona voluntate." Sed si non est volentis velle, neque currentis currere, sed Dei moventis ad hoc hominem, videtur quod homo non sit dominus sui actus, quod pertinet ad libertatem arbitrii. Et ideo dicendum est, quod Deus omnia movet, sed diversimode, inquantum scilicet unumquodque movetur ab eo secundum modum naturae suae. Et sic homo movetur a Deo ad volendum et currendum per modum liberae voluntatis. Sic ergo velle et currere est hominis, ut libere agentis: non autem est hominis ut principaliter moventis, sed Dei.' The *Eudemian Ethics* passage (1248a16-29) runs as follows: 'This, however, one might question, whether fortune is the cause of just this, namely desiring what and when one ought. But will it not in this case be the cause of everything, even of thought and deliberation? For one does not deliberate after previous deliberation, but there is some starting point; nor does one think after thinking previously to thinking, and so *ad infinitum*. Thought, then, is not the starting point of thinking nor deliberation of deliberation. What, then, can be the starting point except chance? Thus everything would come from chance. Perhaps there is a starting point with none other outside it, and this can act in this sort of way by being such as it is. The object of our search is this – what is the commencement of movement in the soul? The answer is clear: as in the universe, so in the soul, it is god. For in a sense the divine element in us moves everything. The starting point of reasoning is not reasoning but something greater. What, then, could be greater than knowledge and even intellect but god?' On Thomas and the 'good fortune' moment of the *Eudemian Ethics*, T. Deman, 'Le "Liber de Bona Fortuna" dans la théologie de S. Thomas d'Aquin', *Revue des Sciences Philosophiques et Théologiques* 17 (1928), 38-59.

in the historical order that brings us to the heart of Dante's problem
with the kind of Augustinianism decisive for the substance and tone
of the grace questions of the *Prima secundae*; for Dante, prepared as he
was to countenance lovelessness as a condition of the human spirit (for
lovelessness is of man rather than of God), could never settle for its
unloveability, unloveability, as a property of whatever *is* in the world in
consequence of the original and abiding *fiat*, at once calling into question
the efficacy of that *fiat* and the ardour of the One from whom it proceeds.

2. The fundamental option for the individual living in the moment between
the first and second coming of the Christ is the option either for or against
him, and it is an option which impinges upon that individual as soon as he
comes of age, with the dawning of critical self-awareness. This, Thomas
thinks, is the key moment. Emerging from adolescence into adulthood,
and sensing at last something of the problematic nature of his presence
in the world as a creature of moral and eschatological accountability, the
individual is called upon to move one way or the other, to opt either for
a resolution of self in the other-than-self which is God, which is the way
of self-finding and of lasting happiness, or for a resolution of self in and
through self itself, which is the way of self-losing and of lasting sadness:

> Cuius ratio est quia antequam ad annos discretionis perveniat,
> defectus aetatis, prohibens usum rationis, excusat eum a peccato
> mortali, unde multo magis excusat eum a peccato veniali, si committat
> aliquid quod sit ex genere suo tale. Cum vero usum rationis habere
> inceperit, non omnino excusatur a culpa venialis et mortalis peccati.
> Sed primum quod tunc homini cogitandum occurrit, est deliberare
> de seipso. Et si quidem seipsum ordinaverit ad debitum finem, per
> gratiam consequetur remissionem originalis peccati. Si vero non
> ordinet seipsum ad debitum finem, secundum quod in illa aetate est
> capax discretionis, peccabit mortaliter, non faciens quod in se est. Et
> ex tunc non erit in eo peccatum veniale sine mortali, nisi postquam
> totum fuerit sibi per gratiam remissum.

> (*ST* Ia IIae.89.6 resp.)[5]

[5] The reason for this is because before a man comes to the age of discretion, the lack
of years hinders the use of reason and excuses him from mortal sin, wherefore, much
more does it excuse him from venial sin, if he does anything which is such generically.
But when he begins to have the use of reason, he is not entirely excused from the guilt
of venial or mortal sin. Now the first thing that occurs to a man to think about then is to
deliberate about himself. And if he then direct himself to the due end, he will, by means
of grace, receive the remission of original sin: whereas if he does not then direct himself
to the due end, and as far as he is capable of discretion at that particular age, he will
sin mortally, for through not doing that which is in his power to do. Accordingly, there

Now it rarely happens in Thomas that attention is turned to anything like the drama of being in its positive unfolding, to the travail of the spirit – of this or that individual spirit – under the conditions of time and space. And perhaps even here we do not move far in this direction. But there is even so a sense from time to time of the urgency of it all, of the need on the part of the adolescent or as yet unformed spirit to look with all haste in God's direction as the condition of its properly human well-being; so, for example, in addition to the passage just quoted and the following *ad tertium*, these lines from the *De malo* (5.2 ad 8 and 7.10 ad 8), similarly eloquent in respect of what it means to come of age as a creature of moral determination:

> quia defectus aetatis quamdiu excusat a peccato mortali, multo magis excusat a peccato veniali propter defectum usus rationis. Postquam vero usum rationis habent, tenentur salutis suae curam agere: quod si fecerint, iam absque peccato originali erunt, gratia superveniente: si autem non fecerint, talis omissio est eis peccatum mortale ... Quia ante usum rationis puer excusatur a peccato mortali, ita ut si etiam committat actum qui de genere suo sit peccatum mortale, non incurrat reatum mortalis peccati, eo quod nondum habet usum rationis; unde multo magis excusatur a reatu peccati venialis; quia quod excusat maius peccatum, multo magis etiam excusat minus. Sed postquam habet usum rationis, peccat mortaliter, si non facit quod in se est ad quaerendum suam salutem; si autem faciat, gratiam consequetur, per quam immunis erit ab originali peccato.[6]

cannot thenceforward be venial sin in him without mortal, until afterwards all sin shall have been remitted to him through grace.

[6] for a lack of maturity, since it sometimes excuses from mortal sin due to lack of the use of reason, far more excuses from venial sin. And after persons attain the age of reason, they are obliged to attend to their salvation. And if they have done this, they will now be free from original sin with the advent of grace, and if they have not done this, such omission on their part will be a mortal sin ... a child before having the use of reason is excused from mortal sin, so that it does not incur the punitive liability of mortal sin even if it should commit an act that is by reason of its kind a mortal sin, since the child does not yet have the use of reason. And so much more is the child excused from the guilt of venial sin, since what excuses the greater sin much more excuses the lesser sin. But the child, after it has the use of reason, sins mortally if it does not do what lies in its power to acquire its salvation, and if it should do so, it will obtain the grace whereby it will be free from original sin. The *ad tertium* to Ia IIae. 89. 6 runs as follows: 'Ad tertium dicendum quod ab aliis peccatis mortalibus potest puer incipiens habere usum rationis, per aliquod tempus abstinere, sed a peccato omissionis praedictae non liberatur, nisi quam cito potest, se convertat ad Deum. Primum enim quod occurrit homini discretionem habenti est quod de seipso cogitet, ad quem alia ordinet sicut ad finem, finis enim est prior in intentione. Et ideo hoc est tempus pro quo obligatur ex Dei praecepto affirmativo, quo dominus dicit, "convertimini ad me, et ego convertar ad vos", Zachariae I.'

or these from the even earlier *Scriptum* (II, dist. 42, qu. 1, art. 5 ad 7) with
their sense once again of the arduousness of age, of maturity as a matter
of knowing self in the moral accountability of self:

> Sed imperfectio aetatis excusat peccatum mortale, ut puer nondum
> usum liberi arbitrii habens peccati mortalis reus non habeatur, etiam
> si actum faciat qui ex genere peccatum mortale sit; unde multo
> amplius excusat infantia ne peccatum veniale imputetur; et ideo non
> potest esse quod homo venialiter peccet ante illud tempus quo usum
> rationis habet, ut jam mortaliter peccare possit. Statim autem ut ad
> tempus illud pervenit, vel gratiam habet, vel in peccato mortali est:
> quia si facit quod in se est, Deus ei gratiam infundit; si autem non
> facit, peccat mortaliter: quia tunc est tempus ut de salute sua cogitet,
> et ei operam det.[7]

Here, then, distributed across the spectrum of Thomas's work, is a
more or less developed sense of, again, the urgency of it all, of maturity
as a matter of the need for resolution. To suppose otherwise, Thomas
seems to be saying, is to linger on the plane of adolescence, of a kind of
dreaming innocence. But there is a difference here, for whereas at the
time of the *Scriptum* Thomas was confident that man as ungraced could
from out of himself turn towards God and prepare himself for the gracing
of his spirit, by the time of the *Prima secundae* he is of the opinion that
this now is down to God alone, to the God who not only perfects man
but moves him to desire that perfection in the first place; so, for example,
112.2, committed both explicitly and emphatically to the referability of
free will to a movement of grace as to its origin:

> Sed si loquamur de gratia secundum quod significat auxilium Dei
> moventis ad bonum, sic nulla praeparatio requiritur ex parte hominis
> quasi praeveniens divinum auxilium, sed potius quaecumque
> praeparatio in homine esse potest, est ex auxilio Dei moventis
> animam ad bonum. Et secundum hoc, ipse bonus motus liberi arbitrii
> quo quis praeparatur ad donum gratiae suscipiendum, est actus liberi
> arbitrii moti a Deo, et quantum ad hoc, dicitur homo se praeparare,
> secundum illud Prov. XVI [v. 1], *hominis est praeparare animum*. Et

---

[7] Yet lack of age excuses mortal sin, for a child not having the use of free will will not
carry the guilt of mortal sin, even if what he does falls into the category of mortal sin;
whence an infant is all the more excused from the charge of venial sin. A man cannot
therefore sin venially before such time as he has the use of reason, the reason by which he
is able already to sin mortally. As soon as he arrives at that stage, however, he lives either
in grace or in mortal sin, for inasmuch as he does what he can God breathes grace into
him. Inasmuch, however, as he refuses to do what he can, he sins mortally, for this is the
moment in which he considers his soul and applies himself to doing something about it.

est principaliter a Deo movente liberum arbitrium, et secundum
hoc, dicitur a Deo voluntas hominis praeparari, et a domino gressus
hominis dirigi.

(*ST* Ia IIae.112.2 resp.)[8]

Here too, therefore, the dialectic in human experience of gracing and
willing is resolved in favour of the former, at which point the question
which most concerns us here, and which most concerned Dante as he
himself thought the issue through with a view to accommodating as
equitably as possible its at once various and variously conflicting emphases
is again acute; for if grace as but the *love-encompassing* is all, and nature
as but the *love-encompassed* is nothing, then there is a sense in which each
alike is abolished, theology at once delivering itself to its own effrontery.

---

[8] But if we speak of grace as it signifies a help from God to move us to good, no
preparation is required on man's part, that, as it were, anticipates divine help, but rather,
every preparation in man must be by the help of God moving the soul to good. And thus
even the good movement of the free-will, whereby anyone is prepared for receiving the
gift of grace is an act of the free will as moved by God. And thus man is indeed said to
prepare himself, according to Proverbs 16: 'It is the part of man to prepare the soul'; and
yet preparation is principally from God, who moves the free will. Hence it is said that
man's will is prepared by God, and that man's steps are guided by God.

Appendix C
Dante on Acquisition

Chapter 1 above turned on a sense in Dante of the coalescence of divine and human willing at the core itself of existence, a notion both presupposing and in turn confirming that of grace as operative, not over against, but from out of the economy of nature, from – in the case of man – out of the recesses of personality. Following on from this, however, is a no less characteristic commitment in Dante to the notion of acquisition, of man's laying hold of his proper good by way of his ordinary power to moral determination. Take, for example, the following lines (52-60) from Canto VIII of the *Purgatorio*, settled in their sense of the soul's achieving its proper good *ex seipso*, from out of the powers and potentialities of historical selfhood:

> Ver' me si fece, e io ver' lui mi fei:
> giudice Nin gentil, quanto mi piacque
> quando ti vidi non esser tra ' rei!
>   Nullo bel salutar tra noi si tacque;
> poi dimandò: "Quant' è che tu venisti
> a piè del monte per le lontane acque?".
>   "Oh!", diss' io lui, "per entro i luoghi tristi
> venni stamane, e sono in prima vita,
> ancor che l'altra, sì andando, acquisti".[1]

The journey, then, is acquisitive in kind, man, by virtue of his status as a new creation in Christ, of the power to resurrection made his by way of the cross, laying claim to his inheritance from out of his original and now renewed capacity for seeing and doing aright. And what applies in Canto VIII of the *Purgatorio* applies also in Canto XVII, where it is a question,

---

[1] He moved toward me and I toward him. Noble judge Nino, how I rejoiced to see you there, and not among the damned! No fair salutation was silent between us; then he asked, "How long is it since you came to the foot of the mountain over the far waters?" "Oh", I said to him, "from within the woeful places I came this morning, and am in the first life, albeit by this my journeying I gain the other".

however, less of the power, than of the perseverance of acquistion, of the
endless and endlessly energetic state of mind required of the individual
as he contemplates the fundamental structures of his existence, enters
the fray (the 'contende' of line 129), and, here as before, seeks from out
of himself to realize his proper finality as a creature of historical and
eschatological accountability:

> Questo triforme amor qua giù di sotto
> si piange: or vo' che tu de l'altro intende,
> che corre al ben con ordine corrotto.
>   Ciascun confusamente un bene apprende
> nel qual si queti l'animo, e disira;
> per che di giugner lui ciascun contende.
>   Se lento amore a lui veder vi tira
> o a lui acquistar, questa cornice,
> dopo giusto penter, ve ne martira.

(Purg. XVII.124-32)[2]

If, then, to this passage we add these lines (130-35) from *Paradiso*
XXIII on the treasure acquired by the suffering spirit in consequence of
its long exile:

> Oh quanta è l'ubertà che si soffolce
> in quelle arche ricchissime che fuoro
> a seminar qua giù buone bobolce!
>   Quivi si vive e gode del tesoro
> che s'acquistò piangendo ne lo essilio
> di Babillòn, ove si lasciò l'oro.[3]

or these (40-45) from *Paradiso* XXVII on the acquistion among the old
martyrs of the living joy ('viver lieto') of paradise as the point of arrival in
respect of their striving under the conditions of time and space:

> Non fu la sposa di Cristo allevata
> del sangue mio, di Lin, di quel di Cleto,
> per essere ad acquisto d'oro usata;

---

[2] This threefold love is wept for down here below. Now I would have you hear of the
other, which hastens towards the good in faulty measure. Each one apprehends vaguely
a good wherein the mind may find rest, and this it desires; wherefore each one strives to
attain thereto. If lukewarm love draws you to see it or to acquire it, this terrace after due
repentance torments you for it.

[3] O how great is the abundance which is heaped up in those rich coffers, who were good
sowers here below! Here they live and rejoice in the treasure which was acquired with
tears in the exile of Babylon, where gold was scorned.

ma per acquisto d'esto viver lieto
e Sisto e Pïo e Calisto e Urbano
sparser lo sangue dopo molto fleto.[4]

then a distinctive pattern of seeing and speaking begins to emerge, a
pattern at every point determined by Dante's sense of human nature as
empowered in respect of its proper good, as attuned to *acquisition* as a
principle of self-interpretation. Thomas, though, is doubtful. Given the
distinction to be drawn, he thinks, between the imperfect happiness of
this life and the perfect happiness of the next life, we have no alternative
but to put a limit on *acquiring* as a way of seeing and understanding the
human situation, the notion of acquisition extending (though even here
with some qualification) to the former, to what can be done here and now,
but not to the latter:

> beatitudo imperfecta quae in hac vita haberi potest, potest ab homine
> acquiri per sua naturalia, eo modo quo et virtus, in cuius operatione
> consistit, de quo infra dicetur. Sed beatitudo hominis perfecta, sicut
> supra dictum est, consistit in visione divinae essentiae. Videre autem
> Deum per essentiam est supra naturam non solum hominis, sed etiam
> omnis creaturae, ut in primo ostensum est. Naturalis enim cognitio
> cuiuslibet creaturae est secundum modum substantiae eius, sicut de
> intelligentia dicitur in libro de causis, quod 'cognoscit ea quae sunt
> supra se, et ea quae sunt infra se, secundum modum substantiae
> suae'. Omnis autem cognitio quae est secundum modum substantiae
> creatae, deficit a visione divinae essentiae, quae in infinitum excedit
> omnem substantiam creatam. Unde nec homo, nec aliqua creatura,
> potest consequi beatitudinem ultimam per sua naturalia.
>
> (*ST* Ia IIae.5.5 resp.)[5]

---

[4] The spouse of Christ was not nurtured on my blood and that of Linus and of Cletus to
be employed for gain of gold; but for the acquiring of this happy life Sixtus and Pius and
Calixtus and Urban shed their blood after much weeping.

[5] imperfect happiness that can be had in this life can be acquired by man by his natural
powers, in the same way as virtue, in whose operation it consists; on this point we shall
speak further on [qu. 63]. But man's perfect happiness, as stated above [qu. 3, art. 8],
consists in the vision of the divine essence. Now the vision of God's essence surpasses the
nature not only of man, but also of every creature, as was shown in Part I (12. 4). For the
natural knowledge of every creature is in keeping with the mode of his substance. Thus
it is said of the intelligence in the *Book of Causes* [prop. viii] that 'it knows things that are
above it, and things that are below it, according to the mode of its substance'. But every
knowledge that is according to the mode of created substance falls short of the vision
of the divine essence, which infinitely surpasses all created substance. Consequently
neither man, nor any creature, can attain final happiness by his natural powers. Aquinas
on acquisition generally, *ST* Ia 19.2 resp. (on the inclination of things generally to acquire

Now lest, as far as Dante is concerned, we be tempted to see in this an expression of theological naïveté, we must take care to perspectivize his discourse at this point, to locate it within the context of grace as, for him too, the enfolding and the empowering; for it is precisely this sense of grace as the enfolding and the empowering – as that whereby man is equipped from beforehand for the business of acquisition – that enables him to think and speak in this way. Quickened by grace, in other words, as operative at the still centre of his being, man as man is able to embark on the way of significant self-implementation, of reaching out in the power of what he always was, and now is again in and through the spiritual potentiation that is his in Christ, for his proper good, at which point it is correct to speak of his 'acquiring' that good, of his laying hold of it as his proper inheritance.

their proper perfection): 'Res enim naturalis non solum habet naturalem inclinationem respectu proprii boni, ut acquirat ipsum cum non habet, vel ut quiescat in illo cum habet'; Ia.62.1 resp. (on the discursive or progressive nature of man's acquiring perfection): 'Sic igitur dicendum est quod, quantum ad primam beatitudinem, quam Angelus assequi virtute suae naturae potuit, fuit creatus beatus. Quia perfectionem huiusmodi Angelus non acquirit per aliquem motum discursivum, sicut homo, sed statim ei adest propter suae naturae dignitatem'; Ia 85.5 resp., etc.

Bibliography

PRIMARY WORKS
Dante
Rime, ed. K. Foster and P. Boyde in *Dante's Lyric Poetry*, 2 vols (Oxford: Clarendon Press, 1967).

Detto d'Amore and *Fiore*, ed. G. Contini in *Il Fiore e Il Detto d'Amore attribuibili a Dante Alighieri* (Milan: Mondadori, 1984).

Vita nuova, ed. D. De Robertis in *Opere minori*, 2 vols (Milan-Naples: Ricciardi, 1984), vol. 1, part 1, pp. 1-247.

Il Convivio, ed. G. Busnelli and G. Vandelli, 2 vols (Florence: Le Monnier, 1934-37); 2nd edn, updated and with an appendix by A. E. Quaglio (Florence: Le Monnier, 1964 and reprints).

Convivio, ed. C. Vasoli and D. De Robertis in *Opere minori* (Milan-Naples: Ricciardi, 1988), vol. 1, part 2, pp. 3-1108.

Convivio, ed. F. Brambilla Ageno, 3 vols (Florence: Le Lettere, 1995).

De vulgari eloquentia, ed. P. V. Mengaldo in *Opere minori* (Milan-Naples: Ricciardi, 1979), vol. 2, pp. 1-237.

Monarchia, ed. P. G. Ricci (Milan: Mondadori, 1965).

Monarchia, ed. B. Nardi in *Opere minori* (Milan-Naples: Ricciardi, 1979), vol. 5, part 2, pp. 239-503.

Monarchia, ed. and trans. P. Shaw (Cambridge: Cambridge University Press, 1995).

Epistole, ed. A. Frugoni and G. Brugnoli in *Opere minori* (Milan-Naples: Ricciardi, 1979), vol. 5, part 2, pp. 505-643.

Egloge, ed. E. Cecchini in *Opere minori* (Milan-Naples: Ricciardi, 1979), vol. 5, part 2, pp. 645-89.

Quaestio de aqua et terra, ed. F. Mazzoni in *Opere minori* (Milan-Naples: Ricciardi, 1979), vol. 5, part 2, pp. 691-880.

La commedia secondo l'antica vulgata, ed. G. Petrocchi, 4 vols (Verona: Mondadori, 1966-67).

Dante Alighieri, La Commedia, ed. A. Chiavacci Leonardi, 3 vols (Milan: Mondadori, 1991-97).

Aquinas
Leonine edition (Rome, 1892-).

Summa theologiae, ed. T. Gilby and T. C. O'Brien, 60 vols (London: Eyre and Spottiswoode, 1964-73).

S. Thomae Aquinatis, *Opera Omnia*, ed. R. Busa, 7 vols (Stuttgart: Frommann-Holzboog, 1980).
S. Thomae de Aquino, *Opera omnia* (http://www.corpusthomisticum.org/iopera.html).

SECONDARY WORKS
Medieval philosophy and theology generally
Bianchi, L., *Il vescovo e i filosofi. La condanna parigina del 1277 e l'evoluzione dell'aristotelismo scolastico* (Bergamo: Lubrina, 1990).
Bianchi, L. and E. Brandi, *Le verità dissonanti. Aristotele alla fine del Medioevo* (Bari: Laterza, 1990).
Chenu, M. -D., *La théologie au douzième siècle*, 3rd edn (Paris: Vrin, 1976).
D'Onofrio, G. (ed.), *Storia della teologia nel medioevo*, 4 vols (Casale Monferrato: Piemme, 1992-2003).
Evans, G. R. (ed.), *The Medieval Theologians* (Oxford: Blackwell, 2001).
Gilson, E., *The Spirit of Mediaeval Philosophy* (London: Sheed and Ward, 1936).
Knowles, D., *The Evolution of Medieval Thought* (London: Longmans, 1962; 2nd edn ed. D. E. Luscombe and C. N. L. Brooke, 1988).
Kretzmann, N., A. Kenny and J. Pinborg, J. (eds), *The Cambridge History of Later Medieval Philosophy* (Cambridge: Cambridge University Press, 1982).

Ethics, grace, soteriology and election generally in the Middle Ages
Bougerol, J. -G., *La Théologie de l'espérance aux XIIe et XIIIe siècles*, 2 vols (Paris: Etudes augustiniennes, 1985).
Cessario, R., *The Godly Image: Christ and Salvation in Catholic Thought from St. Anselm to Aquinas* (Petersham, MA: St Bede's Publications, 1990).
Dilman, I., *Free Will: An Historical and Philosophical Introduction* (London: Routledge, 1999).
Farrelly, M. J., *Predestination, Grace and Free Will* (London: Burns and Oates, 1964).
Froehlich, K., 'Justification, Language and Grace: the Charge of Pelagianism in the Middle Ages', in E. A. McKee and B. G. Armstrong (eds), *Probing the Reformed Tradition. Historical Studies in Honor of Edward A. Dowey, Jr* (Louisville, Ky: Westminster-John Knox Press, 1989), pp. 21-47.
Gunton, C. E. (ed.), *God and Freedom: Essays in Historical and Systematic Theology* (Edinburgh: T. and T. Clark, 1995).
O'Connor, W. R., *The Eternal Quest. The Teaching of St Thomas Aquinas on the Natural Desire for God* (New York: Longmans, Green and Co., 1947).
idem, *The Natural Desire for God* (Milwaukee: Marquette University Press, 1948).

DANTE
Dante in general
Anderson, W., *Dante the Maker* (London and Boston: Routledge and Kegan Paul, 1980).
Ascoli, A. R., *Dante and the Making of a Modern Author* (Cambridge: Cambridge University Press, 2008).

Barolini, T. and H. Wayne Storey (eds), *Dante for the New Millennium* (New York: Fordham University Press, 2003).

Bemrose, S., *A New Life of Dante* (Exeter: University of Exeter Press, 2000).

Bloom, H., *Dante* (New York: Chelsea House, 1986).

Boyde, P., *Dante, Philomythes and Philosopher: Man and the Cosmos* (Cambridge: University Press, 1981).

idem, *Human Vices and Human Worth in Dante's 'Comedy'* (Cambridge: Cambridge University Press, 2000).

idem, *Perception and Passion in Dante's 'Comedy'* (Cambridge: Cambridge University Press, 1993).

Cachey, T. J., Jr (ed.), *Dante Now. Current Trends in Dante Studies* (Notre Dame, Ind.: University of Notre Dame Press, 1995).

Cogan, M., *The Design in the Wax. The Structure of the Divine Comedy and its Meaning* (Notre Dame, Ind. and London: University of Notre Dame Press, 1999).

Malato, E., *Dante* (Rome: Salerno, 1999).

Reynolds, B., *Dante. The Poet, the Political Thinker, the Man* (London and New York: I. B. Tauris, 2006).

Scott, J. A., *Understanding Dante* (Notre Dame, Ind.: Notre Dame University Press, 2004).

Dante, philosophy and theology

Allan, M., 'Two Dantes: Christian versus Humanist', *Modern Language Notes* 107 (1992), 18-35.

Armour, P., *Dante's Griffin and the History of the World. A Study of the Earthly Paradise (Purgatorio, cantos XXIX-XXXIII)* (Oxford: Clarendon Press, 1989).

idem, review of A. C. Mastrobuono, *Dante's Journey of Sanctification* (Washington D.C.: Regnery Gateway, 1990), *Modern Language Review* 88 (1993), 219-20.

idem, *The Door of Purgatory. A Study of Multiple Symbolism in Dante's Purgatorio* (Oxford: Clarendon Press, 1983).

Aversano, M., *Dante cristiano. La 'selva', Francesco, Ulisse e la 'struttura' dell'Inferno* (Rome: Il Calamaio, 1994).

Barbi, M., *Problemi di critica dantesca*, 2nd series (1920-1937) (Florence: Sansoni, 1941 and 1975).

Barblan, G. (ed.), *Dante e la Bibbia. Atti del convegno internazionale promosso da 'Bibbia', Firenze, 26-28 settembre 1986* (Florence: Olschki, 1988).

Barolini, T., 'Medieval Multiculturalism and Dante's Theology of Hell', *Italiana* 9 (2000), 82-102; subsequently in *Dante and the Origins of Italian Literary Culture* (New York: Fordham University Press, 2006), pp. 102-21.

eadem, *The Undivine Comedy: Detheologizing Dante* (Princeton NJ: Princeton University Press, 1992).

Basile, B., 'Il viaggio come archetipo. Note sul tema della "peregrinatio" in Dante', in *Letture classensi* 15 (Ravenna: Longo, 1986), pp. 9-26.

Battaglia, S., 'Teoria del poeta teologo', in *Esemplarità e antagonismo nel pensiero di Dante*, 2 vols, 2nd edn (Naples: Liguori, 1967-74), vol. 1, pp. 271-301.

Battistini, A., '"Se la Scrittura sovra voi non fosse . . . ". Allusioni bibliche nel canto XIX del Paradiso', *Critica letteraria* 59 (1988), 2, 211-35.

Bemrose, S., *Dante's Angelic Intelligences. Their Importance in the Cosmos and in Pre-Christian Religion* (Rome: Edizioni di Storia e Letteratura, 1983).

Berretta, G., '"Fortuna" e responsabilità umana in Dante', *Filologia e letteratura* 12 (1966), 243-52.

Biffi, I., *La poesia e la grazia nella 'Commedia' di Dante* (Milan: Jaca Book, 1999).

Boffito, G., *Saggio di bibliografia Egidiana*, with a preliminary essay on *Dante, S. Agostino ed Egidio Colonna* (Florence: Olschki, 1911).

Boitani, P., 'Il poema di Dante e la cristianità', in *Dante poeta cristiano* (Florence: Edizioni Polistampa, 2001), pp. 1-17.

Bonifaxi, D., 'Filosofia, teologia e poesia di Dante nella critica d'oggi', *Aquinas* 11 (1968), 385-98.

Bosco, U., 'Teologia e ultra-teologia negli ultimi canti del *Paradiso*', in *Altre pagine dantesche* (Caltanissetta and Rome: Sciascia, 1987), pp. 61-92.

Bottagisio, T., *Il Limbo dantesco. Studi filosofici e letterari* (Padua: Antoniana, 1898).

Botterill, S., *Dante and the Mystical Tradition: Bernard of Clairvaux in the Commedia* (Cambridge: Cambridge University Press, 1994).

Boyde, P., 'Predisposition and Prevenience: Prologomena to the Study of Dante's Mind and Art', *Proceedings of the British Academy* 69 (1983), 327-54.

Busnelli, G., *Cosmogonia e antropogenesi secondo Dante Alighieri e le sue fonti* (Rome: Civiltà Cattolica, 1922).

idem, 'La colpa del "non fare" degl'infedeli negativi', *Studi Danteschi* 23 (1938), 79-97.

Cambon, G., 'Dante's Noble Sinners: Abstract Examples or Living Characters?', in *Dante's Craft. Studies in Language and Style* (Minneapolis: University of Minnesota Press, 1969), pp. 67-79.

Cioffari, V., *The Conception of Fortune and Fate in the Works of Dante* (Cambridge, Mass.: Dante Society of Cambridge, Mass., 1940).

Colilli, P., 'Harold Bloom and the Post-Theological Dante', *Annali d'italianistica* (monographic volume entitled *Dante and Modern American Criticism*) 8 (1990), 132-43.

Collins, J., *Pilgrim in Love. An Introduction to Dante and his Spirituality* (Chicago: Loyola University Press, 1984).

Comollo, A., *Il dissenso religioso in Dante* (Florence: Olschki, 1990).

Consoli, A., 'Dante anticlericale?', in *Dante ecumenico. Letture e postille* (Naples: Conte, 1973), pp. 20-24.

Corti, M., *Dante a un nuovo crocevia* (Florence: Sansoni, 1981).

eadem, *La felicità mentale. Nuove prospettive per Cavalcanti e Dante* (Turin: Einaudi, 1983).

Costa, D. J., 'Dante as a Poet-Theologian', *Dante Studies* 89 (1971), 61-72.

Cotter, J. F., 'Dante and Christ: the pilgrim as "Beatus Vir"', *Italian Quarterly* 107 (1987), 5-19.

Crevenna, C., 'Retorica e teologia negli *exempla* del *Purgatorio*', in F. Spera (ed.), *La divina foresta. Studi danteschi* (Naples: D'Auria, 2006), pp. 201-84.

Di Ceglie, R., 'Dante Alighieri e la filosofia cristiana nell'interpretazione di Etienne Gilson', *Rivista di Filosofia Neo-scolastica* 97 (2005), 627-49.

Di Scipio, G., *The Presence of Pauline Thought in the Works of Dante* (Lewiston, Queenston and Lampeter: Edwin Mellen, 1995).

Esposito, V., *La Commedia dantesca tre fede e dissenso* (Pescara: Tracce, 1999).

Fallani, G., *Dante: poeta teologo* (Milan: Marzorati, 1965).

idem, *L'esperienza teologica di Dante* (Lecce: Milella, 1976) (with 'Dante e S. Tommaso' at pp. 205-38).

idem, *Poesia e teologia nella 'Divina Commedia'*, 2 vols (Milan: Marzorati, 1959-1965).

Fortin, E. L., *Dissidence et philosophie au moyen âge: Dante et ses antécédents* (Montréal: Bellarmin and Paris: Vrin, 1981) (*Cahiers d'études médiévales* 6), with an English translation by M. A. Lepain, *Dissent and Philosophy in the Middle Ages: Dante and his Precursors* (Lanham, Md.: Lexington Books, 2002).

Foster, K., O.P., *God's Tree: Essays on Dante and Other Matters* (London: Blackfriars, 1957).

idem, *The Two Dantes and Other Studies* (London: Darton, Longman and Todd, 1978).

idem, ad voc. 'Teologia' in the *Enciclopedia dantesca*, 6 vols (Rome: Istituto dell'Enciclopedia Italiana, 1970-78), vol. 5, pp. 564-68.

Franke, W., *Dante's Interpretive Journey* (Chicago: Chicago University Press, 1996).

Freccero, J., *Dante: The Poetics of Conversion*, ed. R. Jacoff (Cambridge, Mass. and London: Harvard University Press, 1986).

Garin, E., 'Dante e la filosofia', *Il Veltro* 18 (1974), 4-6, 281-93.

Ghisalberti, A., 'Dante Alighieri: la teologia del poeta', in *Storia della teologia nel medioevo, III: La teologia delle scuole* (Casale Monferrato: PIEMME, 1996), pp. 301-323.

idem, *Dante e il pensiero scolastico medievale* (Milan: Edizioni di Sofia, 2008).

idem, 'Dante filosofo e teologo', *Vita e pensiero. Rassegna italiana di cultura* (2000), 6, pp. 556-65.

idem (ed.), *Il pensiero filosofico e teologico di Dante Alighieri* (Milan: V&P Università, 2001).

Gilson, E., *Dante et Béatrice: études dantesques* (Paris: Vrin, 1974).

idem, *Dante et la philosophie* (Paris: Vrin, 1939) (in English, trans. D. Moore, *Dante the Philosopher*, London: Sheed and Ward, 1949, and New York, Evanston and London: Harper and Row, 1963 as *Dante and Philosophy*).

Guardini, R., *Dantes 'Göttliche Komödie'. Ihre philosophischen und religiösen Grundgedanken (Vorlesungen)*, ed. H. Mercker (Mainz Paderborn: Grünewald-Schöningh, 1998).

Harwood-Gordon, S., *A Study of the Theology and the Imagery of Dante's Divina Commedia. Sensory Perception, Reason and Free Will* (Lewiston, Queenston and Lampeter: Edwin Mellen, 1991).

Hawkins, P. S., 'All Smiles. Poetry and Theology in Dante', *Publications of the Modern Language Association of America* 121, 2 (2006), 371-87.

Hollander, R., 'Dante *Theologus-Poeta*', *Dante Studies* 94 (1976), 91-136 (subsequently in *Studies in Dante* (Ravenna: Longo, 1980), pp. 39-89).

Iannucci, A. A., ad voc. 'Theology' in *The Dante Encyclopedia*, ed. R. Lansing (New York and London: Garland, 2000), pp. 811-15.

idem, 'Dante's Theological Canon in the *Commedia*', *Italian Quarterly* 37 (2000), 51-56.

Imbach, R., *Dante, la philosophie et les laïcs; initiation à la philosophie médiévale* (Paris and Fribourg: Editions universitaires and Paris: Cerf, 1996).

Livi, F., *Dante e la teologia. L'immaginazione poetica nella Divina Commedia come interpretazione del dogma* (Rome: Casa editrice Leonardo da Vinci, 2008).

Mandonnet, P., *Dante le théologien* (Paris: Desclée de Brouwer, 1935).

Mattii, N., *Teologia e Dante Alighieri* (Montegiorgio: Finucci, 1912).

Mazzeo, J. A., *Structure and Thought in the Paradiso* (Ithaca NY: Cornell University Press, 1958).

Mazzotta, G., *Dante, Poet of the Desert. History and Allegory in the Divine Commedy* (Princeton NJ: Princeton University Press, 1979).

idem, *Dante's Vision and the Circle of Knowledge* (Princeton NJ: Princeton University Press, 1993).

idem, '"Teologia ludens". Angels and Devils in the *Divine Comedy*', in K. Brownlee and S. Walter (eds), *Discourse of Authority in Medieval and Renaissance Literature* (Hanover and London: University Press of New England, 1989), pp. 216-35, subsequently in *Dante's Vision and Circle of Knowledge* (Princeton: Princeton University Press, 1993), pp. 219-41, and, in a revised form, A. Paolella et al. (ed.), *Miscellanea di studi danteschi in memoria di Silvio Pasquazi*, 2 vols (Naples: Federico & Ardia, 1993), vol. 2, pp. 507-17.

Meersseman, G. G., 'Dante come teologo', in *Atti del Congresso internazionale di studi danteschi (Florence, 20-27 April, 1965)*, vol.1 (Florence: Sansoni, 1965), pp. 177-95 (see also vol. 2, pp. 59-64).

Miller J., 'Introduction: Retheologizing Dante', in J. Miller (ed.), *Dante and the Unorthodox. The Aesthetics of Transgression* (Waterloo (Ontario-Canada): Wilfrid Laurier University Press 2005), pp. 1-60.

Moevs, C., *The Metaphysics of Dante's 'Comedy'* (Oxford and New York: Oxford University Press, 2005).

Montemaggi, V. and M. Treherne (eds), *Dante's Commedia. Theology as Poetry* (Notre Dame, Ind.: University of Notre Dame Press, 2010).

Moore, E., *Studies in Dante*, four vols (Oxford: Clarendon Press, 1968; originally 1896-1917).

Nardi, B., 'Filosofia e teologia ai tempi di Dante in rapporto al pensiero del poeta', in *Saggi e note di critica dantesca* (Milan and Naples: Ricciardi, 1966), pp. 3-109.

Nuttall, G. F., *The Faith of Dante Alighieri* (London: SPCK, 1969).

Ozanam, F., *Dante and Catholic Theology in the Thirteenth Century*, trans. L. D. Pychowska, 2nd edn (New York: The Cathedral Library Association, 1913).

Pietrobono, L., 'Filosofia e teologia nel *Convivio* e nella *Commedia*', *Giornale Dantesco* 41 (1938), 13-71.

Robiglio, A. A., 'Filosofia e teologia di Dante Alighieri. A proposito di studi recenti', *L'Alighieri. Rassegna dantesca* 43, n.s. 20 (2002), 127-38.

idem, 'Il pensiero filosofico e teologico di Dante Alighieri', in *Rivista di Storia della Filosofia* 4 (2000), 73-98.

Russo, V., *Il romanzo teologico. Sondaggi sulla 'Commedia' di Dante* (Naples: Liguori, 1984).

Sarteschi, S., *Il percorso del poeta cristiano. Riflessioni su Dante* (Ravenna: Longo, 2006).

Schaff, P., 'Dante's Theology', in *Papers of the American Society of Church History*, vol. 2 (January 1890), 53-73.

Schnapp, J. T., *The Transfiguration of History at the Center of Dante's Paradise* (Princeton NJ: Princeton University Press, 1986).

Singleton, C. S., *Dante's Commedia: Elements of Structure* (Cambridge MA: Harvard University Press, 1954).

idem, *Dante's Journey to Beatrice* (Cambridge MA: Harvard University Press, 1958).

Toussaint, S., 'Dante tra neoscolastica e teologia poetica: Curtius, Maritain, Maurras, Gilson', in *Dante e la cultura del suo tempo. Dante e le culture dei confini. Atti del Convegno Internazionale di Studi Danteschi, Gorizia, ottobre 1997* (Gorizia: Società Dante Alighieri, 1999), pp. 81-90.

Valensin, A., S.J., *Le Christianisme de Dante* (Paris: Aubier, 1954).

Vasoli, C., 'Filosofia e teologia in Dante', in *Otto saggi per Dante* (Florence: Le Lettere, 1995), pp. 13-40.

Williams, A. N., 'The Theology of the *Comedy*', in R. Jacoff (ed.), *The Cambridge Companion to Dante*, 2nd edn (Cambridge: Cambridge University Press, 2007), pp. 201-17.

Dante, ethics, grace, soteriology and election

Allan, M., 'Does Dante Hope for Virgil's Salvation?', *Modern Language Notes* 104 (1989), 1, 193-205.

idem, 'Much Virtue in "Ma": *Paradiso* XIX, 106, and St. Thomas's "Sed contra"', *Dante Studies* 111 (1993), 195-211.

idem, 'Two Dantes: Christian versus Humanist?', *Modern Langage Notes* 107 (1992), 1, 18-35.

Bandini, L., *Misericordia e carità. La manifestazione della grazia nella Divina Commedia* (Florence-Monsummano: Carla Rossi Academy Press, 2003 (as an e-book, http://www.cra.phoenixfound.it).

Barolini, T., 'Q: Does Dante hope for Vergil's Salvation?', *Modern Language Notes* 105 (1990), 1, 138-44 and 147-49 (and in *Dante and the Origins of Italian Literary Culture* (New York: Fordham University Press, 2006), pp. 151-57).

Berretta, G., '"Fortuna" e responsabilità umana in Dante', *Filologia e Letteratura* 12 (1966), 243-52.

Biffi, I., *La poesia e la grazia nella Commedia di Dante* (Milan: Jaca Book, 1999) (especially 'Un viaggio che parte dalla grazia', pp. 29-35).

Bufano, A., 'Applicazione della dottrina del libero arbitrio nella Commedia', in A. Paolella et al. (ed.), *Miscellanea di studi danteschi in memoria di Silvio Pasquazi*, 2 vols (Naples: Federico & Ardia, 1993), vol. 1, pp. 193-99.

Busnelli, G., 'La colpa del "non fare" degli infedeli negativi', *Studi Danteschi* 23 (1938), 79-97.

Cacciaglia, N., '"Per fede e per opere" (una lettura del tema della salvezza nella *Divina Commedia*)', in *Critica Letteraria* 115-16 (2002), 2-3, 265-74 (also in *Annali dell'Università per Stranieri di Perugia* 29 (2002), 123-31).

Cambon, G., 'Dante's Noble Sinners: Abstract Examples or Living Characters?', in *Dante's Craft. Studies in Language and Style* (Minneapolis: University of Minnesota Press, 1969), pp. 67-79.

Camilli, A., 'La teologia del Limbo dantesco', *Studi Danteschi* 30 (1951), 209-14.

Cannavò, G. (ed.), *Regnum celorum vïolenza pate. Dante e la salvezza dell'umanità. Letture Dantesche Giubilari, Vicenza, October 1999 - June 2000* (Montella (Avellino): Accademia Vivarium Novum, 2002).

Capéran, L., *Le Problème du salut des infidèles*, 2 vols, revised edn (Toulouse: Grand Séminaire, 1934).

Cherchi, P., '"Da me stesso non vegno" (*Inf.* X, 61)', in *Rassegna europea di letteratura italiana*, 18 (2001), 103-106.

Chiampi, J. T., 'The Role of Freely Bestowed Grace in Dante's Journey of Legitimation', *Rivista di Studi Italiani* 17 (1999), 1, 89-111.

Cioffari, V., *The Conception of Fortune and Fate in the Works of Dante* (Cambridge, Mass.: Dante Society of Cambridge, Mass., 1940).

Coletti, V., '"Cognitio Dei" tra *Convivio* e *Commedia*', in *Omaggio a Gianfranco Folena* (Padua: Editoriale Programma, 1993), pp. 409-18.

Colish, M. L., 'The Virtuous Pagan: Dante and the Christian Tradition', in W. Caferro and D. G. Fisher (eds), *The Unbounded Community. Papers in Christian Ecumenism in Honor of Jaraslov Pelikan* (New York: Garland, 1996), pp. 43-91.

Cremascoli, G., 'Paganesimo e mondo cristiano nel commento a Dante di Benvenuto da Imola', in P. Palmieri and C. Paolazzi (eds), *Benvenuto da Imola, lettore degli antichi e dei moderni* (Ravenna: Longo, 1991), pp. 111-25.

Cristaldi, S., 'Rimedio del peccato', in *Dante di fronte al gioachimismo. I. Dalla 'Vita Nova' alla 'Monarchia'* (Caltanisetta and Rome: Salvatore Sciascia, 2000), pp. 73-222.

Dunning, T. P., 'Langland and the Salvation of the Heathen', *Medium Aevum* 12 (1943), 45-54.

Fenn, R. K., 'Testing Claims to Grace', in *The Persistence of Purgatory* (Cambridge: Cambridge University Press, 1995), pp. 1-38.

Filosa, C., 'La "virtù" dei romani nel giudizio di S. Agostino e di Dante', in *Atti del congresso internazionale di Studi Danteschi* (Florence: Sansoni, 1965), pp. 195-210.

Forti, F., 'Il limbo dantesco e i Megalopsicoi della *Etica nicomachea*' in *Fra le carte del poeta* (Milan: Ricciardi, 1965; originally 1961), pp. 9-40 (subsequently in idem, *Magnanimitade. Studi su un tema dantesco*, with an introduction by E. Pasquini, (Rome: Carocci, 2006), pp. 9-48).

Frank, M. E., 'La "concreata e perpetua sete" del *Paradiso*', *Esperienze Letterarie* 18 (1993), 3, 41-56.

Frezza, M., *Il problema della salvezza dei pagani (da Abelardo al Seicento)* (Naples: Fiorentino, 1962).

Frye, J., 'Reason and Grace: Christian Epistemology in Dante, Langland, and Milton', in T. K. Rabb and J. E. Seigel (eds), *Action and Conviction in Early Modern Europe. Essays in Memory of E. H. Harbison* (Princeton NJ: Princeton University Press 1969), pp. 404-22.

Gigante, C., '"Adam sive Christus": creazione, incarnazione, redenzione nel canto VII del *Paradiso*', *Rivista di studi danteschi* 8 (2008), 2, 241-68.

Godenzi, G., 'Il viaggio spirituale di Dante dal peccato alla grazia', in *Quaderni Grigionitaliani. Rivista trimestrale delle valli Grigionitaliane* 56 (1987), 3-4, 234-39.

Grabher, C., 'Il Limbo dantesco e il nobile castello', *Studi danteschi* 29 (1950), 41-60.

Grandgent, C. H., '"All men naturally desire to know"', in *Discourses on Dante* (Cambridge, Mass.: Harvard University Press, 1924), pp. 95-123.

Hahn, T. O'H., 'I "gentili" e "un uom nasce a la riva / de l'Indo" (*Par.* XIX, vv.70 sgg.)', *L'Alighieri* 18 (1977), 2, 3-8.

Harent, S., 'Infidèles, Salut des', *Dictionnaire de Théologie Catholique*, 15 vols, ed. P. Moraux et al. (Paris: Letouzey et Ané, 1909-46), vol. 7, ii, cols 1726-1930.

Hartung, S., 'Guido Guinizzelli e la teologia della grazia', in F. Brugnolo and G. Peron (eds), *Da Guido Guinizzelli a Dante : nuove prospettive sulla lirica del Duecento. Atti del Convegno di Studi Padova-Monselice 10-12 maggio 2002* (Padua: Il Poligrafo, 2004), pp. 147-70.

Iannucci, A. A., 'Il limbo dei bambini', in L. Coglievina and D. De Robertis (eds), *Sotto il segno di Dante. Scritti in onore di Francesco Mazzoni* (Florence: Le Lettere, 1998), pp. 153-64.

idem, 'Limbo: The Emptiness of Time', *Studi danteschi* 52 (1979-80), 69-128.

Iliescu, N., 'Will Virgil be saved?', *Mediaevalia* 12 (1986), 93-114 (and as 'Sarà salvo Virgilio?' in C. Franco and L. Morgan (eds), *Dante. Summa medievalis. Proceedings of the Symposium of the Center for Italian Studies, SUNY Stony Brook* (Stony Brook, N.Y.: Forum Italicum, 1995), pp. 112-33).

Inglese, G., 'Il destino dei non credenti. Lettura di *Paradiso* XIX', *La Cultura. Rivista trimestrale di filosofia letteratura e storia* 42 (2004), 2, 315-29.

Jacomuzzi, A., 'Il Canto XIX del *Paradiso*', *L'Alighieri* 14 (1973), 2, 3-24 (and in *L'imago al cerchio e altri studi sulla Divina Commedia* (Milan: Franco Angeli, 1995), pp. 250-73).

Lanza, A., 'Giustizia divina e salvezza dei 'senza fede', in *Dante eterodosso* (Bergamo: Moretti Honegger, 2004), pp. 113-24.

Maillard, J.-F., 'Libero arbitrio, predestinazione e provvidenza nel poema dantesco di Francesco Giorgio Veneto', in L. R. S. Tarugi (ed.), *L'uomo e la natura nel Rinascimento* (Milan: Nuovi Orizzonti, 1996), pp. 227-41.

Marshall, W. W., 'Dante and the Doctrine of Original Sin. A Theological Gloss on *Purgatorio* XVI, 80-105 and *Paradiso* XXVII, 121-41', *Dante. Rivista internazionale di studi su Dante Alighieri* 3 (2006), 21-40.

Martinelli, B., 'Canto XIX', in G. Güntert and M. Picone (eds), *Lectura Dantis Turicensis. Paradiso* (Florence: Cesati, 2002), pp. 281-305 (revised with the title 'La fede in Cristo. Dante e il problema della salvezza (*Paradiso* XIX)', *Rivista di Letteratura Italiana* 20 (2002), 2, 11-39 and in *Dante. L'"altro viaggio"* (Pisa: Giardini, 2007), pp. 289-319).

Mastrobuono, A. C., *Dante's Journey of Sanctification* (Washington D.C.: Regnery Gateway, 1990).

Montanari, F., ad voc. 'Limbo', in the *Enciclopedia dantesca*, 6 vols (Rome: Istituto della Enciclopedia Italiana, 1970), vol. 3, 651-54.

idem, 'Natura, civiltà, grazia', in *L'esperienza poetica di Dante*, 2nd rev. edn (Florence: Le Monnier, 1968), pp. 250-72.

Morghen, R., 'Dante tra l'"umano" e la storia della salvezza', in *L'Alighieri. Rassegna bibliografica dantesca* 21 (1980), 1, 18-30.

Muresu, G., 'Il tema della predestinazione in *Paradiso* XXI', in V. De Gregorio (ed.), *Bibliologia e critica dantesca. Saggi dedicati a Enzo Esposito* (Ravenna: Longo, 1997), *II. Saggi danteschi*, pp. 197-202.

O'Connell Baur, C., *Dante's Hermeneutics of Salvation. Passages to Freedom in the 'Divine Comedy'* (Toronto, Buffalo and London: University of Toronto Press, 2007).

Padoan, G., 'Il Limbo dantesco', *Lettere Italiane* 21 (1969), 369-88 (and in *Il pio Enea, l'empio Ulisse. Tradizione classica e intendimento medievale in Dante* (Ravenna: Longo, 1977), pp. 103-24).

Panvini, B., 'La concezione tomistica della grazia nella *Divina Commedia*', in *Letture classensi* 17 (Ravenna: Longo, 1988), pp. 69-85.

Pérez Carrasco, M., 'Nota sobre la preeminencia de la moral en el *Convivio* de Dante', *Patristica et Mediaevalia* 27 (2006), 115-20.

Pertile, L., '*Paradiso*: a Drama of Desire', in J. C. Barnes and J. Petrie (eds), *Word and Drama in Dante* (Dublin: Irish Academic Press,1993), pp. 143-80 (also, modified, in *Dante Contemporary Perspectives*, ed. A. A. Iannucci (Toronto: University of Toronto Press, 1997), pp. 148-66 with the title 'A Desire of Paradise and a Paradise of Desire: Dante and Mysticism' and, further modified, in *La punta del disio. Semantica del desiderio nella Commedia* (Florence: Cadmo, 2005), pp. 137-61, with the title 'Desiderio di Paradiso').

Picone, M., '*Auctoritas* classica e salvezza cristiana: una lettura tipologica di *Purgatorio* XXII', in *Studi in memoria di Giorgio Varanini* (Pisa: Giardini, 1992), vol. 1 (*Dal Duecento al Quattrocento*), pp. 379-95.

idem, 'La "viva speranza" di Dante e il problema della salvezza dei pagani virtuosi. Una lettura di *Paradiso* 20', *Quaderni di Italianistica* 10 (1989), 1-2, 251-68.

Pinchard, B., 'La dignité de l'homme et les formes de sa liberté selon Dante', in P. Magnard (ed.), *La dignité de l'homme. Actes du Colloque tenu à la Sorbonne, Paris IV, en novembre 1992* (Paris: Champion, 1995), pp. 41-61.

Quilici, B., *Il destino dell'infidele virtuoso nel pensiero di Dante* (Florence: Ariani, 1936).

Rati, G., 'L'alto e magnifico processo (canto VII del *Paradiso*)', in *Saggi danteschi e altri studi* (Rome: Bulzoni, 1988), pp. 57-80.

Rizzo, G., 'Dante and the Virtuous Pagans', in W. De Sua and G. Rizzo (eds), *A Dante Symposium in Commemoration of the 700th Anniversary of the Poet's Birth (1265-1321)* (Chapel Hill: University of North Carolina Press, 1965), pp. 115-40.

Rossi, S., 'Il trionfo della grazia nell'episodio di Bonconte da Montefeltro', *L'Alighieri: rassegna bibliografica dantesca*, n.s. 3-4, 35 (1994), 83-93.

Ruffini, F., 'Dante e il problema della salvezza degli infedeli', *Studi danteschi* 14 (1930), 79-92.

Ryan, C. J., 'Free Will in Theory and Practice. *Purgatorio* XVIII and Two Characters in the *Inferno*', in D. Nolan (ed.), *Dante Soundings* (Dublin: Irish Academic Press, 1981), pp. 100-112.

idem, 'Grace, Merit and *Buona Volontade*: Studies in the Relationship between the *Comedy* and the *Convivio*', *Italian Studies* 35 (1980), 6-11.

idem, '"Natura dividitur contra gratiam": concetti diversi della natura in Dante e nella cultura filosofico-teologica medievale', in P. Boyde and V. Russo (eds), *Dante e la scienza. Atti del Convegno Internazionale di Studi, Ravenna 28-30 maggio 1993* (Ravenna: Longo, 1995), pp. 363-73.

idem, '*Paradiso* VII: Marking the Difference between Dante and Anselm', in J. C. Barnes and C. Ó Cuilleanáin (eds), *Dante and the Middle Ages* (Dublin: Irish Academic Press, 1995), pp. 117-37.

idem, review of 'A. C. Mastrobuono, *Dante's Journey of Sanctification', Italian Studies* 46 (1991), 110-14.

idem, 'The Theology of Dante', in *A Cambridge Companion to Dante*, 1st edn by R. Jacoff (Cambridge: Cambridge University Press, 1993), pp. 136-52.

Schildgen, B. D., 'Dante and the Indus', *Dante Studies* 111 (1993), 177-93.

eadem, 'Dante's Utopian Political Vision, the Roman Empire, and the Salvation of Pagans', *Annali d'Italianistica* 19 (2001), 51-69.

Scorrano, L., 'Paradiso XXXII. La legge, la grazia', *L'Alighieri: rassegna bibliografica dantesca*, 37, n.s. 7 (1996), 19-36 (subsequently in *Tra il 'banco' e 'l'alte rote'* (Ravenna: Longo, 1996), pp. 103-22, with the title 'La legge, la grazia').

Singleton, C. S., 'Viaggio a Beatrice: La giustificazione nella storia', in *La poesia della Divina Commedia* (Bologna: Il Mulino, 1978), pp. 229-46.

Thompson, D., 'Dante's Virtuous Romans', *Dante Studies* 96 (1978), 145-62.

Trabant, J., '"Gloria" oder "grazia". Oder: Wonach die "questione della lingua" eigentlich fragt', *Romanistisches Jahrbuch* 51 (2000), 29-52.

Turner, R. V., '"Descendit ad Inferos". Medieval Views on Christ's Descent into Hell and the Salvation of the Ancient Just', *Journal of the History of Ideas* 27 (1966), 173-94.

Dante and Aquinas

Adorno, F., 'Dante (1265-1321), tra San Tommaso (1225/26-1274) e San Bonaventura (1221-1274)', in *Letture classensi* 32-34 (2005), pp. 13-22.

Alfano, G., 'Letteratura e filosofia nel pensiero e nell'opera di Dante Alighieri', *Aquinas* 34 (1991), 1, 223-244.

Blum, P. R., 'Sigieri e San Tommaso nel *Paradiso*', in *Verbum. Analecta Neolatina* 3 (2001), 1, 101-109.

Boni, F., 'San Tommaso d'Aquino e Dante', in F. Zangrilli (ed.), *La Ciociaria tra letteratura e cinema. Atti del Convegno di Studi, Ripi 17-20 gennaio 2002* (Pesaro: Metauro, 2002), pp. 327-44.

Bonora, E., '"Di fra Tommaso il discreto latino": sulla lingua del canto di San Francesco', in *Giornale Storico della Letteratura Italiana* 164 (1987), 161-80 (subsequently in *Interpretazioni dantesche* (Modena: Mucchi, 1988), pp. 155-79).

Boyle, M. O., 'Closure in Paradise: Dante Outsings Aquinas', *Modern Language Notes* 115 (2000), 1, 1-12.

Busnelli, G., *Cosmologia e antropogenesi secondo Dante Alighieri e le sue fonti* (Rome: Civiltà cattolica, 1922); reviewed by B. Nardi in the *Giornale storico della letteratura italiana* 81 (1923), 307-34, and reproduced in his *Saggi di filosofia dantesca*, 2nd edn (Florence: La Nuova Italia, 1967), pp. 341-80.

Cao, G. M., 'Appunti storiografici in margine al carteggio Gilson-Nardi', in *Giornale Critico della Filosofia Italiana*, 6th series, 21 (2001), 137-70.

Cordovani, M., O.P., 'Tomismo dantesco', *Xenia Thomistica* 3 (1925), 309-26.

Cornoldi, G. M., *La filosofia scolastica di San Tommaso e di Dante, ad uso dei licei* (Rome: A. Befani, 1889; revised edn 1899).

Costa, G., *Virtù e vizi nella 'Divina Commedia' tomisticamente coordinati* (Vicenza: Consonni, 1964).

Crouse, R. D., 'Dante as Philosopher. Christian Aristotelianism', *Dionysius* 16 (1998), 141-56.

Curcio, G. C., *Amore passione, amore dilezione. Un confronto-intreccio tra san Tommaso d'Aquino e Dante Alighieri* (Rome: Aracne, 2005).

D'Onofrio, T., 'S. Tommaso nella poesia dantesca', in *Tommaso d'Aquino nella storia del pensiero. I. Le fonti del pensiero di S. Tommaso. II. Dal Medioevo ad oggi* (Naples: Edizioni Domenicane Italiane, 1976), pp. 141-48.

Fallani, G., 'Dante e S. Tommaso', in *L'esperienza teologica di Dante* (Lecce: Milella, 1976), pp. 205-38.

Fedrigotti, P., 'Presenze tomiste e bonaventuriane nella concezione dantesca della beatitudine', in *Studi danteschi* 72 (2007), 141-213.

Foster, K., O.P., 'Dante e San Tommaso', *L'Alighieri. Rassegna bibliografica dantesca* 16 (1975), 1-2, 11-26.

idem, 'St Thomas and Dante', *New Blackfriars* 55 (1974), 148-55 (reprinted in *The Two Dantes and Other Studies* (London: Darton, Longman and Todd, 1977), pp. 56-65).

idem, ad voc. 'Tommaso d'Aquino', in the *Enciclopedia dantesca*, 6 vols (Rome: Istituto dell'Enciclopedia Italiana, 1970-78), vol. 5, pp. 626-49.

Gagliardi, A., 'Dante fra Sigieri e Tommaso', in *Tommaso d'Aquino e Averroè. La visione di Dio* (Soveria Mannelli: Rubbettino, 2002), pp. 273-94.

Ghisalberti, A. M., 'Roma antica nei trattati politici da Tommaso d'Aquino a Dante', in *Roma antica nel Medioevo. Mito, rappresentazioni, sopravvivenze nella "Respublica Christiana" dei secoli IX-XIII. Atti del quattordicesima Settimana Internazionale di Studio, Mendola, 24-28 agosto 1998* (Milan: Vita e Pensiero, 2001), pp. 347-64, and in J. A. de Camargo Rodrigues de Souza (ed.), *Idade média: tempo do mundo, tempo dos homens, tempo de Deus* (Porto Alegre: EST Edições, 2006), pp. 429-40.

Giannatale, G. di, 'Dante tra Aristotele e S. Tommaso: l'argomento logico-metafisico dell'*ordinatio ad unum* degli enti', *Sapienza* 34 (1981), 1-2, 175-82.

Giovinazzo, F., 'Il tomismo dantesco nella critica del Novecento', *Asprenas* 28 (1981), 445-56.

Griswold, J., 'Aquinas, Dante and Ficino on Love: an Explication of the *Paradiso*, XXVI, 25-39', *Studies in Medieval Culture* 8-9 (1976), pp. 151-61.

Higgins, D. H., 'Cicero, Aquinas and St. Matthew in *Inferno* XIII', *Dante Studies* 93 (1975), 61-94 (subsequently in *Dante and the Bible. An Introduction* (Bristol: University of Bristol Press, 1992), pp. 115-54 with the title 'The Bible as Palimpsest: Cicero, Aquinas and St. Matthew in canto XIII of Dante's *Inferno*').

Iannucci, A. A., 'Tommaso e il canone teologico in Dante', in F. Zangrilli (ed.), *La Ciociaria tra letteratura e cinema. Atti del Convegno di Studi, Ripi 17-20 gennaio 2002* (Pesaro: Metauro, 2002), pp. 317-26.

Imbach, R., 'Filosofia dell'amore. Un dialogo tra Tommaso d'Aquino e Dante', in *Studi Medievali*, 3rd series, 43 (2002), 2, 816-32.

La Favia, L. M., 'Thomas Aquinas and Siger of Brabant in Dante's *Paradiso*', in P. Cherchi and A. C. Mastrobuono (eds), *Lectura Dantis Newberryana II (Chicago, Illinois, 1985-1987)* (Evaston, Ill.: Northwestern University Press, 1990), pp. 147-72.

Mariani, U., La funzione storica del tomismo in Dante (Florence: Olschki, 1930).

Mastrobuono, A. C., *Dante's Journey of Sanctification* (Washington D.C.: Regnery Gateway, 1990).

Mazzotta, G., 'The Heaven of the Sun: Dante between Aquinas and Bonaventure', in T. Barolini and H. W. Storey (eds), *Dante for the New Millennium* (New York: Fordham University Press, 2003), pp. 152-68.

Metz, W., 'Das Weltgericht bei Dante in Differenz zu Thomas von Aquin', in J. A. Aertsen and M. Pickavé (eds), *Ende und Vollendung. Eschatologische Perspektiven im Mittelalter* (Berlin and New York: Gruyter, 2002), pp. 626-37.

Mongeau, G., 'Dante Alighieri', in D. Berger and J. Vijgen (eds), *Thomisten-Lexikon* (Bonn: Nova & Vetera, 2006), pp. 125-27.

Nardi, B., 'A proposito di "Dante e il buon frate Tommaso" di F. Orestano', *Studi danteschi* 26 (1942), 148-60.

idem, *Dal Convivio alla Commedia: sei saggi danteschi* (Rome: Istituto Storico Italiano per il Medio Evo, 1992; originally 1960).

idem, *Dante e la cultura medievale*, ed. P. Mazzantini (Bari: Laterza, 1983; originally 1942).

idem, *Intorno al tomismo di Dante e alla quistione di Sigieri* (Florence: Olschki, 1914).

idem, *"Lecturae" e altri studi danteschi*, ed. R. Abardo (Florence: Le Lettere, 1990).

idem, *Nel mondo di Dante* (Rome: Edizioni di Storia e Letteratura, 1944), with 'Il tomismo di Dante secondo Fr. Orestano' at pp. 363-67 and 'Il tomismo di Dante' at pp. 368-76.

idem, *Note critiche di filosofia dantesca* (Florence: Olschki, 1938).

idem, *Saggi di filosofia dantesca*, 2nd edn (Florence: La Nuova Italia, 1967; originally 1930).

idem, *Saggi e note di critica dantesca* (Milan and Naples: Ricciardi, 1966), with 'Filosofia e teologia ai tempi di Dante in rapporto al pensiero del poeta' at pp. 3-109.

Orestano, F., 'Dante e "il buon frate Tommaso"', *Sophia* 9 (1941), 1-19 (reprinted in *Opera omnia*, 5 vols (Padua: Cedam, 1960-69), vol. 3, pp. 66-80).

O'Rourke Boyle, M., 'Closure in Paradise: Dante Outsings Aquinas', *Modern Language Notes* 115 (Jan. 2000), 1-12.

Pinchard, B., 'Thomas d'Aquin, Dante, deux visionnaires de la prudence', in J. -Y. Chateau (ed.), *La Vérité pratique. Aristote, 'Ethique à Nicomaque', livre VI* (Paris: Vrin, 1997), pp. 317-33.

Poletto, G., *Dizionario dantesco di quanto si contiene nell'opere di Dante Alighieri con richiami alla Somma Teologica di San Tommaso, con l'illustrazione dei nomi proprj, mitologici, storici, geografici e delle questioni più controverse* (Siena: S. Bernardino, 1885-87).

idem, *Libertà e legge nel concetto di Dante Alighieri e Santo Tommaso* (Prato: Ranieri Guasti, 1883).

Ricklin, T., 'L'image d'Albert le Grand et de Thomas d'Aquin chez Dante Alighieri', *Revue thomiste* 97 (1997), 129-42.

Sargent, D., 'Dante and Thomism', *The Thomist* 5 (1943), 256-64.

Stump, E., 'Dante's Hell, Aquinas's Moral Theory, and the Love of God', *Canadian Journal of Philosophy* 16 (1986), 2, 181-98.

Sweeney, E., 'Aquinas' three levels of divine predication in Dante's *Paradiso*', *Comitatus. A Journal of Medieval and Renaissance Studies* 16 (1985), 29-45.

Vettori, V., 'S. Tommaso e Dante oggi', in *Tommaso d'Aquino nella storia del pensiero. I. Le fonti del pensiero di S. Tommaso. II. Dal Medioevo ad oggi* (Naples: Edizioni Domenicane Italiane, 1976), pp. 149-51.

Wicksteed, P. H., *Dante and Aquinas* (Honolulu: University Press of the Pacific, 2002) (facsimile of the original, London: Dent and New York: Dutton, 1913).

Yearley, L. H., 'Genre and the Attempt to Render Pride: Dante and Aquinas', *Journal of the American Academy of Religion* 72, 2 (2004), 313-39.

Yrjönsuuri, M., 'The Soul as an Entity: Dante, Aquinas, and Olivi', in H. Lagerlung, *Forming the Mind: Essays on the Internal Senses and the Mind/Body Problem from Avicenna to the Medical Enlightenment* (Dordrecht: Springer, 2007), pp. 59-92.

AQUINAS
Aquinas in general

Busa, R., *Index Thomisticus* (Stuttgart: Frommann-Holzboog, 1974-80).

Copleston, F. C., *Aquinas* (London: Harmondsworth, 1955 and reprints).

Davies, B., *The Thought of Thomas Aquinas* (Oxford: Clarendon Press, 1992).

Donagan, A., *Human Ends and Human Actions: An Exploration in St. Thomas's Treatment* (Milwaukee: Marquette University Press, 1985).

idem, 'Thomas Aquinas on Human Action', in N. Kretzmann, A. Kenny and J. Pinborg (eds), *The Cambridge History of Later Medieval Philosophy* (Cambridge: Cambridge University Press, 1982), pp. 642-54.

Dunn, J. and I. Harris (eds), *Aquinas*, 2 vols (Cheltenham: Elgar, 1997).

Elders, L. J., 'Les citations de saint Augustin dans la Somme Théologique de saint Thomas d'Aquin', *Doctor Communis* (1987), 40, 115-67.

idem, 'Thomas Aquinas and the Fathers of the Church', in I. Backus, *The Reception of the Church Fathers in the West from Augustine to the Maurists*, 2 vols (Leiden: Brill, 1997), vol. 1, pp. 337-66.

Gilson, E., *Thomism: the Philosophy of Thomas Aquinas*, trans. L. K. Shook and A. Maurer (Toronto: Pontifical Institute of Mediaeval Studies, 2002; from *Le Thomisme: introduction à la philosophie de Saint Thomas d'Aquin*, 6th edn rev., Paris: Vrin, 1965).

Hibbs, T. S., *Dialectic and Narrative in Aquinas. An Interpretation of the 'Summa contra Gentiles'* (Notre Dame, Ind.: University of Notre Dame Press, 1995).

Jaffa, H. V., 'Thomism and Aristotelianism. A Study of the *Commentary by Thomas Aquinas on the 'Nicomachean Ethics'* (Chicago: University of Chicago Press, 1952; and Wesport, Conn.: Greenwood Press, 1979).

Kenny, A., *Aquinas* (Oxford: Oxford University Press, 1980).

Kretzmann N. and E. Stump (eds), *The Cambridge Companion to Aquinas* (Cambridge: Cambridge University Press, 1993).

O'Meara, T. F., *Thomas Aquinas. Theologian* (Notre Dame, Ind.: University of Notre Dame Press, 1997).

Torrell, J. -P., *Initiation à saint Thomas d'Aquin: sa personne et son oeuvre*, 2 vols (Fribourg: Editions universitaires, 1993).

Van Nieuwenhove, R. and J. P. Wawrykow (eds), *The Theology of Thomas Aquinas* (Notre Dame, Ind.: University of Notre Dame Press, 2005).

Vanni Rovighi, S., *Introduzione a Tommaso d'Aquino*, 3rd edn (Bari: Laterza, 1986).

Aquinas, ethics, grace, soteriology and election

Bernard, Ch. -A., *Théologie de l'espérance selon saint Thomas d'Aquin* (Paris: Vrin, 1961).

Bouillard, H., *Conversion et grâce chez s. Thomas d'Aquin: étude historique* (Paris: Aubier, 1944).

Bradley, D. J. M., *Aquinas on the Twofold Human Good: Reason and Happiness in Aquinas's Moral Science* (Washington, D.C.: Catholic University of America Press, 1997).

Celano, A. J., 'The Concept of Worldly Beatitude in the Writings of Thomas Aquinas', *Journal of the History of Philosophy* 25 (1987), 215-26 (reprinted in J. Dunn and I. Harris (eds), *Great Political Thinkers* (Cheltenham: Elgar, 1997), vol. 7, pp. 394-405).

Cessario, R., 'Is Aquinas's Summa only about grace?', in C. -J. P. De Oliveira, *Ordo sapientiae et amoris: Image et message de saint Thomas d'Aquin* (Fribourg, Suisse: Editions universitaires, 1993), pp. 197-209.

Deman, T., 'Le *Liber de Bona Fortuna* dans la théologie de S. Thomas d'Aquin', *Revue des Sciences Philosophiques et Théologiques* 17 (1928), 38-59.

Dhont, R. -C., *Le Problème de la préparation à la grâce: Débuts de l'école franciscaine* (Paris: Editions franciscaines, 1946).

Ernst, C., O.P. (ed.), *Thomas Aquinas, Summa theologiae*, vol. 30 (*The Gospel of Grace: ST 1a 2ae. 106-14*), (London: Eyre and Spottiswoode, 1972), pp. xv-xxvii.

Finili, A., 'Natural desire', *Dominican Studies* 1 (1948), 313-59.

idem, 'Natural desire', *Dominican Studies* 2 (1949), 1-15.

idem, 'New Light on Natural Desire?', *Dominican Studies* 5 (1952), 159-84.

Finnis, J., *Aquinas: Moral, Political and Legal Theory* in the series *Founders of Modern Political and Social Thought* (Oxford: Oxford University Press, 1998).

Flick, M., *L'attimo della giustificazione secondo S. Tommaso* (Rome: Apud aedes Universitatis Gregorianiae, 1947).

Garrigou-Lagrange, R., O.P., *Grace. Commentary on the Summa theologica of St Thomas, Ia IIae, q. 109-14* (London: B. Herder, 1957).

idem, *La Prédestination des saints et la grâce: doctrine de Saint Thomas comparée aux autres systèmes théologiques* (Paris: Desclée de Brouwer, 1936).

Geenen, J. G., 'Le fonti patristiche come "autorità" nella teologia di san Tommaso', *Sacra Doctrina* 77 (1975), 7-67.

Goris, H. J. M. J., *Free Creatures of an Eternal God: Thomas Aquinas on God's Infallible Foreknowledge and Irresistible Will* (Leuven: Peteers, 1996).

Jenkins, J. I., *Knowledge and Faith in Thomas Aquinas* (Cambridge: Cambridge University Press, 1997).

Jordan, M. D., *The Alleged Aristotelianism of Thomas Aquinas* (Toronto: Pontifical Institute of Mediaeval Studies, 1992).

Korolec, J. B., 'Free will and free choice', in N. Kretzmann, A. Kenny and J. Pinborg (eds), *The Cambridge History of Later Medieval Philosophy* (Cambridge: Cambridge University Press, 1982), pp. 629-41.

Ladrille, G., 'Grâce et motion divine chez saint Thomas', *Salesianum* 12 (1950), 37-84.

Landgraf, A. M., 'Das Axiom "facienti quod in se est Deus non denegat gratiam"', in *Dogmengeschichte der Früscholastik*, 4 vols (Regensburg: Pustet), vol. 1, pp. 249-63.

Laporta, J., *La Destinée de la nature humaine selon Thomas d'Aquin* (Paris: Vrin, 1965).

idem, 'Pour trouver le sens exact des termes *appetitus naturalis, desiderium naturale, amor naturalis* etc. chez Thomas D'Aquin', *Archives d'histoire doctrinale et littéraire du moyen âge* 40 (1973), 37-95.

Lawler, M. G., 'Grace and Free Will in Justification: a Textual Study in Aquinas', *The Thomist* 35 (1971), 601-30.

Lonergan, B. J. F., S.J., *Grace and Freedom: Operative Grace in the Thought of St Thomas Aquinas*, ed. F. E. Crowe and R. M. Doran (Toronto: University of Toronto Press, 2000).

Piclin, M., 'La nature et la grâce', in *Philosophie et théologie chez saint Thomas d'Aquin* (Paris: Klincksieck, 1983), pp. 131-60.

Ruini, C., *La trascendenza della grazia nella teologia di San Tommaso d'Aquino* (Rome: Università Gregoriana, 1971).

Seckler, M., *Instinkt und Glaubenswille nach Thomas von Aquin* (Mainz: Matthias-Grünewald-Verlag, 1961).

Vanneste, A., 'La nécessité de la grâce selon Saint Augustin et selon saint Thomas', in *Nature et grâce dans la théologie occidentale: dialogue avec Henri de Lubac* (Leuven: Leuven University Press, 1996), pp. 293-304.

Von Hertling, G., 'Augustinus-Zitate bei Thomas von Aquin' (Munich: Sitzungberichte der Bayerischen Akademie der Wissenshaften, 1904), 535-602.

Wawrykow, J. P., *God's Grace and Human Action. 'Merit' in the Theology of Thomas Aquinas* (Notre Dame, Ind.: University of Notre Dame Press, 1995).

idem, 'Grace', in R. Van Nieuwenhove and J. Wawrykow (eds), *The Theology of Thomas Aquinas*, (Notre Dame, Ind.: University of Notre Dame Press, 2005), pp. 192-221.

idem, 'On the Purpose of "Merit" in the Theology of Thomas Aquinas', *Medieval Philosophy and Theology* 2 (1992), 97-116.

Wippel, J. F., 'Natur und Gnade (*S.th.* I-II, qq. 109-114)', in A. Speer (ed.), *Thomas von Aquin: Die Summa theologiae. Werkinterpretationen* (Berlin: de Gruyter, 2005), pp. 246-70.

Index of Names

www.ingramcontent.com/pod-product-compliance
Lightning Source LLC
Chambersburg PA
CBHW070442090426
42735CB00012B/2441